W9-BUL-092

"Biallas departs from the usual historical method of world religions textbooks and follows an unusual and refreshing story approach. For each religion, he uses two representative stories to weave a pattern of religious assumptions, beliefs, values, and practices.

"Biallas thoughtfully introduces, analyzes, and applies each story. In the process, by emphasizing the power of faith stories to transform adherents spiritually, he invites Christian students to open themselves to a greater awareness of their own spiritual heritage and to learn from others what may have been overlooked in their own tradition.

"Discussion questions, a reading list, a full index, and extensive photos add to the value of this book as a text. Unlike the typical textbook, this one is readable and relevant to students' own spiritual quests."

Henry N. Smith
Southwestern Journal of Theology

"At a time when world boundaries are all next door through TV, it is important to have knowledge of and a feeling for world religions. That is well provided in *World Religions: A Story Approach* by Leonard J. Biallas. An experienced teacher, Biallas discusses the setting, the faith, the writings, and two major stories for Judaism, Christianity, Islam, Hinduism, Confucianism and Taoism, Buddhism, Maya (Mexico), and Baganda (Uganda). Becoming aware of the beliefs of other religions invites one to deepen one's understanding of one's own faith."

Prairie Messenger

"*World Religions: A Story Approach* offers a refreshing alternative to the standard survey textbook. Dr. Biallas has selected stories from several traditions and invites students to 'read' these stories as transformative, not merely informative. In addition to brief summaries highlighting features of each faith, references to contemporary issues and statistics on the current status of major traditions are included.

"*World Religions* is an excellent supplemental text that will enliven the introductory world religions survey course."

Christopher Chapple
Loyola Marymount University

"This is a fascinating approach to the study of world religions. Stories capture the culture in marvelous ways, enriching the reader with new understanding."

John Catoir
The Christophers

LEONARD J. BIALLAS

W O R L D
RELIGIONS

A Story Approach

✠
XXIII
TWENTY-THIRD PUBLICATIONS
Mystic, Connecticut

Third printing 1998

Twenty-Third Publications
P.O. Box 180
185 Willow Street
Mystic, CT 06355
(203) 536-2611
800-321-0411

ISBN 0-89622-493-7
Library of Congress Catalog Card No. 91-65738

Photo Credits

PREFACE

I have written this book for everyone who appreciates the strength and beauty of religion in its diverse manifestations both in history and in our contemporary human community.

World Religions: A Story Approach is a general introduction to the major living religious traditions of the world. It differs from other books in two significant ways. First, I give the place of honor to the stories found in the sacred writings of each religious tradition. When readers have finished the book, they will be able to summarize the major themes of the world's religions by telling two stories from each of the religions. Second, I show how the stories help effect a spiritual transformation in the lives of the readers, even though the stories come from different religious traditions. The sacred stories are so rich that they transcend their own contexts. They have so much to offer to our human experiences, if we will only open our eyes, reflect on what they are telling us, and make them a part of our own stories.

There are any number of introductions to the world's religions, ranging from the comprehensive to the barest of outlines. Why add to the list? Because I find that students of religion do not retain much from those that emphasize religions' philosophy and history, nor do they find these disciplines very useful for their own spiritual lives. Students of religion need a new way to approach rituals, ethics, communities, expressions of salvation and faith, and other basic themes of religion. I am convinced that an approach to the religions through their stories is very beneficial.

99131

Most textbooks on world religions today treat each tradition as a social-religious entity bearing a distinctive creed and each religious individual as a member of one or another of these mutually exclusive groups. Often encyclopedic in nature, the books present such a vast amount of factual information on philosophical movements and historical dates that readers are overwhelmed. The dominant concern for garnering pure facts and data has sapped the religions and their gods of their strength, reducing them to bloodless symbols. In emphasizing the external phenomena of the religions, the books pay scant attention to how religious beliefs shape the spiritual lives of humans. There is little or no dynamic interrelation between scholarly detachment and personal involvement, or between academic objectivity and subjective participation.

What students of religion need is material that will correlate with their own pertinent contemporary questions—stories do that. Some students will approach this book from a background that sees religions other than Christianity as somehow inferior. What they need is material that will challenge those assumptions—stories do that. Some will come to this book with no background in religion. What they need is a simple beginning that builds on a sense of wonder—stories do that.

I have found that when people talk about inner spiritual experiences they grow closer together, sharing insight after insight, but polarization results when the conversation turns to religious doctrines or religious politics. I am convinced that an appreciation of the richness and diversity within the religions is crucial for our global concerns today—not only economic and political, but especially environmental and ecological. Studying the stories helps us tap the brightest and best aspects of our human creativity and opens us to new inspiration. Most of all, studying the stories brings us closer together by showing us what the religious traditions have in common.

I have not aimed at innovative scholarship. There are no footnotes, but I do acknowledge my sources for each chapter in the suggested readings at the end of the book. I deliberately mention the major themes in each religion just briefly. Where this book is used for college courses, I assume that professors will supplement the text with their personal accents and modifications, with their own strengths—whether theological, historical, or philosophical. Because my concern is more with archetypal themes than historical and doctrinal development, I have kept dates and names of major historical figures to a minimum. The chapters are independent of each other and can be read in any sequence.

I want to thank many people from Twenty-Third Publications. Neil Kluepfel and Pat Kluepfel offered their encouragement and friendship, John van Bemmel worked patiently to make the manuscript revision a pleasant experience, Stephen B. Sharper shared his imaginative reflections and enthusiasm for the project for so long before leaving to continue his own religious and spiritual quest, and Deborah McCann edited the copy with great skill.

I owe much to John J. Lakers, O.F.M., for providing stimulating suggestions and perceptive criticism, and to Thomas Brown, O.F.M., for making available his superb collection of original photos. Martha Gott Sankey and Duncan Sankey found time to escape from their little demon Mara to make many helpful suggestions. Mike Chase has my respect for helping me to recover from computer difficulties on more than one occasion and for bringing his own empirical insights on spirituality. A special word of appreciation goes to Daniel R. Barry for his gentle prodding and good-natured opinions. I am grateful to William Grosnick, Robert Webb, Joseph Cha, T.J. Salgia, and many others who offered valuable suggestions and new perspectives on specific parts of the book. I am also grateful to my students who stimulate and challenge me by their questioning looks and who confront my assumptions with their own experiences. The members of the Council (John Ernst, Dan McLaughlin, Jim Rinella, Mike McLaughlin, Matt Ehrhart, and Carl Craven) encouraged me with their high-spirited discussions of many of the archetypal themes. Without them, I would have found the writing of this book all work and no play. Though Martha Weedman Biallas laughingly calls herself my chief paper-sorter, she is really loving friend, patient wife, and creative teacher. This book is for her.

Contents

Studying stories about Sun and Rain gods can bring greater knowledge and insights into the mysteries of life, death, and the universe.

INTRODUCTION

Stories are at the heart of the world's religious traditions. They touch universal chords of our human experience and invite us to take part in their telling. Their living symbols operate within us at a deeper level than our rational consciousness. Sacred places and monuments may enshrine and root a religion, and rituals and ethics may reflect the pragmatic features of a religion, but it is the stories of a religion that work magic on our hearts. The images and metaphors of stories influence beliefs and behavior more than concepts and doctrines do. Stories have the power to challenge us and change our cultures.

The stories in the sacred writings of the world's religions highlight and color the basic human experiences of our individual and social existence. They grace our existence with acceptance and forgiveness and they fill us with joy and healing. These stories extend our horizons, alter our perspectives, and make us take notice of things beyond our immediate needs and desires. They empower us for service and caring.

By studying the images and symbols of the stories in world religions, we gain a greater knowledge of those religions and their insights into the mysteries of life, death, and the universe. More than that, the stories bring us into touch with our own spirituality.

Goal 1: Greater Knowledge of World Religions

I have a friend who finds occasions—at a business breakfast, at intermission at a concert, even on the golf course—to pester me in an amicable way with religious questions. Given the death and ruin that Saddam Hussein brought to so many people in Kuwait and Iraq, was his talk of a holy war justified? Why do the religious conflicts of the Muslims with Jews, or with Hindus, or with their fellow Muslims continue over the generations? Was there any religious motivation in the revolt of the Chinese students in Tian An Men square in Beijing or was it a political demand for more freedom of expression? How could a novel such as *The Satanic Verses* really be an insult to a religion and lead to so many protests, demonstrations, and even threats of death? Why does the fighting continue for so long in Northern Ireland?

Mercifully, he doesn't point to other similar situations throughout the world. I cannot give him any totally satisfactory answers, of course, because these questions are not uniquely religious. The roots of so much of the historical bitterness between religious groups are primarily political and cultural rather than religious. Studying the world's religions will not give direct answers to questions like these, but it does put those questions in a broader context. By studying the stories of the different peoples we see what role religion does play in their lives.

That is one goal I have in this book: I want to bring people to a better knowledge of the world religions and a better sense of global awareness. Our world is no longer limited to the territory we traverse in our daily activities or the events we experience firsthand. Our global reality becomes more apparent with each advance in communications technology, with each revolutionary upheaval, and with each environmental impact study. Everyone and everything is increasingly connected, though not unified, economically and culturally. No longer can we carve up the world into "us" and "them." Greater awareness of the visions and value systems of the world's traditions may not explain religious tensions, but it does provide a common approach to issues of social injustice and environmental threats. The religions emphasize that purposeful interdependence with the human community and with nature are the basis of ultimate happiness and fulfillment. By approaching the world's religions in their diversity, unity, and complementarity, we enlarge our sense of global awareness. We learn much from studying their key themes—how they express their faith in Absolute Reality (God) and how they represent human salvation. We examine their various communities, their approach to modernity in the twentieth century, and the expression of their basic beliefs and experiences in their rituals. Exploring the religions from these different perspectives, we increase our knowledge of the world views of the religions and we gain, in the words of Henry James, "the power to guess the unseen from the seen, to trace the implication of things, to judge the whole piece by the pattern."

By approaching the world religions through their stories, we find an even more fruitful basis for greater knowledge and understanding. The stories open up fresh channels of thought into the essence of the different traditions. They maintain the philosophical and theological depth of the religions without losing us in scholarly fog. The stories are timeless, illuminating the various doctrines, rituals, ethics, and religious lifestyles that have nourished people's convictions through many generations.

Goal 2: Greater Spiritual Awareness

Creating Awareness

A young soldier stationed abroad wrote me that he has been searching everywhere for a book that will help bring him out of his doldrums. He has scoured many books on Christianity and other world religions looking for spiritual answers. Yet every book he opens is a can of worms for him, an encyclopedia of facts and foreign words that make no sense. "Where do I start looking for meaning?" he asks. "How can I make sense of all that's happening around me?" He feels stuck in a mind rut, going backward instead of forward. He is searching for something to grab hold of, yet he doesn't know what it's like to be drawn toward a goal. He puts on a happy face for everyone else to see, but he has just about run out of smiles.

The second goal I have in this book is to show the soldier—and many others—that the stories in the world's religions can increase our awareness of the spirituality of those religions. This, in turn, can empower people to experience a sense of personal vitality and authenticity. Stories educate us and lead us out of that narrow, stifling individualism that is the universal prison of humans. The heroes who decorate the stories in the sacred writings of world religions illustrate the discovery that becoming fully human is an ongoing process that entails moving beyond present insights and accomplishments. Stories about and by great religious figures such as Jesus, Buddha, and Moses capture our imagination and attention because their lives are vivid, concentrated, focused, and integrated. Their stories trigger experiences in us that support our personal growth and spiritual rebirth. Their stories enliven the fundamental meaning and values of our activities and our lives, meshing us with their interests, passions, and achievements.

Whenever our lives become more complicated than our world-views allow us to understand, we humans are driven to reexamine our vision of life. We seek explanations when we encounter frustration, failure, or novelty, and where our personal freedom is restricted. When we detect insecurity we struggle to maintain and enhance our self-esteem, our sense of competence and well-being. Our natural curiosity compels us to make some sense out of our world. We seek to find meaning in the midst of those problems that come deeply and pervasively into our lives, bewildering our attempts to love well and work well.

When the yearning to find meaning also extends to the mysteries in our lives—when we ask, for example, why there is suffering or death in the world—we are engaged in a spiritual quest. We are restless in the face of mystery, never satisfied with the apparent nor tamed by the accepted limits. We push at the boundaries of life and death and puzzle over strategies of good and evil. Our tireless pursuit for meaning, our impulse to achieve self-identity, and our willingness to share this search with others all develop our spirituality.

Many people have looked for greater spiritual awareness to Jerusalem, the site of the core stories of many religious heroes.

Our spirituality grows as we become aware of the complex feelings and emotions that we experience in our relationships with others. It is expanded and deepened by our encounter with other religious traditions. Religious stories present new perspectives for grappling with our hopes and despairs, our sadness and joys, our fears and expectations, our certainties and doubts. Our spirituality develops deeper convictions and a firmer base as it searches for and integrates new insights. Spiritual strength and spiritual quest are essential, not merely compatible, to each other.

By approaching and studying the classical stories in the sacred writings, we find new treasures that bless us and those we meet in our everyday lives. The stories launch us on our own heroic quest or voyage, where we are challenged by new visions of spiritual wholeness. When we take on new spiritual insights from the stories, we return as changed persons, with new gifts that we can contribute to our community. The convictions we appropriate through our quest awaken our inner selves to bring a new sense of relationship with God, the world, and society into our range of experience.

"How can I find meaning?" the soldier asks. We have no simple answers for this momentous question. There are no shortcuts on our spiritual quests. Yet the religious stories yield some understanding to help end his confusion. They point to patterns beneath the confusion of everyday experience. They proffer knowledge and healing that render our selves healthy and whole. The stories stimulate us to find a ruling passion, something around which we can organize our lives. They help us experience the joy of heightened consciousness, the actualization of our potentialities, the broadening of our experiential horizons, and the attainment of the greatest love and freedom of which we are capable. The stories, however, will not simply hand over these treasures. They can be gained only when the stories in the religions and our personal experiences shed light on one another.

Enhancing Awareness

The stories can be just as powerful for those who are not going through some kind of personal spiritual crisis. I know an elderly woman with more than seventy years of perfect Sunday church attendance. She says that the fellowship gives her a spiritual boost: It supplies her the energy to share her memories with others. As a young girl she went to church in snow three feet deep after persuading her uncle to hitch a horse to a sleigh to get her through the drifts that blocked access to the church. To keep her record intact, she has attended the services of dozens of different denominations throughout the United States and other countries. She even spent one Sunday in the Upper Room in Jerusalem. It is a shame, she remarks, that we have so many different religions because "the Sunday school lessons and the people are just about the same everywhere." "We're all aiming for the same place," she says, "we're just taking different roads."

She is a woman with much spiritual wisdom. God is very real in her life. She knows and lives her own religious tradition very intensively and very deeply. Still, she can learn much from the rich abundance of experiences and perspectives that are available in the stories of other religious traditions. Just hearing the stories of the different religions can be a source of wisdom. There is a certain joy in picking up a story from another religion and being able to say: "I like this story even better than some of my stories. This is really my story." Stories in other traditions stimulate deeper experiences in the Christian tradition. The stories can have the unexpected effect of making my elderly friend take a renewed interest in her own heritage.

The ritual of the Eucharist is a thanksgiving feast that reenacts the Christian story of God's generous love and gifts of forgiveness and freedom.

For her, the master story of the life, ministry, death, and resurrection of Jesus answers the questions of what life is all about and how she has to live to make her life worthy and good. The story of Jesus bolsters her stance toward life and the way she relates to the world and other people. What I am suggesting is that the stories from other religions can, either consciously or unconsciously, enhance the master story by which she and all Christians operate. The stories transcend their formulations in any single religion and compel Christians to reflect critically and seriously on the faith they have chosen or inherited. Challenged to examine their values, they often find that long-forgotten elements of their religion tug at their memory. This challenge appears again and again in these pages, not only in reading the stories, but in studying how the stories are magnified (by still other stories), exemplified (in the stories of other human witnesses), and appropriated.

Stories from other religious traditions can help her develop spiritual experience of transcendent reality and make her aware of the affinity she has with the spiritual giants in other religions. Indeed, the stories can open the vision of wider horizons to all Christians, bringing their lives clarity and enrichment. The stories are a nectar delighting and quenching their spiritual thirst. The stories give life to their religious identification and tradition, vivifying their beliefs, theology, and churches.

Stories about conversion and martyrdom, about sacrifice and detachment, about relationships to nature and to ancestors, prompt insights that operate more deeply than the level of concepts and ideas. Stories about trials in the passages of life, about death and resurrection, touch archetypal dimensions of existence. The stories work on our imaginations, exciting and driving us to personal commitment. They bring us an experience of joy, wholeness, and harmony at the moments when our behavior and our belief come together. When this happens we act from our hearts; in turn, our commitment energizes the world anew.

Religion and Spirituality

While religion and spirituality both describe a way of life that relates our selves to the realms of the sacred, other people, and the natural world, they are not the same thing. We study the religious dimension when we objectively examine the institutional and intellectual aspects of the world's religions. We study the spiritual dimension when we explore the experiential and emotional side of the religions. Institutions can be religious, people spiritual.

When we delve into spirituality we look *subjectively* at how we can apply insights from the religions to our own experiences. We are determined to live by the highest values and attain the highest goals we can see. We are concerned with the possibilities for human wholeness through self-transformation and self-transcendence. The spiritual component transcends our minds and bodies to bring us into contact with a reality beyond the world of immediate experience. Spirituality is an existential dimension of human life, the quest for ultimate meaning when confronted with questions about the meaning of life and the universe. It is a way of life oriented to God, the Absolute Reality that transcends, wraps around, and permeates humanity and the world. Though spirituality is often described in terms of contemplation and prayer, it includes social justice as an essential aspect. A spirituality that does not confront realities of injustice, oppression, and exploitation is emaciated.

When we look *objectively* at how the different religious communities relate their teachings (doctrines) and practices (rituals and ethics) to what they regard as sacred, we study their religious side. We look at how the stories in the religions have become intellectualized and institutionalized. We study how their symbols express a total system of involvement with the realm of the sacred in thought, action, and social forms. We examine how humans move from isolation and self-absorption to unite their lives with others in the community who share their ultimate values. We study how the religions exercise authority and establish institutional and intellectual guidance in the practical elements of religion.

Stories are the link between spirituality and religion. They are the foundation that generates the behaviors and beliefs of each religion and they are the foundation that best enables us to understand those behaviors and beliefs. Indeed, stories show how the spiritual and religious dimensions have to be balanced for wholeness. They have to be closely integrated and kept in constant balance, mutually enriching each other, for a full human life.

The greatest obstacle to wholeness is a withering of either of these dimensions, when they exist in an unconnected fashion, or when one overpowers the other. If the spiritual dimension is atrophied, the practical and cognitive sides of the religious dimension are more limited and more superficial. When the spiritual dimension is strengthened, imagination and feelings come into play and we discern the deeper meaning and value of the institutional community and of our intellectual understanding of our experiences and of the world.

The inner spiritual world cannot be embraced all alone, though. When this happens, we become so absorbed in its mystery and power that we reject the institutional authority and the faith traditions we have received, because we falsely perceive them to be totally inadequate to express the reality we have discovered within. The religious side also has to be developed: We need its cognitive side to understand and articulate our perceptions of the world and our experiences of life in various conscious, intellectual ways, and we need its institutional side to affect and effect our relationships with other people. Only when the spiritual and religious dimensions are interconnected and integrated do they mutually energize each other and elicit mature human life.

Requirements

In this book I include much material on the institutional and intellectual sides of the religious dimension. I pay more attention to the spiritual dimension, though, not because it is more important, but because it is so often quickly dismissed or altogether neglected in textbooks on the world's religions. I am confident that greater awareness of the spiritual dimension will also enhance our knowledge of the religious dimension. When we put it all together, we can then understand the religions in a global context and have a greater awareness of our own spiritual consciousness. Intellectual effort is certainly necessary to carry out this project, but, more important, we need openness, wonder, humor, and self-transformation.

Openness

First of all, we have to be open to what is different and hospitable to a new way of seeing and understanding. Part of our task is to escape our personal and cultural onesidedness by giving each tradition's stories their due. Prejudices, as Charlotte Brontë has told us, are most difficult to eradicate from the heart whose soil has never been loosened or fertilized by education: They grow there, firm as weeds among stones. Our healthiest encounters are with those whose values, opinions, and beliefs differ significantly from our own. Openness to those who do not accept all the unconscious assumptions we hold about religion leads us to reexamine many of our presuppositions and values. We may reject or alter some, but we reaffirm others with renewed conviction.

Openness indicates hospitality, where both guest and host reveal their most precious gifts and bring new life to each other. When we invite the stranger and the stranger's religion into our lives, then our private spaces are suddenly enlarged. They are no longer cramped and restricted, but expansive and free. Hospitality to the stranger gives us a chance to see our own lives afresh, through different eyes, and to become aware of other spiritual and religious experiences that enlighten, broaden, and deepen our own.

There is a risk in trying to develop and strengthen the mature religious consciousness. Sometimes acquaintance with other religions brings uncertainty about our own religious convictions. This risk is worth taking, though, and the challenge fuels the strength for our own struggles. We are then liberated to discover the real impetus for pondering the meaning and goals of our own lives in our own relig-

Meditation in a Buddhist temple provides a lesson in enlightenment and compassion and can bring about self-transformation.

ious traditions. Then we are ready to discover some real surprises. For example, God is then encountered rather than thought about, experienced from within rather than presented from without. God is loved and lived rather than theorized about and is experienced in action and power rather than in external constraints and discipline.

Wonder

Second, we need a sense of wonder to stimulate us. Though wonder is not commonly thought of as a spiritual virtue, it is perhaps the most fundamental of all; indeed, religion arises out of a sense of wonder. When spiced with imagination, wonder drives us toward the unknown, making us experience our present world under a different set of metaphors. Wonder is central to human consciousness: It pushes us to entertain an alternative world not yet visible.

Wonder embraces what John Dunne has called "passing over." This is the process of sympathetically entering into the feelings of persons in other religions. There we become receptive to images that give expression to our feelings and attain insight into those images. We then come back to our own religion enriched by new insights that guide our lives into the future. The intellectual work required for this passing over and return excites the imagination. We may never attain definitive answers to life's mysteries through the process, but we arrive at answers that are better informed and more effective in our lives. New insights are born and our horizon of knowledge expands in an exhilarating pursuit of understanding, not in a nervous pursuit of certainty.

Humor
Third, we need a sense of playful humor to free us from the ties of the status quo. We can turn our entire world upside down when we are able to wink at our seriousness. Without a sense of amused detachment, we suffer the consequences of taking our present ambitions, our opinions and beliefs, our situations and achievements with ultimate solemnity. Humor is essential for our sense of spiritual well-being. Unfortunately, we all too frequently picture God as grave, supremely grave, as if Absolute Reality must be characterized by absolute seriousness. Too often we regard humor as a failure to take religion with proper seriousness, as if we understand ourselves most religious and reverential when we are at our dreariest and dullest. Our problem, though, is the loss of laughter, not the loss of seriousness.

Humor is a type of play, and play is prayer. Humor is the very expression of the human role in the universe—the display of the unique image of God. There is a necessary connection between play and creativity. As C.G. Jung reminds us: "All creative individuals whatsoever owe all that is greatest in their lives to play; without this playing with fantasy no creative work has ever yet come to birth." When we playfully allow the creative activity of our imagination to express itself, we free ourselves from our bondage to the "nothing but." We create a different aspect of the divine face, divine hands, and divine humor by the ways we choose to live out our spirituality.

Self-Transformation
Finally, the enrichment of religious and spiritual consciousness comes not merely through information, but through personal transformation. Self-transformation is more important than self-fulfillment: This is a fundamental insight of all religions. The force of religion derives from the demand it makes on us to become more than we naturally want to be. It drives us to transcend the goals that we can set and achieve by ourselves.

The encounter with the stories in the world religions awakens our inner selves to experience the Absolute Reality. If we separate this experience from the concrete activities of our daily lives, then it is meaningless. We also have to bring a concern for the human community and the world of nature into the fundamental center of our existence. This is self-transformation, and it is achieved to the extent that we appropriate the stories and make them our own.

Plan of the Book

The first two chapters are introductory. In Chapter One I present four different approaches to the world's religions. While the approaches through diversity, unity, and complementarity are geared more to the religious dimension, the approach through awareness and appropriation of stories is more of a creative aid in our own process of spiritual transformation. Chapter Two presents an overview of the role of sacred writings in world religions and of the three major kinds of stories that we will be considering in the various sacred writings: narrative history, parable, and myth. I also discuss some considerations regarding interpretation of the stories.

In the remaining chapters I present the broad strokes of each of the world's major religious traditions. I examine the objective, content-oriented dimension of the religions in their major teachings, their faith in Absolute Reality, their way of salvation, and their twentieth-century expression in community, human rights, and ritual. I examine the subjective, spiritual dimension of the religions through two classical stories from their basic sacred writings that encapsulate the essence of the religions at their origin and still provide the foundation for their words, deeds, and lifestyles today. I elaborate the spiritual dimension in the sections on the magnification, exemplification, and appropriation of the stories as well as in the sections on other stories and human witnesses.

The lions in the court of the Alhambra palace in southern Spain guard the spiritual riches of the Islamic religion.

Chapter One

APPROACHES
TO RELIGION

We can take many different approaches on our quest for greater knowledge of world religions and greater awareness of their spiritual dimension. The irony—and joy—of making this long, arduous, dangerous trip into the remote strongholds of the other world religions is that we discover that the real treasures of religion are never far away. There are spiritual riches buried in the innermost recesses of our own religions that are only opened up to us when we encounter what is strange and different in the other traditions.

Excessive Baggage
For the voyage of discovery to be fruitful, however, we have to lighten our load by discarding some baggage. We hinder ourselves and bog down our quest whenever we feel compelled to compare other religions with our own and whenever we are attracted by the negative aspects of religion.

The Judgmental Load. First of all, we have to leave behind the tendency to appraise or judge the other religions in relation to our own. In the past few decades, dialogue between members of the different world religions has been very worthwhile, especially to the extent that it has been able to avoid two extremes. One extreme attempts to make people all belong to one same religion and asserts that all religions represent only different levels of the one universal truth. The other extreme insists that Christianity is the only religion and that it alone has a lock on truth.

Christians, for example, do not have to cling to the idea that their religion has an ultimacy and normativity meant to embrace and ful-fill all the others, even while respecting the dignity and value of all religious paths. When they feel this way, they relegate other relig-ions to a lower or a partial knowledge of the truth in such a way that their own religion, from the outset, is raised to the status of a super-system. When they then smugly dismiss the stories in the oth-er religions as irrelevant and superfluous, they miss the treasures those stories have to offer.

There are many true religions and many spiritual paths to salva-tion. Parallels and similarities between the religions do appear, but so do fundamental differences. The world's major religions have different views of what reality is, how truth is to be known, and what the aims of life are. It is beneficial to listen carefully to these different, yet critical, nuances. Approaching the religions with dis-criminating empathy makes us more aware of the many responses they have made to the questions that both plague and inspire hu-mans in their efforts to become whole persons. The trick is to look at the other religions in a way that is free of superiority and chauvin-ism, while remaining academically respectable.

The Negative Load. For our quest to be successful we also have to leave behind a fascination with the negative elements in world re-ligions. There is no question that all major religions have functioned in a profoundly ambiguous manner. While religious beliefs have been offered as the true basis for harmony and salvation, they have served equally well as a basis for alienation, hostility, and destruc-tion. The religions are world-creating powers that have released both beneficial forces and demonic realities. One of the terrible iro-nies of history is that religions have been a primary source of brutal and tragic conflict between people. As Pascal said: "Humans never do evil so completely and cheerfully as when they do it from relig-ious conviction."

In Christianity, religious fanaticism (the Crusades), witch hunts, unscrupulous profiteering (indulgence-selling), persecutions of the Jews, mass suicide of cultic followers, and exploitation of the poor have all left their scars. In traditional Eastern cultures, lethargy in

Occupying a sacred place in the religious stories of the Hindus, the cow symbolizes a certain detachment from worldly progress.

relation to social and economic problems, lack of economic progress
(and consequent poverty) are heavily influenced by religious motives. Much ruthless killing, warfare, pain, starvation, exploitation,
slavery, dishonesty, and grasping for wealth and power can be
traced to religious conviction. Bloody conflicts without pity—
whether in Northern Ireland, Palestine, the Persian Gulf, India, or
elsewhere—are done in the name of God.

While we have to recognize these negative features, we do not
have to dwell on them. Because the tragic and painful aspects of human nature and human experience are all parts of life, the dark side
cannot simply be excluded. While recognizing this radically destructive underside of religion, we find it fruitful to concentrate on
the positive and creative side. The celebration of the glorious side of
the human spirit—as creators, builders, visionaries—is much more
constructive. Allowing the stories in the religions to shed light on
and help overcome chaotic and meaningless lives is much more important and productive than dwelling on their shadowy and negative elements.

Comfort Zone
We need a comfort zone in our quest of greater knowledge and
awareness of the other religions. When we leave the familiarity of our
home environments—the cultural values of our own religion and the

moral teachings of our families—we are inevitably startled and have trouble juggling the elements to arrive at a satisfactory mental destination. We find information and ideas that momentarily jar us out of the circle of our everyday thinking and we encounter depth charges that stir up our spiritual unconscious. The French philosopher Diderot once advised an explorer friend: "Put on the costume of the country you visit, but keep the suit of clothes you will need to go home in." So, our minds need ideas that they can serenely take for granted, ideas that seem certain and remain unchallenged. Likewise, our spirits have to have familiar surroundings. With their firm grounding, the comfort zones of our own religious traditions have a powerful and reassuring appeal.

Those with a Christian background and foundation in the Christian Scriptures find comfort in their beliefs and practices. Still, we are discovering today that we can learn much from other religions without always having to be defensive and on guard or aggressive and hostile. When Christians study other world religions, they do not have to give up their own religion and embrace another. Indeed, before they can expand their own vision with new insights, they have to begin by acknowledging their particular allegiance to the historical Jesus.

Approach 1: Diversity

The most common approach to world religions highlights their diversity. The religions are examined from outside in an objective and academic manner, then differences in the specific and concrete forms of expression are discussed. This approach contrasts, for example, how the various religions relate to the Absolute Reality (God, or Yahweh, or Allah) and express their ultimate commitment and highest goal in life. Thus, for example, the Absolute Reality is diversely personal or impersonal, transcendent or immanent, numinous or mystical. It is variously manifested in nature, society, or individual experience.

The approach through diversity contrasts how the religions describe human nature and the human condition. It compares how the religions express their meaning of life and death, destiny, extent of love, involvement, and compassion, and how they relate these aspects of life to other aspects such as jobs, politics, and families. Again, the approach examines the diversity of external phenomena (symbols, doctrines, theologies, philosophies, rituals, prayers, moral codes, values, community traditions, churches, paintings, sculptures, festivals).

The approach investigates the personal quests of religious founders to discover a fulfilling and liberating way of life. Or perhaps it illustrates the divergences by studying the rites-of-passage ceremonies (initiations, weddings, funerals) that guide individuals through the crises and turning points of life. It also makes distinctions between religions on the basis of how they perceive the truth or how they tackle wider cultural issues, such as human rights.

The approach through diversity provides a great understanding of the world's religions. Though it tends to be encyclopedic and fairly tedious, it has contributed much to our stock of global knowledge of the religions.

Approach 2: Unity

A second approach to religions attempts to find their unity. It studies religions to discover what they all share. By this I don't mean finding something bland like "All life is sacred, all humans are one, Absolute Reality does exist, and humans are more likely to find truth and happiness in a quiet and receptive state of mind, as religious people—Jesus, Lao Tzu, Buddha—have been claiming for thousands of years." This is too simplistic to be meaningful.

Most often the approach through unity detects common ground in such spiritual experiences of and responses to Absolute Reality as faith, surrender, duty, awakening, or devotion. The unity of religions lies in their identical mystical core; the particular formation of symbols, moral laws, rituals, and practices is just a different crystallization of that same spiritual experience. The same Absolute Reality is revealed in many ways precisely because different cultures, languages, and experiences provide a variety of modes of expression and understanding. This Reality is universally self-revealing to those who are attentive: in human conscience, in the variety of human experiences and relationships, in nature about us, and in the traditions of faith and worship that the peoples of the earth build out of their characteristic ethnic histories and languages.

Another approach through unity claims that all religions share the affirmation of the value and immense potentialities of the individual human spirit—here and now, not just in the future. Again, it finds a universal dimension of all religions in their social and natural compassion, that is, their common concern for the outcasts and the heartbroken and their common concern for the world of nature, embraced down to each drop of water. The different variations on this approach through unity each contribute academically and objectively to increase our global knowledge of the religions.

Those who find some kind of unity in the religions tend to make all religions the same or to claim that they are all just different forms of some one universal world religion. They point to this oneness of all religions with many different metaphors and images. A Japanese poem articulates it this way: "Though paths for climbing a mountain from its foot differ, we look up at the same moon above a lofty peak." Again, as a Hindu tradition has it, "A river passes through many countries and each claims it for its own; still, there is only one river." And, by reversing this image: "All the separate rivers and rivulets of faith draw on a single mighty reservoir."

In one of his more playful moments, the great mythologist Joseph Campbell used the metaphor of computer software to describe the functions of individual religions. Each religion, he said, can be likened to distinct software, with its own set of signals or symbols that work for the user. Any of this software, each in its own limited way, can be put into the mainframe to enable the user to get at the Mystery of Being. Campbell's software metaphor is humbling: It admits the possibility of other systems working for other people and it suggests that the Mystery we seek is bigger than all of us. The software metaphor can be helpful for those approaching other religions, but it can also dull our respect for the power of commitment to one system.

These first two approaches to religion, either bringing out their diversity or stressing some fundamental unity or universal vision, are powerful tools in enlarging religious consciousness. I find it curious, though, that while looking at the very same phenomena, some scholars will bring out diversity in the religious traditions, while others will find unity there. Both approaches can be very deceiving. When we approach the world religions in their diversity we presume that it is possible to look at them from an objective point of view, freeze-framing and capturing them in a moment of time. Too often, the next step is to judge from that static standpoint whether one religion is better than another. On the other hand, when we approach the world religions in their unity we are forced to look at them from the same perspective and we rob them of their uniqueness—the very element that makes them vibrant. Irreconcilable differences do exist between the great religious traditions and even between major communities within the same religion. These differences matter, perhaps even more than the similarities.

Approach 3: Complementarity

Using a third approach, the way of complementarity, we pick up valuable insights from the religions without either trying to show what they have in common or how they differ from each other. With this approach we neither have to hide differences nor trumpet similarities. Turning the kaleidoscope of the religions we find a multifaceted spectacle that is brilliant and very exquisite. The world's religious traditions open our eyes to the divine color and significance that are our true environment. Holding the religions at different angles, we let them illuminate different parts of our existence. They startle us with new insights and acquaint us with facets that have escaped us. Their continually changing forms and shifting patterns all illuminate one another. By reflection we find new patterns.

Exploring religions through their complementarity is particularly productive and resourceful when we look at expressions of faith and salvation.

Faith

While most approaches to expressions of faith explore the content of an abstract body of truths and examine objective beliefs, it is more fruitful to study instead the subjective faith of the persons who experience the Absolute Reality in their lives. Faith in this instance is personal, not propositional; it is an active verb, not a static noun. Following the lead of the philosopher of religion Wilfred Cantwell Smith, we recognize that religious persons, not texts, are primary. Faith is found in humans and in the different forms—such as surrender, duty, awakening, or devotion—that faith takes in their rituals, sacred stories, and customs. It nourishes and supports their value systems. By their faith, people determine the course of their history and the success of their search for fulfillment. People express their faith, in the words of the novelist John Updike, "not merely to dismiss from one's life a degrading and immobilizing fear of death, but to possess that Archimedean point outside the world from which to move the world."

By distinguishing between faith and belief and giving priority to faith, I am not arguing against the importance of theological doctrines as signposts on the way to God, nor against beliefs that are fundamental, life-guiding propositions. It is just that personal experiences of faith, rather than philosophical views and beliefs, are the backbone of the world's religions. No doubt, we understand the faith of others to some extent by studying a collection of beliefs in a creed. Still, creeds are too often polemical tools dividing and separating people. It is by studying personal faith, the existential trust in a Reality beyond the self, that we find that other people take their religion as seriously as we take our own.

The Buddhist bodhisattva is seated atop the lotus of enlightenment and compassion, working ceaselessly for the liberation of all living things.

Faith is a significant way of knowing and experiencing, of capturing our imaginations with the possibilities of reaching out to Absolute Reality. Faith is the basic mode of relatedness to that transcendent Absolute in which life is ordered, deepened, and directed. Faith brings the great confidence and joy that enable human beings to feel at home in the universe and to find meaning in the world and in their own lives. Faith employs imagination to bring diverse impressions into a common landscape and thus brings wholeness.

Faith is meaning-making, the dynamic process by which persons form perspectives on the ultimate conditions of existence and shape their way of relating to self, to others, and to life in relation to those perspectives.

Studying Judaism, Christianity, and Islam, we find that their expressions of faith relate to the Absolute Reality as awesome mystery, active in the world, more than as "wholly other." Jews center their relationship on Yahweh, the living God, the creator who is present and active in human affairs. Christians give their hearts to the personal God who forgives them and offers a share of divine life. Muslim faith is total acceptance of whatever life brings, a total surrender to the transcendent Allah who is truly great and utterly controls the world.

Studying the Eastern religious traditions, we find that their faith expresssions are geared toward the Absolute Reality as impersonal. For Hindus, faith is the affirmation of oneness with Brahman, which is the holy power and source of the universe that pervades all things as total Being, Consciousness, and Bliss. The Chinese express their faith as harmony with a transcendent reality that brings a sense of peace and tranquility in human relationships with each other and with nature. Some Buddhists attempt to supersede faith in the realization of Emptiness, while others have faith in the saving grace of the compassionate Buddha. The Maya people of Latin America and the Baganda (the largest tribe in Uganda) reveal their faith by their sense of awe and wonder, looking for human fulfillment primarily through their relationships with family and the human community.

The faith expressions in these different religious traditions are analogous. Their modes of openness to the transcendent are neither identical nor contradictory: They are universal yet complementary. When we study these faith commitments we become aware of dimensions of experience and reality to which we have been insensitive.

Salvation

Another way to approach the world religions through complementarity examines their systems of salvation or liberation. Each religion both affirms the immense innate potentialities within individual human spirits that liberate them from some initial discontent and provides the spiritual resources for the actual transformation of human existence. The religions all invite their followers to actualize and expand their horizons and to realize their deeper human potential by transcending and transforming their present existence through voluntary renunciation of their self-centeredness.

John Hick is one scholar of religion who has studied these transitions from an unsatisfactory selfish state to a limitlessly better selfless state. In his view, the possibility of transformation of human existence away from self-centeredness is manifestly taking place within the religions. This transformation occurs in different forms according to the various perceptions of Absolute Reality and achieves fulfillment in Reality-centeredness. The common model or pattern for this salvation in the major religious traditions consists of a problem, a strategy, and a solution. Again, the forms of this model are neither identical nor contradictory, but complementary.

The Problem. The first component of the salvation model is the problem. In general terms the problem is usually a form of self-centeredness that is the source of acquisitiveness, dishonesty, injustice, and exploitation. It may also be the realization that humans are limited and finite and do not now enjoy the goal of life. Conversely, the problem may be people's refusal to accept their finiteness. The problem may be perceived as alienation from the source of life, or commingling of the forces of good and evil, or disobedience to God. It may be forgetfulness of the will of God or negligence of the divine nature that is dormant in every human being. It may be immersion in a world of meaningless change, or a life pervaded throughout by suffering, or entrapment in a web of illusion or chaos.

The Strategy. The second element in the salvation model is the strategy. This defines the way of overcoming the problem, usually through some form of voluntary relinquishing of self-centered existence. The strategy involves a self-giving to, or self-losing in, the Absolute Reality, thus bringing acceptance, compassion, and love for all humans—indeed for all life. Humans realize their deeper human potential by transcending, not perpetuating, their present self-enclosed individual existence. Through self-renunciation they build the larger corporate life of perfected humanity. The strategy includes the mystical way of contemplation and knowledge, or the practical way of action in the world, or the way of loving personal devotion to the Absolute Reality. In fact, each of the major world religions includes all these ways, though in different proportions. Whatever humans do, their activity is usually coupled with openness to the assistance coming from the Absolute Reality, the gratuitous divine gift that is sometimes both necessary and sufficient for overcoming the problem.

For Christians, the strategy includes loving others as they love themselves, giving and forgiving without limit. It includes participation in the rituals of the guiding and nurturing community and in the activity of Jesus, the God-man, who is the way, the truth, and the life. It involves openness to the activity of a God who, out of compassion and graciousness, reaches out to do for humans what they cannot do on their own.

Though other strategies in the world religions may vary according to personality and individual taste, they all work to transform consciousness and liberate humans from attachment to selfishness. Strategies might include living in complete obedience to a divine law and total submission to the will of God, or personal commitment in crying out against the injustices done to the poor and the defenseless. They might be such moral and spiritual disciplines as ritual, meditation, and prayer that awaken consciousness and bring detachment from worldly pursuits. Discipline, devotion to family, hard work, and education all generate the inner dynamics of human relationships that extinguish selfish desires, secure inward transformation, and produce compassion and harmonious human order. Generous living and loving, here and now in the course of day-to-day existence, also contribute to the development of human potential in its fullness.

The Solution. The final element in the salvation model is the solution or goal. This may be the eventual reunion with a limitlessly loving and merciful God, or the triumph of good over evil that humans look forward to, and which they can, to some extent, anticipate during their lives. Christians recognize that they are already children of God, made in the divine image: They already experience their new life in conscious relationship to God. In other traditions the solution may be union in wisdom with the Way of Life or participation in that Infinite Being, Awareness, and Joy that are the resolution of frustration, futility, and boredom. Most often it is depicted as some form of life in a heaven or paradise.

There is something to be said for the complementary models of salvation. We humans do suffer—physically, emotionally, and spiritually. This is inherent in the very notion of what it means to be human. It is also true that when we are in pain we seek relief: We know that something is wrong that should be made right. We are sustained by our sense that there is release from suffering. What the religious traditions tell us is that the possibility for actual change is available, whether through devotion, ritual, prayer, obedience, work, meditation, study, or social action. The change is a liberation that consists of a new and limitlessly better quality of existence. If all humans practiced the complementary ethical ideals in their traditions, a universal human community would be realized on earth. Such a possibility makes the study of the various complementary systems of salvation in the world's religions worthwhile.

I will use this approach to describe the dimensions of faith and salvation for each of the major world religions. Along with the first two approaches, the way of complementarity increases our knowledge of these traditions.

Approach 4: Awareness and Appropriation

While the first three approaches help us appreciate the world's religions in an abstract and objective fashion, there is another, more effective approach for making us aware of the spiritual dimension of the religions and aiding us to develop our own spirituality. In this fourth approach, awareness and appropriation, we study the religions through the stories in their sacred writings. This approach calls for growth in self-awareness and for appropriation of the stories, challenging us to go beyond the other three primarily intellectual and academic approaches. To use this approach properly and effectively, it is not enough to learn the stories: We have to integrate them into our own spiritual commitment. This approach helps us discern the driving forces of our own Christian religion and provides valuable intuitions that strengthen our spiritual development within it. Far from destroying our own spirituality or religion, this approach enriches it, bringing extra depth and dimensionality to our lifestyle and responsibilities.

The transformation that the approach of awareness and appropriation calls for is not just in technique or practice, as if we were to say: "Now I use Zen for my work" or "I'm into karmic vibrations for my prayer." As the religion scholar John Cobb explains this transformation, it combines unqualified openness to other faiths with fidelity to Christ: "Christ is the way that excludes no ways." Christians are not to be neutral with respect to all values, but to perceive everything through their deeper understanding of the mission and message of Christ. Their spirituality continues to involve emulation of the vision and lifestyle of Jesus, and the new insights they gain from other religions inspire them to continue the never-finished task of making the kingdom of God present. When Christians come to realize how limited their experience and reality are, they must allow themselves to be continually changed and creatively transformed by virtue of their very Christian commitment. To better understand this approach, I want to examine briefly how stories can be appropriated as models or paradigms in two different ways. The spiritual value and truths of a story are exemplary for those within the story's religious tradition; the spiritual value and truths of the story are transformative for those outside its tradition.

Exemplary Models

Religious stories are exemplary for those within the tradition. Even though they originated in the past, they address and ring true in the lives of the present generation. The stories function as eternal and ideal models for human behavior and goals and anchor the present generation in a meaningful, significant past. Indeed, the stories are timeless, and each generation has to approach and consult them anew, bringing its own set of problems and its own inevitable questions. The stories infuse experience at its roots, linking individual consciousness with both the ultimate powers in that religion and the inner lives of others within that tradition. People over the centuries have found commitment, liberation, and transcendence through them in their day-to-day existence and brought their ultimate concerns into focus.

The stories describe the whole of reality and furnish the structure of reality for those within the tradition. This structure keeps people away from chaos by establishing a framework where everything has a proper fit. Stories function as a selector of goals and operate as a style guide for proper responses in concrete situations. They supply the structure that organizes intellectual and physical experiences and they reveal the convictions, beliefs, values, and conduct that the religion prizes. The stories tell what sort of questions can be asked about the world.

Stories help people within the tradition as they vacillate between a desire to discover a way of their own and a need to follow a way already known. They yield a pattern for spiritual growth and development that is distinctive to that religion, yet as predictable as the physical growth of children into adulthood. The people react to the stories with pride and humility: They accept the challenge to imitate the lives and follow in the footsteps of their heroes and saints, yet they worry that somehow they will not be able to do so.

Christians who are attempting to use the approach of awareness and appropriation gain fresh insights by studying their own stories.

By studying the parable of the prodigal son, for example, they become aware that persons who cannot forgive others or themselves are blocked from wisdom and growth. From the story of Paul's conversion they learn that surrender of the will to a Higher Power brings a surge of power, confidence, peace, and joy. In appropriation, they forgive others out of a sense of compassion and interdependence. Experiencing their own conversion, they turn away from a life characterized by selfishness to answer the call to transform the world and to witness to God's activity by their joy.

Transformative Models

Stories are transformative for those outside the religious tradition. Thus, for Christians, the stories from the other major world religions present the challenge to imagine what might follow from taking up and acting on one set of convictions rather than another. The stories make us ponder the difference between the certainties we are born with in our own tradition and the situations we encounter in the other traditions. The stories are so powerful precisely because they communicate across cultures and traditions through archetypal spiritual experiences. Awareness and appropriation trigger a new intensity of conviction for our doctrinal statements and ritual expressions. These then feed into practical action in our life situations. Religious stories are classics because they communicate their message over the widest barriers of time, space, and language. They produce some insight into the human situation that escapes the limits of our individual ideologies. As we recognize the universal patterns in the stories, we discover ourselves in them—part of our hearts, our aspirations, our humanity.

Stories from other religious traditions bring us into a new world of gods, heroes, and saviors. Our lives are touched by the playfulness of Krishna, the zeal of Muhammad, the finesse of Confucius, the wit of Lao, and the peace of Gautama. The stories grant us one insight after another into community harmony, reciprocity with nature, realism in facing death, hope in striving to better the human condition, and a laughing sense of life's absurdity.

When we appropriate the stories, we are forced to deliberate yet again the ironies, paradoxes, and complexities of human nature. We find layer upon layer of meaning that confirms our understanding and points us yet further to new inward horizons. The stories push us to sustain a vision of transcendence and plunge to the depths of spiritual experience. In the face of mystery, we find our struggles broadened and heightened. The figures, allusions, and images in the stories shed light on our actions and motives and make them plain, revealing the deepest hopes, desires, fears, potentialities, and conflicts of our human wills. When this happens, the stories reawaken our bounce and make our dance pulsate to a new rhythm.

When we appropriate the stories, we may go on doing the same things, but we learn to view them differently. Though we may travel the same road, we use a different map. If we stumble onto a story that expresses the life that we are already living, it better equips us to recognize what is happening. If the story is different enough, it might even impel us to change both our view of the world and our behavior, moving us off our own treadmill onto an entirely new path.

The Western Wall of the Temple in Jerusalem is a holy place where people express humility and reverence in the presence of God.

When Christians approach the religions through awareness and appropriation, they become involved in the process of transformation. The story of Moses, for example, makes us aware that the proper attitudes in the presence of the holy are humility and reverence. From David we learn that external success, whether political, social, or economic, does not necessarily mean success in our private lives. In appropriation, we realize that anything is possible if we do not try to go beyond our human limitations, and that we surely fail if we try to do everything alone. We no longer divide the world into heroes and failures, for there is a complex relationship between success and failure.

When we study Muhammad's story we learn that the jihad (holy war) is an internal struggle to establish God's design in the world. Through Husain's story we acknowledge that martyrdom accents the highest degree of self-sacrifice for the sake of religious principles. Appropriating the struggle against evil, we are ready to die for our faith and witness for those who are poor or oppressed.

By studying Krishna's advice to Arjuna we learn that liberation from the world is achieved by abandoning all attachment to it. The story of the elephant-god Ganesha's beheading alerts us that sacrificial death is the beginning of restoration to divine intimacy. When we appropriate the stories, we give our undivided consent to whatever we are doing while remaining open to unexpected possibilities. Rather than living with tragic seriousness, we find spontaneous joy in life, recognizing that everything is gift and grace.

Mencius makes us aware that humaneness is the full commitment to wanting what is best for all, and Chuang Tzu shows the serenity and poise that accompany acting with the flow of nature and its rhythms. Appropriating their stories, we base our human relationships on reciprocity and complementarity and we make the harmonious interplay of opposites a focal point of our lives.

The story of Vessantara's generosity brings new insights into compassion and self-forgetfulness, and Hui-Neng's mirror-wiping story teaches that meditation awakens the latent wisdom that comes through self-forgetfulness. When we appropriate these stories, our generosity goes hand in hand with our gratitude and sense of interdependence. We accept the eternal fullness of each situation and each moment.

Studying the myths of the Maya in Latin America and the Baganda people in Uganda, we gain a refreshing outlook on sacrificial death and rebirth and we become aware of the importance of the present moment. By appropriation, we make sacrifices in our own lives, we accept death as inevitable, and we recognize that each moment of time is fragile in its sweetness.

Conclusion

Most books on world religions approach them through their diversity. Contrasting their concrete forms of expression, they examine the religions from outside, objectively and academically. Other books approach the religions by searching for their mystical core and find a certain unity in religions. Still another approach to religions, complementarity, brings new insights and acquaintance with facets of human religion that may have escaped us. Christians who study productive and resourceful religious expressions of faith in Absolute Reality and of salvation, for example, gain a greater knowledge of the world religions and also discover insights that enhance and clarify their most basic spiritual commitments.

In this book we will concentrate on a fourth approach, the creative way of awareness and appropriation. This method studies the world religions through stories drawn from their sacred writings. This approach explores those aspects of experience and reality that each religion accents more deeply than the others and that encapsulate the essence of that religion. We then examine how we might integrate these aspects into our own life situations and actions and thus bring new insights into our spiritual lives. The approach leads to enriched self-understanding and discernment of the driving forces of our own religion. This, in turn, aids the process of self-transformation into spiritual wholeness.

Discussion Questions

1. Why does the study of world religions have to acknowledge the tragic and painful aspects of human nature and human experience?

2. What is the appeal of having a comfort zone in studying world religions?

3. What are the positive and negative elements in studying religions in their diversity and their unity?

4. Explain the distinction between faith as personal and faith as propositional.

5. Explain the approach by way of complementarity that studies religions as systems of salvation in terms of a problem, a strategy, and a solution.

6. Describe the approach of awareness and appropriation and show how stories from each of the world's major religions can effect transformation of self.

7. Discussion Starter: "If persons are really involved in a religion, they better stay with the software they have got. But a chap like my-

self, who likes to play with the software—well, I can run around, but I probably will never have an experience comparable to that of a saint." (Joseph Campbell)

8. Discussion Starter: "Life is either a daring adventure or nothing. To keep our faces toward change and behave like free spirits in the presence of fate is strength undefeatable." (Helen Keller)

9. Discussion Starter: "No religious tradition has a monopoly on the living waters of salvation; and we should not water down the tenets of any authentic religion in order to reach religious concord." (Raimundo Panikkar)

10. Discussion Starter: "The pedagogy of the oppressed is instructive not only to the oppressed, but to the oppressor as well. The white community has much to learn about itself from the black; males may be instructed about the significance of masculinity from women writers; if Western societies were receptive to Eastern cultures their self-consciousness could not but be enhanced." (Paulo Freire)

At the feet of a spiritual master, a disciple hears stories on the relationship of human nature and the underlying moral order of the universe.

Chapter Two

STORIES IN SACRED WRITINGS

The Sacred Writings

Communities in many religious traditions and cultures have for thousands of years treated particular groups of texts in a strikingly special way, with great consequences. The writings are a body of literature that the religious communities accept as sacred and authoritative. People discover in them illumined teachings that provide a coherent explanation of the mysterious character of the universe. They find ways to live and to understand their lives in the context of Absolute Reality. These diverse sacred writings are often referred to as "scriptures" (this was originally a Western concept specifying the Bible as revered by Jews and Christians). Sometimes they are called "classics" or "traditions," though these terms do not have any religious connotation, nor do they convey a sense of religious authority.

In some fashion, the sacred writings occupy a position of central importance in each of the historical world religions. They act as a repository of material for the spiritual life of believers. They contain dominant images that shape religious consciousness. The underlying dimensions of human existence are all there—trust, wonder, loyalty to a cause greater than self, fascination, healing, fulfillment, peace, anxiety, death. In these texts we find much about the religious adventure that is wonderful and illuminating. All the challenges, possibilities, and joys of a mature spiritual life find their expression in them. Reading and studying them is a refreshing, delightful, and stimulating experience.

Canon

The relationship between the religious communities and their sacred writings is vital and mutual. By connecting people in the present with the community's traditions, the sacred writings define and enhance the community and ensure the continued survival of those traditions. Most of the world's religions have their own particular canon or set of norms that grant official recognition to the writings. The sacred writings serve as a measure against which the truth of certain ideas and the rightness of certain practices can be assessed and valued. This canon can neither judge nor be judged by the canons of other religions.

There are levels of canon. In the Jewish sacred writings, for example, the Torah, Prophets, and Writings have the place of honor, followed by the writings in the Talmud (the legal, ritual, and exegetical commentaries that have developed right down to contemporary times). In Islam, the Qur'an has higher status than the Hadiths (collections of the life and teachings of Muhammad). The Hindu Shruti (writings "heard by the sages") have higher status than the Smriti ("remembered writings"). Sometimes the canon is closed after having developed over hundreds of years, as in both Christianity and Judaism; sometimes it is still open all the way to contemporary times (e.g., the Puranas in the Hindu canon). Sometimes certain schools and movements later add to their collections of definitive classics, as in both the Mahayana Buddhist and Confucian traditions.

Authority

In some religious traditions, the sacred writings are a record of the revelations of Absolute Reality and are therefore directly binding, with unconditional authority (e.g., the Qur'an for Muslims and the Bible for Christian fundamentalists). Without discounting whether the origins of sacred writings may be through direct divine inspiration or conceived in the fertile mind of a great religious leader, their authority still derives primarily from the fact that they are the most pervasive and enduring expressions of spiritual experience. It is this experience that inspires and produces sacred writings and gives them their authority and reliability. Their authority does not derive from the authors, for in most cases we simply do not know who composed the sacred books: Most of the writings are anonymous or pseudonymous.

Forms

The sacred writings of the world's religions contain dozens of different literary forms. There are oracles, prayers, hymns, koans, mantras, and rituals. There are laws, philosophic discourses, aphorisms, oaths, and theologies. The writings are spiced with histories, chronicles, biographies, legends; with poems, proverbs, apocalyptic prophecies, and divination. The most common form in all the sacred writings is story. It is extremely valuable to study these stories. The stories, carefully selected, supply the background and raw experience for the doctrines, rituals, ethics, and other expressions of the religions. It is not possible to fully appreciate the religions through their stories alone, of course, but they are most useful for their power to affect people's lives today.

Ringing the bell outside a shrine, a Chinese monk calls to awareness the teachings of Confucius on becoming a wise and generous public servant.

Master Stories and Core Stories

At the heart of each major religious tradition is a basic experience that gave birth to that religion and continues to be available to its members in succeeding generations. The story of this experience is the religion's master story. By telling this master story, the people not only preserve their different religious traditions but reaffirm the story's value as a pattern for their lives. In Christianity, for example, the master story elaborates Jesus' birth, his ministry, preaching, his death, resurrection, and sending of the Spirit. The master stories in other religious traditions relate the Hebrew exodus and establishment of the covenant, Muhammad's night of power and flight from Mecca, Confucius' life and hard times, the search for enlightenment by Lao Tzu and Gautama, the Buddha. They also include the Hindu story of the defeat of illusion and the Chinese search for harmony with community and nature.

The core stories are another group of stories found alongside the master stories in the sacred writings. These may be stories within the master stories or variations on the themes of the master story told at a much later date. These core stories are often as familiar as the master stories. They continuously re-create the spiritual mood proper to each particular religion and at the same time impart their own distinct character to the manifestations of that religion. Indeed, the vitality of the religions depends on their capacity to put people today in touch with these core stories. The core stories are the heart of the communication system that links the members of each religion together with their roots, beliefs, practices, traditions, and institutions. Through recourse to these core stories the religions resolve their recurrent crises and regenerate themselves in the face of new challenges.

In the following chapters I will develop a few of these core stories for each religion. I will incorporate the essence of the master stories in developing the broad context of each religion, but I will give more emphasis to the core stories, because I feel that they exhibit facets of the religions in a way that is new and fresh.

Stories and Truth

The sacred stories come from and lead to spiritual experience. They are the raw material for religious reflection. Both the master stories and the core stories in the world religions add existential interest to our search for answers to practical and unavoidable questions. Asking who we are and what we must be about is both a path to truth and the task that comes with our very breath. We attempt to order and organize our experiences around stories, shaping them by the images and symbols that our religious heritage makes available.

With the need for order, theology (and religious philosophy) makes its appearance, for experience demands rigorous reflection and critique. Systems begin to grow out of stories. The result is sometimes loss rather than gain, because the stories become removed from our daily lives and decisions; religion then becomes a matter for specialists. Theology and story are both essential approaches to religious truth and both serve a common mystery: One probes with questions; one spins out tales. While theology restrains unbridled imagination, story disparages theology's critical restraint. They rejoice only partially in each other's gifts.

Sacred writings approach truth both through the imagination of stories and through the rational propositions and proofs of theology. Theology and story are two different expressions of experience. One is objective and rational, engaging the intellect; the other is subjective and emotional, engaging the heart. Theology follows the Joe Friday school ("Just the facts, ma'am"); story looks to wit, affection, and humor. The logic of theology is a path to truth, limited yet secure; the imagination of story is another path to truth, often disturbing and challenging. We sometimes disparage imagination in our modern dedication to facts and hard-headed objectivity. We accuse imagination of getting us away from "reality" and tainting our work with subjectivity. Worst of all, we often take imagination as the "frosting" to life rather than as the solid food. Yet imagination is not fancy decoration at all, but the fountainhead of human experience. Imagination rises out of deeply felt experiences of creativity and gives us the powers most central to our human fulfillment. Imagination uncovers what is hidden or disowned, sheds new light on what is already known and, just as important, teaches a way of living with the unknown and understanding its crucial role in our spiritual existence.

The stories in sacred writings not only report or describe reality; they excite our imagination to engage us in and help us redefine it. Stories link us with the achievements of personal maturity. They conduct us across those difficult thresholds of transformation that demand a change in the patterns of our conscious and unconscious lives. Through the stories we develop awareness of our own strengths and weaknesses in a manner that equips us for the arduous tasks with which life confronts us. Stories surprise and challenge us with experiences that expand the sense of what is possible, sometimes eventually transforming us as we discover anew the nature and meaning of life. The stories remind us that we can lift our lives above the customary trails our nature has cut for itself through the ages. We see in them the magic of love and the power of hate, poignant expressions of the joy of success and the tribulation of failure.

Stories in sacred writings express in an imaginative form precisely those convictions about the human person, culture, the world, and Absolute Reality that cannot be adequately expressed in theological or philosophical language. Through their use of imagination, they touch universal chords and invite us to take part in their telling. We ignore imagination only at our own peril: As William Blake expressed it, "Imagination denied, war ruled the nations."

Types of Religious Stories

We are heirs to many different stories and our lives involve partial commitments and limited responses as we act on the basis of one, and then another, of our stories. Our lives are a tangle of stories— stories to which we only aspire, stories that seduce us, stories that others have felt to be reliable indicators of who we are, even though we may never put them into words. Each type of story—historical novels, Shakespearean plays, detective stories, jokes—has its own character, its own aims, and its own limitations. There are as many stories to tell as there are lives lived or imagined. They are "only a story," but because of this, they are dangerous and powerful. Stories are told in the best of times and in the worst of times. Sometimes the stories are told with delight, sometimes with horror; sometimes they have profound import, sometimes little.

The stories in the sacred texts of world religions have always been treated with reverential love and accorded a place of honor. They exert a special force on their believers when they ponder them and reenact many of them in their sacred rites. The stories evoke a powerful spiritual experience, a path to enlightenment, a way of salvation. The stories in the sacred texts are classics. They are valid for every generation, but valid differently for different generations; they are shaped by their times yet bear witness to the present moment.

There are treasures for us to find in stories from other religions, not the least of which is a way of helping us break through the barriers that stand in the way of understanding and appropriating our own stories. Stories from unfamiliar religions tell us things that no one else knows, things that our own stories neither envision nor reflect on. But they also reveal to us that what seems unusual in our own stories, and even in our private dreams, may not in fact be as strange as we fear it to be. Because they are different, the stories provoke and intensify a shock of recognition when we identify the patterns of our own lives from an unanticipated angle.

There are three major types of stories in the sacred texts of the world religions. In one type, narrative history, the stories are about historical figures, but often told in archetypal form. These narratives provide not only knowledge but wisdom. They challenge the readers to share the normative message and activities of the exemplary religious figures. The second type, parable, includes stories by the religious figures that call our comfortable assumptions into question. They bring an unexpected turn to everyday experiences, forcing us to look through the commonplace to a new view of reality. The third type, myth, describes the order of the world and the relationship of gods and humans. Myths embrace stories of gods and humans to illustrate how a community has come to understand and relate to what it holds to be the ultimate meaning of reality. Mythic themes are cosmic and universal, transcending any one religion.

Narrative Histories

Religions contain narratives of the historical experiences of their heroic figures in their sacred writings both to hold on to their history and to disclose the nature of their relationship with the sacred. The Jews, for example, relate that Yahweh spoke through Abraham and Isaac and Jacob and the prophets and gave them their essential identity and mission in a covenant. Christians assert that Jesus performed miracles and that, after he suffered and died, he was raised again from the dead and appeared a number of times to his followers. Muslims affirm that Muhammad was visited regularly by the angel Gabriel who revealed to him the contents of the Qur'an. Buddhists maintain that Gautama, after following various teachers and almost dying from undertaking the path of extreme asceticism, eventually came to enlightenment as to the nature, causes, and solution to the problem of suffering.

We know too little about the great religious figures of the past. Still, the value of the stories of their rich spiritual experiences does not depend on their historical origins and veracity, but lies in what the religious heroes tell us: What they know and do, they know and

Gargoyles on medieval Gothic churches warn those who cross the threshold that they are leaving the profane world and are entering into sacred space.

do for us. Certainly, their stories contain information and insights worth remembering, but, more important, they present us the challenge to emulate their models and share their experiences. To our openness in the face of questions for which explanations are simply not sufficient, their stories pose another question: "It's like this, isn't it?" What then follows is a narrative with characters and plot, rather than philosophical reflections or collections of laws. Their plots mirror and identify our experiences: Through the stories we see what they saw and we view the world as they did. When we tell their stories, we feel their power affecting our lives.

Narrative stories deal with the most jealously guarded attributes of our spiritual lives and our daily experiences, our unpredictable changes of mood and inner elations, our moments of despair and illumination. Their value lies in the world they open up, the pictures of self, others, nature, history, and God that they suggest. They create a world with dangers lurking within, but a world that also holds out new possibilities. The stories fire our imagination and nurture our spirituality. We gain a fuller way to order and unify our lived experience, with all its tensions, surprises, reversals, and triumphs when we make these historical narratives the basis for our aspirations for the future.

In this book we will look at the narrative histories of Moses and David from the Jewish tradition, Paul from the Christian story, Husain from Islam, and Hui-Neng from Buddhism.

Parables

Parables are much more than easy-to-understand pictures instructing us in correct moral behavior. Some parables are short stories, with plot, motion, and characterization. Other parables are aphoristic, with dense, compact, and jarring language. In either case they are stories that use familiar situations or actions to illustrate religious ideas and transcendental truths. They are fresh, unique stories born out of religious experience that disclose insight directly to the imagination. Parables evoke experiences we have never had and instill awareness of realities not even guessed at before. Whether as stories told to their followers by Jesus, Mencius, or Gautama, as the koans ("mental puzzles") of Buddhist masters, or as tales of the Sufi mystics, they require our participation as they tease our minds out of familiar channels and into a different view of the world.

Parables disclose the most profound dramas at the root of human experience. They never lose their power or their freshness, but continue to speak to our elementary human striving, frustration, and—sometimes—unexpected fulfillment. Parables reveal a meaningful order in which both our human perceptions and our human actions are significant. They enlarge our scope of awareness, illustrating a sense of life that includes both inner and social, bodily and visionary, ethical and philosophical dimensions.

We not only learn about reality by paying attention to parables, we are invaded by it. Parable stories arouse our sluggish consciences and dormant awareness, coercing us to see things as they are. They present unexpected turns and twists and have the power to compel our imagination, shock us into making new judgments, and come to new decisions. Through extravagant exaggeration, paradox, or surprising development, they make us think of things in a new way. Parables have a way of lurking below the surface of our minds, demanding a decision or judgment. They lead us into a strange world where everything is familiar yet radically different. They undermine our dominant social realities, teasing us toward new social possibilities. When we submit to the parables we enter their world, make ourselves vulnerable, and admit that we do not know at the outset where they will lead us.

In this book several of the core stories are parables: Christ's prodigal son, Muhammad's seven youths, Chuang Tzu's Cook Ting, and Mencius' Bull Mountain.

Myths

Myths are symbolic expressions of deep spiritual and religious experiences, the privileged narratives that convey perceptions of deep and abiding truths about the human condition.

When used in a religious context, the term "myth" has no pejorative association with lies, fictions, or fables. Myths retain nothing of the sense of falsehood, unreality, or specious fabrication.

In myths we listen to the stories of gods, heroes, and saviors and recall their deeds to make them live again in our minds and hearts. Their lives enrich our lives, their existence ennobles our existence, and their paths illuminate our paths. Religions use myths to illustrate and explain something about their worldview and how they correlate the divine and the human. In their images myths reveal our deepest hopes, desires, fears, potentialities, and conflicts. Myths structure consciousness, encourage attitudes, and suggest behaviors. They bring insight to certain archetypal elements of human experience, call attention to patterns present in reality, and entice us to relate to that reality through those patterns. Myths embody and promote values that are absolutely necessary to creative human functioning.

Though myths are timeless, they become familiar through repetition. They enlarge our consciousness to grasp the common dimensions of human activities and involvements, no matter how widely separated in time, space, or cultures. Myths address our basic, timeless human dilemmas. They are the detector of the long, slow rhythms of human behavior drumming beneath the staccato beats of temporality. Myths picture history not as a series of isolated events, but as a continuum, a pulse that moves beneath our episodic ups and downs.

In this book the core stories include the myths of the Hindu gods Krishna and Ganesha, the Buddhist Vessantara, the heroic twins of the Maya, and Kintu, the ancestor of the Baganda people.

Interpretation of Stories

To enlarge our global knowledge of the world religions through the truths of the stories, we cannot leave them frozen within their texts. We have to engage in the process of interpretation to exercise our creative awareness and appropriation and allow the power of the stories to transform our own spirituality. The stories are but a finger pointing to the moon: If we notice only the finger, we miss the beauty of the moon. Interpretation is a delicate process and we have to keep several factors in mind for it to be effective.

Selection

Interpretation begins with the very process of selecting the texts, a process that is not without its difficulties. No single text is the ultimate story of any religion; on the other hand, not every text points to the essence of the religion. No long text, given in short paraphrase, can communicate all of what it would feel like to live and die within the ambience of the religion. The stories are all culture-bound, otherwise they would not reflect and effectively speak to the people in their culture. They are proportionately limited in effectiveness to those outside the religious tradition because of the cultural differences resulting from variations in geography, time, class, and ways of knowing. On the other hand, the stories we choose have to be archetypal to some degree in order to effect any transformation in our spiritual lives.

Not everyone would choose the same stories from the sacred writings as the best examples of those narratives that have shaped a religion's identity. For example, some people within the Jewish tradition might embrace the story of Adam and Eve, others Abraham's sacrifice of Isaac, and still others the giving of the covenant to Moses. Scholars in religion might choose still different Hebrew narratives. From the Qur'an, some Muslims might select Muhammad's night of transformation, or his flight to Medina. Scholars might select still other episodes. Some might choose Lao Tzu's departure from China and disappearance into Tibet on a water buffalo or Confucius' difficulties as a petty government official for their study of Chinese religions rather than later stories by Chuang Tzu and Mencius.

Perhaps the most exemplary stories of a religious tradition are not even those found in the canonical sacred writings. The Sufi tales of the dervishes, the medieval hagiographies in Christianity, and the Hasidic tales in the Jewish tradition have all had a transformative effect on many persons.

In religions without official sacred writings, we are dependent on the records of missionaries and explorers, of anthropologists and ethnologists. These records routinely contain deficiencies due perhaps to prejudice on the part of the gatherers, to lack of religious sensibility and background, to reluctance of the religious people to reveal their most sacred experiences, or to a kind of overspecialization that obscures the essence of the religion in an abundance of details.

Not even a long, impressive, and varied set of footnotes would totally convince anyone that the stories I have selected from the sacred writings capture the true spirit of each religion. Nor can I prove that any of these stories will have a transforming effect on anyone's spirituality. The proof of the stories is in their telling. In the telling they have the power to touch those dimensions of reality that go beyond the empirical and facilitate our attempts to come into contact with the transcendent. In the telling their different strands interweave the organic fabric of cosmos, the social fabric of ethos, the individual fabric of self-fulfillment, and the deep fabric of eschatology.

Context

No stories can be properly interpreted apart from their original setting and context. Yet these settings and contexts are not static entities, but living movements, sometimes changing even within the sacred writings as they were composed over several centuries. The layers of experience and imagery in the stories sometimes block or reject earlier signals and symbols, making it possible to misunderstand the texts.

The modern context also has to be taken into account: What the stories mean in the present, for example, might not be absolutely identical with what they meant in their original historical context. Sacred stories are meaningful for every generation, but they can be meaningful differently for different generations. These interpretations, then, stand in creative tension. To give just one example, in studying the Qur'an we have to recognize where and how Islamic worldviews are inculcated. Normative attitudes toward religious duties, kinship patterns, transfer of women and property, social governance, and human obedience to the divine will are socially reproduced in the pedagogical and ritual transactions of the mosque, home, and marketplace. It is very difficult to walk the tightrope between the original texts and their meaning in Muslim communities today.

The perspective of the ordinary people of the religious tradition is also very important. The people should be able to recognize

Prohibited from pictorial representation, Muslims use ornate decoration in the mithrab, the niche in each mosque that points in the direction of Mecca.

themselves in the interpretations. They may challenge all the assumptions that scholars have of their culture and insist on an alternative interpretation. Even though we consult all the commentaries of scholars both within and outside the tradition, we ultimately have to come back to the people: The stories are to be lived, not endlessly studied.

We have to recognize honestly that the original context of some of these stories was oral, and that recitation in a ritual environment in a prescribed manner is crucial to their interpretation. While we can never reproduce that setting, we must conscientiously consider all the forms that the people believe to be religious and engage in as part of their religious activity. We have to take into account their prayers, songs, architecture, art, language, and any other essential instruments by which their life acquires meaning and value.

Feminine Dimension

Many scholars go so far as to say that the entire substance and import of the major traditions from the past are so trapped in a patriarchal complex as to be unredeemable. Indeed, the great majority of religious figures in the stories are male and the stories all display to some extent a view of males as dominant and somehow more significant than females. I have deliberately tried to plumb the depths of past discoveries and draw fresh water from the wells of tradition in order to include stories about women where possible and to look at religious figures whose respect for the feminine is exemplary. I know the attempt to find these stories and figures in the sacred writings has been shamefully inadequate.

One main reason for my choice of the two core stories for each religious tradition is that they transcend the stereotypes of masculine and feminine. The spiritual insights of the world's great religious leaders apply as readily to a woman's humanity as to a man's. For too long the ideal self has commonly been understood as hard, independent, detached, autonomous, capable of distancing itself from other people and from its own emotions. Still, responsibility and care for the well-being of others represent qualities at least as desirable as the ones associated with the traditional image of the self. The self gains spiritual strength not by accumulating power but by becoming part of a web of relationships. Our entire conception of the spiritual self has to be revised in the light of what we learn from women's experiences. Their quest for full humanity is a critical and fundamental part of the process of interpretation.

Multiple Interpretations

Various communities of a religious tradition often disagree about the correct interpretation of a story. Theravada Buddhists in Sri Lanka, for example, have totally different explanations from Zen Buddhists in Japan. Indeed, they have different master stories. Again, if we compare interpretations of the master stories and core stories in Christianity among the American mainline Protestant denominations with televangelical ministries we often find different values and meaning proclaimed. Sacred stories are potentially open-ended: This is part of their power. Interpretation is a risky and perilous affair, and the conflict of interpretations is normal and healthy.

Various scholars might also find differences of interpretation. Some approach the stories in depth: They learn the language and take serious account of the interpretations offered by the experts who live within the tradition. Others approach the stories in breadth: They apply insights they have gained from their vast knowledge of the entire gamut of world religions rather than one particular tradition. Because the religious stories are so complex, both approaches are necessary and mutually beneficial.

Even though the stories form part of the sacred record for a particular religious culture, insight into the texts is not limited solely to persons within that tradition. Perhaps outsiders are in an even better position to struggle with the texts than the believers themselves. Insiders sometimes have extra filters—from their own experiences, their codes of interpretation, or other parallels in the tradition—that distort or twist the message into fixed patterns. Familiarity with the texts, language, and cultural inheritance often conditions the insiders not to experience the full richness of the stories. This is particularly true when they simply are not familiar with and have not studied their own sacred writings, instead depending on others for interpretation.

The stories are elaborately condensed products. No matter how many layers we peel off there will still remain much to be explained. We try to uncover as many contributory strands as possible. The moment we abandon an attitude of wonder and awe toward these stories and begin to feel certain and smug about their proper interpretation, we deprive ourselves of their quickening contact, and we forfeit our proper humility and open-mindedness before the unknown. When we classify their interpretation under familiar heads and categories, we prevent the emergence of any new meaning or fresh understanding and we blunt the possibility of new challenges and increased expectations.

The Personal Dimension

When we approach the stories to strengthen our own spiritual lives and clarify our own value systems, we do not have to rely entirely on the interpretations of others. In fact, in the process of making these stories a part of our own individual experience, we must not depend on such interpretations. The stories are so powerful because they contain certain universals of human experience that extend beyond and across cultures. When we study a story from another religious tradition for the first time, we want to find something recognizable in it. But we also need something that is foreign to our experience. Much of the delight in approaching the narratives and trying to find personal meaning in them arises from the tacit comparison that is carried on between our familiar world and what is new, from the recognition of how our familiar world is being altered or subverted by this narrative. Thus there is a paradox in interpreting and appropriating the stories into our own spiritual lives. We want a familiar explanation of what we hear and read, but if we slot the text into already predetermined and controlled categories, we kill the story.

Rather than always beginning with an advanced set of instructions for interpreting what a text means and has meant, it is sometimes more fruitful to initially wrestle with a text from our own frame of reference and only then acquaint ourselves with the larger context.

Conclusion

The sacred writings of the world's religions contain stories that present coherent explanations of the mysterious character of the universe, enhance the community, and make core spiritual experiences available to its members in succeeding generations.

There are three major types of these sacred stories. Narrative histories are stories that provide knowledge and wisdom through the exemplary patterns and normative examples of religious figures. Parables are stories that bring an unexpected turn to everyday experiences and force readers to look through the commonplace to a new view of reality. Myths are stories that illustrate how a community has come to understand and relate to what it holds to be the ultimate meaning of reality.

In making these stories our own, we have to pay attention to the context of the stories we select, to their feminine and personal dimensions, and to their multiple valid interpretations. Then the stories increase our knowledge of the world religions and transform our spiritual lives.

Discussion Questions

1. What is meant by the canon of sacred writings? Why do you think we have to take the canon into consideration when interpreting the stories?

2. What are the differences in approaching sacred writings through stories and imagination rather than through reason and theology?

3. How important is it that narrative histories be factually verifiable?

4. What does it mean to say that parables have the power to shock and transform us?

5. What does it mean to say that myths are timeless and archetypal?

6. Why do we have to take into account the context of stories when we attempt to interpret them?

7. Explain: "Perhaps outsiders are in an even better position to interpret a sacred text than the believers themselves."

8. Discussion Starter: "Stories would not even exist or be heard through if human nature did not look to them avidly for illumination of its homelessness in time and circumstance. It is just because life is a labyrinth that we follow eagerly for clues and traces, the impasses and detours and open-sesames of a myth or tale. The world of our story is our own world in a higher register." (Amos Wilder)

9. Discussion Starter: "If cattle and horses or lions had hands, or could draw with their feet, horses would draw the forms of god like horses." (Xenophanes)

10. Discussion Starter: "It is our inward journey that leads us through time—forward or back, seldom in a straight line, most often spiraling. Each of us moving, changing, with respect to others. As we discover, we remember; remembering, we discover." (Eudora Welty)

For thousands of years Jews have made pilgrimages to the Western wall in Jerusalem to ask Yahweh for forgiveness.

Chapter Three

JUDAISM
Presence and Hope

Setting the Scene

The Western Wall

Jews throughout the world wept with joy when the Israeli army recaptured and liberated the Western Wall of the temple in Jerusalem in the 1967 War. Jews everywhere hold this wall in particular affection as a token of their glorious past and as a reminder of their hope for its restoration and for a promised messianic future. Considered a holy place, the Western Wall is that section of the supporting wall that has remained intact since the Romans destroyed the Second Temple in 70 C.E.

Jews have struggled to be close to this wall for almost 2000 years. It is referred to as the "wailing wall," a term given by non-Jewish travelers who noticed the habit of pious Jews visiting the wall to lament and weep over the destruction of Yahweh's (that is, God's) sanctuary. For many Jews it is the object of a prayerful longing to return to the Holy Land and to Jerusalem, the city that David chose as the capital of Israel, the loftiest of summits to which the hearts of Israel are directed.

King Solomon (tenth century B.C.E.), famous for his wisdom, wealth, and building projects, had erected the first monumental sanctuary on Zion hill in Jerusalem. This temple housed the ark of the covenant, the sacred chest containing the implements of the Mosaic faith, and symbolized the continuing presence of God. The Jews believed that the glorious presence of Yahweh dwelt in its innermost room, the Holy of Holies. Until its destruction, the temple was a focus of the life of the nation. Its connection with the presence of Yahweh maintained Jewish solidarity for centuries. As the "dwelling place" of the Divine Presence, the temple symbolized the entire universe, and services held there were considered to be a source of blessing to all the nations. Devout pilgrims made sacrificial offerings there to express their ongoing relationship of intimacy with God and to restore that intimacy whenever it was disrupted by human failings.

Today, with Israel again politically sovereign, the Jews stick their prayers in the cracks of the remaining wall. They pray for forgiveness and for the numberless Jewish dead of the centuries, for whom persecution and suffering have flowed with their mothers' milk. For the world's seventeen million Jews, the wall is a symbol of their astonishing strength and extraordinary endurance. It signals the Jews' ability to accommodate powerlessness in their politics and in their personal lives. The wall is a symbol of their ability to draw heavily on the dark colors of defeat, despair, and despondency. It signifies their ability to endure in hope and to survive one enemy after another throughout their history. Most of all, the temple wall is a symbol of their election by God and their covenant with God.

Covenant and Election

From the beginning, the Jews (also called Hebrews, that is, "foreigners," and the people of Israel, that is, "those who struggle with God") have been identified by their sacred covenant with God. This covenant was made with God during the Exodus in the thirteenth century B.C.E., when the Jews were liberated from slavery in Egypt. The Exodus is the master story of the Jews, the determining event in their history. The covenant is central and critical in Jewish spiritual life, comprising its moral, political, and social customs. It is the focus of their understanding of both the natural world and human history. Their covenant with God has always been a unique demonstration of God's personal intervention on their behalf. "I bore you on eagles' wings and brought you unto myself," God tells them. "If you listen to my voice and keep my covenant, then you shall be my treasure from among all peoples, for all the earth is mine."

The covenant is an agreement between the Jews and God: The Jews will worship and be faithful to God and follow the divine law; God will preserve the Jews throughout history. This covenant gives Jews their essential identity and mission: They are chosen by God to serve God and other humans. They are chosen not because they are superior or more deserving than others, but because they have been summoned by God to witness to divine love for all creation. By their election the Jews are the servants of God, a light to radiate to all people. They are chosen to reveal God's attributes of justice and love and to make them effective in human lives.

By keeping the covenant—giving God their hearts—they experience the divine presence to a degree greater than that of other peoples. Obedience to the covenant law is not slavery, then, but the way of regular encounter with God. Law in Judaism is not the enemy of mystical experience; it is that experience. God's continual presence implies that they should live their lives with joy and enthusiasm, with wonder and gratitude.

Israel's election has not brought with it any particular reward or security. The Jews have had to survive and endure through centuries of destructive persecution. Their election has been a double-edged sword, for in being called as an example for other nations, they are judged all the more sorely for their transgressions. As their prophet Amos told them, their covenant election means that they have to do more and to suffer more than others. The covenant carries a burden: to be God's chosen people is a merit and a distinction, but it is also the basis for Jewish adversities. The source of their sublimity has also been the source of their tragedy.

Faith and Yahweh

Jewish faith centers on involvement in the historical narration of the unique covenant relationship Jews have with their God. Their faith is expressed in actions that highlight their personal commitment and trust in a God whose divine nature is freely and spontaneously revealed in historical events. Their God, Yahweh ("Being Itself, Source of Life"), is a God who says "I will be—I come in new ways" or "I shall be there as I there shall be." The name "Yahweh" reflects a God who does indeed exist. More than that, this God can be relied upon to be responsive in history, to be present with the people in their suffering. This God declares that radical novelty and surprise are possible in the spiritual lives of the faithful. This God offers new possibilities in living tradition. The Jewish faith is expressed from two perspectives: They feel surprise, wonderment, and openness to what new prospects may arise; at the same time they feel totally claimed by the vision of their ancestors.

Jewish faith in God is summarized in the Shema: "Hear, O Israel, the Lord our God, the Lord is One," words still repeated every morning and evening by practicing Jews. The Shema is a prayer that affirms God as the sole ruler over life. It proclaims the struggle against idolatry, against letting anything take priority over God's sovereignty. Yahweh is the one God of all peoples, a God who responds in mercy to human injustices rather than personifying the awesome powers of nature. This one God Yahweh has no limitations of space, time, knowledge, or power.

Because God's greatness is above all worldly greatness, and because the sacred name is considered too holy for humans to pronounce, Jews have often preferred to use the term Adonai ("Lord") when addressing their God. Relative to this God, all human beings, even the most successful and powerful and polished, are as nothing. Still, God makes demands on humans and has expectations of them. As Redeemer, God forgives and shows mercy when humans repent of their shortcomings and selfishness. As supreme wisdom, God is the unknowable source of the universe, creating through the divine "word" alone, continually preserving and watching over the world, giving life and breath to all.

Paradoxically, while God is "other," far above and beyond the created world, God is Presence itself. The divine presence (Shekinah) fills all the world. God is present through history, individually and in community. Yahweh's sovereign power is immediately present and active within history. God has deepfelt emotions for the people, caring for them at all times with passionate love. All God's actions are prompted by the will to save.

Human Salvation

The Problem: Oppression

Jews are on an eternal quest for an explanation of human suffering. Why is there so much evil and suffering in the world? What sense can be made of it? How can humans make innocent people suffer? How can the rest of the world let it happen? Why has there been such hatred of the Jews? Why have they been so persecuted and misunderstood over the centuries? Why have they faced economic limitations, forced conversions, communal expulsions, and compulsory ghetto life? Why have they been a target for national enmity and class hatred? Jewish history is the story of longing for liberation from such injustices done to the poor and the defenseless. The horrors of the Nazi Holocaust in World War II have only intensified such questions and brought them to the consciousness of the Jewish people in ways previously unimaginable.

For whatever reasons—inherited prejudice, religious intolerance and narrowmindedness, common commercial rivalry, cruel sport—the Jews have endured political and racist isolation throughout their history. A pessimistic and serious note vibrates as a dark undertone in their experiences, which are paradoxical because they suffer as God's chosen people. "The days of our years are three score years and ten, or even, by reason of strength, four score years; yet our pride is but labor or sorrow." This is the prayer they have echoed through the centuries to show their tears and express their affliction and oppression.

Judaism teaches that, within limits, humans are creators like God. Created "in the image and likeness of God," all humans are God's representatives in creation, commissioned to sanctify earthly life and not to fall into idolatry, that is, not to let anything take priority over God's sovereignty. Still, they sometimes forget their limitations as humans and consequently risk the danger of self-destruction. Too often, forgetting that they too are part of nature, they use nature for their own ends, leading to chaos. Evil, then, is the squandering of life's potential by using it for selfish ends. It is the sadness of paths not taken, of relations neglected or refused, of opportunities dissipated out of selfishness. Life is a continuing struggle to act in the image of God, to turn the evil inclinations to neglect human potential around so as to live in a positive, life-affirming way.

The Strategy: Obedience to the Torah

What do the Jews believe they can do to overcome evil? God has revealed the Torah (the Law) as the total design for the good life. Jews have a role in their salvation, in their constant and passionate protest against idolatry in any form. Their role is to serve God the creator and fulfill the divine will in the world. Life is to be lived here and now, under God—a life guided by the Torah and fulfilled in the covenant community. Jews achieve their calling as the chosen people through fidelity to the covenant. They are thus not autonomous individuals pursuing their own selfish ends, but part of the human community, seeking the welfare of the whole.

The Jews have a sense of the concrete and practical character of the way to salvation. Their prophet Micah stated it simply: "What does the Lord require of you but to do justice, and to love kindness, and to walk humbly with your God?" They face the world with the will to change it and with the commandment to realize the good in it. The divine will is the law of the Jewish people, and the rules of practice of this law are Halakah. Halakah are prescriptions for conduct for all human activity, not just in business ethics, ritual activities, and sexual relationships. The original 613 laws of the Torah were ethical and ritual injunctions for the life of the people, aimed at ensuring that the Jews lived together in harmony, and seeing that justice and social responsibility were carried out at the community level. Though most of the precepts in the original Torah are no longer operative, the purpose of the Torah remains the same for all time: to promote compassion, loving kindness, and peace in the world. In this way Jews can help overcome evil.

The Solution: Messianic Age

The Jews believe that salvation is possible here and now. No matter what it is called—atonement with God, the restoration of fellowship between God and humans, the move from bondage to freedom, or the overcoming of suffering—salvation can be achieved in this world. True hope for this salvation centers on Yahweh who is present in the midst of the people wherever they find themselves. In every fresh here and every new now, the power can shift, the nations can tremble, the peasant women can dance, and a new world can begin again.

During their formative period in the first century C.E., the rabbis ("master teachers") taught that one day—perhaps today—God would send a deliverer, a Messiah, to restore the people to their land, defeat their enemies, and reestablish their throne. The Messiah would rebuild the temple and reconstitute its cult, institute a world order of justice and compassion, and usher in a time when all the promises of the covenant would be fulfilled. Redemption would follow disaster, and hope would follow despair. Indeed, if everybody in the world would keep the Torah fully for one day, the Messiah would come to rectify evil on earth and initiate an era of joy.

Today some Jews interpret this hope of a Messianic age literally, others figuratively. Some, retaining the idea of a chosen people in a promised land under a divinely sanctioned king, appeal to dreams of glory and expect divinely appointed leadership. For them, the world is a battleground between the forces of good and evil, and they await the day when God will destroy the power of Satan and master the evil that abounds. Others look not for an individual who will renew the world by establishing God's rule forever and everywhere, but for a new era of Jewish political prestige throughout the world. For them, there are messianic overtones in building up the nation of Israel. Land is their central agenda, and the astonishing emergence of the state of Israel gives some meaning to their suffering.

In any case, salvation can be achieved in this life. An oft-repeated saying in Judaism is that the paradise humans imagine in some other world ought to be set on fire, and the hell of their devising ought to be extinguished. The medieval philosopher Maimonides (1135-1204) dismisses as antiquated child's play all the fantasies and sensuous conceptions of a world beyond. The future is to be won here: The world to come is God's kingdom on earth, where God and humans are present to each other.

The Sacred Writings

The Hebrew Scriptures are an autobiography of faith. They possess unique authority, growing out of claims of revelation from and inspiration by God. They are reflections on Jewish history, a very difficult history, with its brief moment of glory under King David, and its long years of defeats and humiliations. When they assembled much of their Scriptures during the Babylonian captivity (sixth century B.C.E.), Jews gradually came to see their history as a history of salvation in and through disaster and tribulation. They began to see their story in terms of liberation from their enemies and oppressors. Twenty-four separate writings, the Tanak (the acronym commonly used by Jews to denote the Hebrew Bible) displays a wide diversity in approaches and literary forms. These forms are historical, legal, and ritualistic; they are prophetic, poetic, and devotional. They include speeches, songs, genealogies, sagas, proverbs, satires, intellectual dialogues, and, especially, narratives.

The Torah
The first major division of the Hebrew Scriptures includes the five

books of the Law (the *Torah*). These books contain the Jewish stories of creation and the patriarchal ancestors (Abraham, Isaac, Jacob, and Joseph). They detail the liberation of the Jewish people from slavery in Egypt, their journey through the desert, and the dramatic effect of the covenant given to Moses by Yahweh on Mount Sinai. A record of ancient oral and written traditions, the Torah was woven together by different editors over the centuries. The Torah records God's commands (rather than proposals or suggestions) for ways to achieve holiness. The commandments are the divinely sanctioned means for experiencing God's presence. The story of Moses and the Exodus in the Torah will form the basis of our first story.

The Prophets

The Books of the *Prophets*, the second major division of the Hebrew Scriptures, begin by describing the Golden Age in the tenth century B.C.E. during the reigns of Kings David and Solomon, a time of vast political and economic power, of unparalleled wealth, fame, and military and diplomatic prowess. The prophets, the embodied voices of conscience, soon appear to condemn the corrupt ways of the Jews and to remind them of the true nature of their religion and destiny. The prophets proclaim again that the Jewish covenant of intimacy with God requires them to practice social justice and compassion: Their moral activity mirrors the sanctifying activity of God's presence in the world.

The message of the prophets is clear: God is a God who suffers when people transgress the covenant and rejoices when they achieve holiness. The prophets point out evils in society and call for moral reform. Amos, Hosea, Isaiah, Jeremiah, and others constantly attack the false securities of the Jewish people, especially their attempts to justify their practice of performing religious rituals to other gods. The prophets mount a devastating attack even on worship of Yahweh when it is invoked as an alibi for the worshipers' indifference to the cry of the oppressed. God's burning desire is to "let justice surge like water, and goodness like an unfailing stream."

The Jewish people are not concerned about the presence of God, however, and do not pay attention to the prophets. The Jewish kingdom comes to its inevitable end in the sixth century B.C.E. when the empire of Babylon overthrows David's royal line and destroys the temple of Solomon. The Babylonians demolish the city walls, loot and burn surrounding villages, and carry off most of the Jewish population to Babylon. The prophets Ezekiel and Second Isaiah buoy the survivors who must live as exiles in a strange land far from Jerusalem. Something new has to be created for this drastic crisis in the history of the Jews, a Jewish community that will be faithful to the covenant under these difficult circumstances. The Jews long for a return to their homeland. They look forward to a new covenant and express their hopes for a Messiah who will bring renewed national autonomy.

The Writings

Returning from exile after fifty years, the Jews rebuild the temple and develop a nationalistic spirit. They increasingly long for a kingly Messiah who will come—perhaps amid cataclysms and cosmic miracles, or perhaps in real political events—similar to their deliverance from captivity. Hopes for this future king focus on a warrior who will defeat Yahweh's enemies in battle and help set up Yahweh's kingdom. These hopes are dashed, however, when the Romans again destroy the temple in 70 C.E. The final group of Hebrew Scriptures, the *Writings*, date from the centuries after the return from exile. The Writings are very diverse in nature, containing philosophy, maxims, psalms, apocalyptic dreams, and much more. Alongside their central message that real wisdom is found in doing God's will, they challenge the traditional Jewish idea of retribution for evil-doing. The jewel of the Wisdom writings is the Book of Job. For many Jews it forms a fundamental part of their master story.

Book of Job. Retribution, the idea that people suffer misfortunes because they have done something wrong, is criticized in the Book of Job. This superb literary masterpiece attacks the prophets' traditional teaching that people will prosper when they keep God's commandments and suffer punishment when they sin. The attack is told through the story of Job, an honorable man who suffers unjustly when his home, family, and possessions are all destroyed. When Job protests his innocent suffering to his friends, they seem unanimously bent on his destruction. "The world is well and fully governed," they exclaim. "If Job suffers, then it is because he is guilty of doing something wrong." Job journeys into the depths of despair and blasphemes God. He wants to take God to court in order to prove his innocence.

At long last, God answers Job from a whirlwind, affirming that the world is well ordered and maintained. God acknowledges the existence of chaotic power in the world, and does not disclaim responsibility for it. Job learns that divine powers are indeed unlimited and that God is never absent from the world. Still, he gets no explanation for his suffering. God simply asserts that there is meaning to the world, and even to Job's suffering, but it is beyond human understanding.

Unlike Job's friends, Yahweh does not ascribe the cause of Job's suffering to his guilt for doing something wrong. Instead, innocent suffering is left enshrouded in divine mystery. When Job experiences the presence of God, he declares himself at peace. He prefers an unjust God who is present in creation to a God who remains apart from creation. The resolution of the story is a subtle acknowledgment of God's splendid rule without crushing Job. Yahweh's integrity is preserved by Job's confession; Job's integrity is vindicated by Yahweh's face-to-face encounter with him.

Talmud

Historically, the Hebrew Scriptures end in the second century B.C.E. and the rabbis close the canon near the end of the first century C.E. The rabbis of the Pharisees, who specialize in instructing what the Torah demands of the people, continue the religion of Judaism in Palestine and beyond. They structure the Jewish religion much as we know it today, teaching that the presence of God is everywhere, in the home and in the heart, and not just in the now destroyed temple. The rabbis put together the *Talmud,* a vast collection of Jewish laws and precise teachings that are flexible enough to be applicable to new times and provide a complete structure for Jewish lives.

A classical text, the Talmud is divided into six "orders" of law—agriculture, festivals, marriage and sexual precepts, legal damages, sacrifices, and ritual purity and impurity. About a third of the texts are law; the rest are a vigorous mingling of myth, theology, memory, poetry, and superstition. Among other things, the Talmud is a great source of wit, with jokes and stories about the rabbis that frequently touch on issues present both in modern intellectual life and Jewish social existence. Certainty is mocked on every page—the Talmud preserves rejected legal opinions, minority dissents, and discredited views. It should be studied, the Jews say, because of its magnificent open-endedness: It is an avenue of access not to the normative, but to the eternal.

The First Story: Moses and Yahweh's Presence

The story of Moses is part of the Exodus narrative. The descendants of Abraham, Isaac, and Jacob are suffering in slavery in Egypt. When they cry out in protest over their oppression, God hears and answers them, pledging to liberate them and bring them to their own land through Moses.

Moses experienced his greatest glory when Yahweh gave him the Law and established the covenant with the Jews at Mount Sinai.

Moses is living in the desert, having fled prosecution as a murderer. His curiosity is aroused one day when he sees a bush that is burning but not consumed in flames. He wants to investigate this fascinating phenomenon more closely, but a voice tells him that the ground he is standing on is holy and that he should not trespass unless he shows respect by removing his shoes. Moses learns that the voice talking to him is God's. Moses is told that he is being given a mission to liberate the Jewish people from their slavery.

"Who am I?" asks Moses with humble fear. He raises a string of objections, refusing to surrender to an unknown deity. When Moses demands "What is your name?" God responds "I am Yahweh"—the source of life who is always present. When Moses shifts his own doubts onto the people, God gives him a magical wand. When he still protests, claiming that he is a stutterer, God tells him his eloquent brother will do the speaking. Three times God invites Moses to accept leadership responsibility, and three times Moses attempts to refuse the call to action.

At last Moses recognizes a power greater than himself, gives up his easy life, and heeds the call. He returns to Egypt and protests the slavery of the Jews to the pharaoh, the Egyptian ruler. The people are finally released, after divine intervention in a series of plagues, but are pursued in their flight by the Egyptians. Moses, raising his rod over the Red Sea (the "Sea of Reeds"), parts the waters and enables the people to go through on dry land. After all the people have passed through, the waters close again and the pharaoh and his forces are drowned. This is a great moment for Moses as leader: He enjoys complete harmony with his people as he leads them on the march to freedom. Moses is at his peak in the exultation of victory.

The passage to the promised land goes through the wilderness. In their years of wandering in the wilderness, they vacillate (by constructing false images), murmur (for better food and conditions), and have doubts ("Are we rushing into the desert only to die?"). It is in this wilderness, though, that they learn the new style of life in code and covenant that will mark them as God's people. Conflicts and crises slowly educate them. Moses continues his majestic leadership, even as the people express a desire to return to Egypt when they realize the many sacrifices they have to make. On their journey, they come to the very mountain where Yahweh was first present to Moses. While Moses goes up the mountain to experience God's presence again, the people worship a golden calf.

Atop the mountain, Yahweh gives the Jews the Law through Moses and establishes the covenant with them. As Moses descends the mountain with the tablets of the Law, his face shines with divine radiance because he has been in the presence of God. The people are afraid to come near or look at him directly. He has to keep putting on a veil when he talks to the people, leaving it on until he goes to speak to God again. As the chosen people continue their journey through the wilderness, Moses stops at a crevice in a rock and prays to see the glory of God: "Let me see who you are." Yahweh does not grant Moses his wish, since "no human can see God and survive."

At the very summit of his spiritual achievements, Moses experiences cruel failure.

The chosen people finally arrive at the edge of Canaan, the promised land. Here, where milk and honey flow, the people will be able to produce the food they need, work for themselves, and have their dignity respected. In another cruel tragedy, however, Moses does not share the joy of entering the promised land with the people. His efforts have been directed toward bringing his people into this promised land, and Canaan has been the summit of his actions and desires. Yet, he comes up against an impassable threshold.

Poor Moses: After forty years in the dry desert, he overlooks the beautiful land of promise from the opposite side of the Jordan and is told by God: "Feast your eyes upon it, but you shall not cross over." Moses is barred from the promised land for his lack of faith. Moses is punished, God tells him, "because you did not believe that I could assert my holiness before the Israelites' eyes." He looks at Canaan from Mount Nebo, but then he has to die—not through old age or with failing abilities, but with his powers at full strength. At the height of his glory with the people, Moses does not attain his chief goal, but instead experiences heartless suffering.

The Story Magnified

Sublimity and Tragedy

The divine presence radiating from Moses' face affirms his special prestige as he descends from Mount Sinai. As God's missionary, acting on behalf of all the people, Moses has the right to dwell in the presence of the Lord. He has an elevated position among the people, and God speaks to him as persons speak to their friends. Yet Moses' status is limited, for he is not allowed to see God's face. Moses is not satisfied with promises that God's presence will go with him among the people: He desires the attainment of absolute knowledge of God. Moses is a mortal like any other, however, and no mortal can see God's face. Though Moses is chosen for a special mission by God, he still suffers tragedy.

The story of Moses is the story of the Jews. He is accorded divine revelations from the start of his mission. He displays supernatural powers with his staff and even draws water from a rock. The glorious national leader on the march to freedom, he takes the Israelites across the Red Sea and delivers them the law on Mount Sinai. Yet when the time comes to enter the Promised Land, Moses again suffers cruel disappointment. The powerful leader is struck down once more. What Yahweh makes explicit to Moses ("It is terrible what I am about to do with you") is a promise that resounds through later Jewish history and continues today.

Suffering

The very heart of Jewish existence is the interplay of the tragic and sublime, of sorrow and hope. Jews have experienced both powerful blessing and distressful suffering throughout their history—"It'll get worse, it'll get better." Even at their wedding celebrations they shatter a glass on the floor, a remembrance of sorrow in the midst of joy. Winning and losing are mixed together. Suffering, it seems, comes to humans independently of their wills; they have to shape it into a part of their lives. Suffering is a test of human power to overcome afflictions. As the rabbis taught, "The best which God gives to Israel, God gives through suffering." Again, "The glory of God draws near to those who are afflicted." Suffering is a "chastisement of love."

We learn in the prophetic book of Second Isaiah that the true meaning of Jewish life is suffering for the sake of others. The Jewish people are "servants of the lord," and their sufferings are more effective than sacrifice for reconciling the world and God. They have suffered for the sake of their individuality from the very beginning. For Jews, the misery of the present and the wealth of the expected future are reconciled as they see and know themselves in the picture of the servant of the Lord. Religion is not a faith in redemption from the world and its demands. It is rather—and this is the realism of Judaism—trust in the world or, to be more precise, the assurance of reconciliation. Reconciliation is the liberating assurance that even now—during human life on earth, while they are coping with what is given and assigned—the faithful are related to God who is present with them. For them, this is the meaning of life.

Presence

The God revealed to Moses is the nameless God of history, the God who is always present. Though wholly beyond human grasp, God is present in an immediate relationship with humans. God is never unrelated to humans; even those who are farthest away from God cannot cut themselves off from the mutual relationship, for God's image and whole existence are embedded in human nature. However faint the divine mark may become, it can never be entirely wiped out.

The essence of the covenant is to realize this mark of divine presence: It brings wholeness to human life. Humans cannot fulfill the covenant obligation of partnership with God with anything less than the whole of life. There is no true human share of holiness without the hallowing of the everyday. Truly religious individuals strive to make present the principles that the nameless, but present, God has come to represent through time: love, truth, and justice.

The Second Story: David and Hope

In the Second Book of Samuel the story of David's affair with Bathsheba and his inability to deal with his rebellious son Absalom are superb examples of the storyteller's art. Public responsibility and power interface with personal temptation and self-deception. In public life David is exalted and all-powerful, the creator of new social, governmental, and religious institutions that help Israel achieve its hopes of a viable political existence. Champion warrior and slayer of Goliath, David is celebrated by the women of Israel who dance in the streets singing his praises. Michal and Jonathan, the daughter and son of King Saul, both love David so much that they help him escape Saul's attempts to kill him. The prophet Nathan finds in him the embodiment of Israel's hopes: Yahweh will build a dynasty for David that will last forever.

His private life is tragic and powerless, though, permeated with manifest imperfections in his dealings with women and with his children. David is the victim of his personal desires and is vulnerable to temptations, passion, and self-deception. He is unable to suppress his personal desires for another man's wife and he is powerless to deal with his manipulative and treacherous son. His intense emotional attachments paralyze him to his public responsibilities.

David seduces Bathsheba, the wife of Uriah, one of his mercenary soldiers out on military campaign. When he later finds out that she is pregnant, David tries to conceal his misadventure by quickly having Uriah furloughed. Uriah refuses to sleep with his wife since his fellow soldiers have to sleep in the battlefields. In desperate fury, David has Uriah stationed at the most vulnerable spot in the front lines where he is quickly slain. David is now free to take Bathsheba for himself.

Nathan, hearing of this intrigue, confronts David with a rather innocent-sounding parable—a story within our story. In a small town, Nathan relates, there are two men, one rich, the other poor. The rich man has flocks and herds in great abundance; the poor man can afford only a single lamb. The poor man lets his lamb eat his bread, drink from his cup, and sleep on his breast. It is like a child to him. When a traveler comes to stay, the rich man refuses to take one of his own herd to provide food for him. Instead he prepares the poor man's lamb for his guest. David, who has been forming opinions and making judgments as he hears the story, is absolutely outraged at the rich man's conduct. "As Yahweh lives," he says to Nathan, "the man who did this deserves to die!" At this point Nathan announces to David, "You are the man."

David created new social, governmental, and religious institutions to help Israel achieve a viable political existence.

This is David's unwitting self-judgment. David has been ridiculing God, for he knows that what he is doing with Bathsheba is offensive to God. And now he is sentenced by Nathan who declares that the sword will never depart from David's house and that evil will be raised up against him out of his own house. To this divine judgment, David responds: "I have sinned against Yahweh." Nobody is immune to God's moral governance, not even a powerful king. David's repentance permits the following settlement: He and

Bathsheba will suffer by losing their child. In turn adulteress, pregnant by her lover, widow, and now bereaved mother, Bathsheba comes to live with David. The Jewish hope for the continuation of the Davidic dynasty comes through the birth of other sons, including Solomon and Absalom. Absalom, though, will not sustain those hopes and will break David's heart.

David's flaws are mirrored in Absalom: He is heir to David's violence, murder, and rebellion. Absalom takes revenge on one of his half-brothers, Amnon, for raping his half-sister Tamar, killing him after getting him drunk at a sheepshearing festival. Because David wants to punish Absalom, he exiles his crown prince. Yet David quickly jeopardizes his decision by permitting Absalom, whom he loves dearly, to return to Jerusalem after three years, if he will live apart for two years. This is a disastrous mistake. During these two years Absalom brashly attempts to seize the crown. He bribes the people who come to David for lawsuit judgments by insinuating himself in David's place and answering their pleas. Gaining the support of disaffected subjects, Absalom takes power away from David and gathers a coterie of supporters who acclaim him king. In full rebellion, the manipulative and treacherous son launches a political uprising against his father.

Absalom's revolt further erodes David's power and forces him to abandon Jerusalem. David makes another mistake: He gives orders not to harm the subversive Absalom, even though his atrocious offense has led the country into civil war. Instead of punishing Absalom or preventing him from increasing his authority, David is paralyzed from acting. A showdown is inevitable, and Absalom dies a tragic death after he is hung up in the branches of a tree by his long hair. David is so overcome with grief that he laments: "O my son Absalom, O my son, my son Absalom. I wish I had died instead of you." David is deeply moved, crying with intense parental love and caring more about the rebel leader than about the loyal troops who saved his kingdom for him at the risk of their lives. David's neglect of his royal obligations blinds him to the destructiveness of his child and brings into jeopardy the Jewish hopes for an everlasting dynasty.

The Story Magnified

Fascination

What makes David so endlessly appealing for the Jews is that he is so human. David excels as leader of his troops and dispenser of justice. He is without peer in dealing with members of his government and with potential enemies. He is in favor with God and all humans. In his outrage with the rich man's conduct in stealing the poor man's lamb, David epitomizes the depth of human feeling. In his deep grief at Absalom's death, David embodies the nature of parental love. His qualities of amazing human tenderness and heartfelt surrender to God form a powerful alliance that the Jewish tradition prizes.

Yet David is powerless when his personal desires and his public obligations come into conflict. Though David is the anointed one, chosen by God to lead the people, he cannot control the tragic suffering in his personal life. Powerful ruler and manipulator of people, he still succumbs to the human weakness of falling for another man's wife and is caught in an impossible struggle with his headstrong son. The deep and unresolvable tension in his life mirrors Jewish life through the centuries. Though they are the people chosen from all the nations, their story has been one of constant persecution and oppression. Yet the Jews find great hope in David, for there is a certain freedom about him. David is a person who emerges, evolves, even undergoes total transformation in the crucible of life. He is the constantly changing product of what he was, what he does, and what he is called to do.

The Ideal David

The Hebrew Scriptures after the Babylonian exile change many of the details in retelling the story of David. In the Books of Chronicles, they reshape the stories, leaving out David's suffering and disappointments. Because David exerts an enormous influence on the future hopes of the Jewish people, the later stories portray a David filled with hope. This permits a community of faith to be sustained in an alien, if not hostile, environment. To counter their powerlessness and hopelessness and loss of identity during the Babylonian exile, they present a David who is shaped by the community both for its religious and its dynastic purposes. In the context of a rebuilt temple, they characterize David as a man who praises Yahweh: He is a pious man performing rituals, his life shaped and enhanced by explicit religious commitment. They present David's love for God reaching great peaks because he is so deeply grateful for his election.

After the Babylonian exile the Jews also look back to the writings of their prophets for their ideal David. In the Book of Isaiah, they find their hope for a messiah expressed as David returning, not in person, but in the restoration of his fallen dynasty and kingdom through a king who will exhibit the traits of the ideal king, which David was thought to have been. The ideal king will be the agent of Yahweh's victories and will inaugurate a universal kingdom of justice and righteousness. He will have the superhuman qualities of wonderful counselor, divine hero, father forever, and prince of peace. He will be a personality of flesh and blood, filled with the spirit of the Lord, the spirit of wisdom and understanding, of counsel and might, of knowledge and the fear of the Lord. This David is not the one whose raw power brought historical scars, but the ideal David who will act under God's power to restore well-being to the Jewish people and bring to life a new covenant written in their hearts.

Hope

The Jews recast David's story of personal suffering to mirror their own hopes in rebuilding the future. They realized after the Babylonian exile that just as God had been faithful to the covenant in punishing the Jews for their sins, so God will respond to their regeneration. This has been a vital part of the Jewish story through the centuries. Though the world is imperfect, it is rich with unfulfilled possibilities. Chastened by their suffering and humbled by God's might, Jews have the power to make their own future, to make a world of peace and justice. They are capable of self-regeneration. Though the time has not come yet to "turn swords into plowshares," the Jews hasten that time whenever they treat fellow humans properly, whenever they enlarge human awareness of the divine presence. When they act compassionately, they are worthy of God's compassion. Then they are that remnant from which God will build a new Israel and the chosen people that God will install in a new Zion under a new David, as the prophet Isaiah has foretold.

The Stories Exemplified

Other Stories

Of the many later stories in Judaism, those of Israel ben Eliezer (1700-1760), the Baal Shem Tov ("Master of the Divine Name"), are perhaps the best known. Called "the Besht," he was a tzaddik, that is, a holy person who carried on the leadership of the Hasidic Jews ("pious ones"). The Hasidic Jews were a revivalist movement that formed close communities among many Jewish groups in Eastern Europe. They were particularly concerned with emphasizing the power of spiritual purification and the preservation of "tradition." The Besht was revered for his intimacy with God, known for his ability to pray passionately, and admired for his loving and joyful compassion. He was acknowledged for the miracles he performed and his humble self-negation, but especially for his gifts as a story-teller. The Besht was not a scholar, and felt most at ease talking to animals and telling stories to children, revealing his message of hope through tales and parables.

In his stories the Besht teaches that individuals can change the world around them and lift their own souls to the presence of God. Rejecting intellectualism and talmudic legalism, his stories emphasize that religious feeling and piety are more important than scholarship. Each individual, no matter how poor or ignorant, can commune with God by self-abandonment. For the Besht, God's grace consists precisely in this: God wants to come to the world through humans. The mystery of human existence, the superhuman prospect for humans, is that God wants to be won by humans. Over the centuries, the Besht's stories have found a welcome audience among the Jewish people who long to be independent and secure. They especially helped the Hasidic Jews live with and eventually turn aside the spate of laws that were designed to make them suffer by denying them the right to lease land, to keep taverns, to settle in rural areas, or to move out beyond the Pale of Settlement.

Human Witnesses

Abraham Heschel. One modern representative of the living out of the Jewish story is Abraham Heschel (1907-1972). He exhibited his intense and personal involvement in religious issues in his anti-war protest marches and his rejection of racism. His books on social justice are grounded in a profound learning, but his style is very close to poetry. He writes that religion has declined not because it has been discredited, but because it has become irrelevant, dull, and oppressive. The message of religion becomes meaningless when faith is completely replaced by creed, worship by discipline, and love by habit. Religion becomes worthless when it speaks only in the name of authority rather than with the voice of compassion. It is empty when faith becomes an heirloom rather than a living fountain.

For Heschel, God is of no importance unless God is of supreme importance. We have different ways of reaching an awareness of the presence of God, he tells us. First, we can align ourselves with God through wonder, as happened to Moses looking at the burning bush. Wonder is radical amazement through which we can become aware of the God who is within and also beyond all finite existence. Second, we can reach awareness of God by delving into the recesses of our own being, realizing that our selves are part of something greater and more comprehensive than our individual existence. Finally, we can experience God by responding to the divine challenge to exercise human freedom to become all that we can be. Perhaps Heschel's most important theme is that God needs humans and that our deepest fulfillment comes through participating in the divine concern.

Etty Hillesum. One person whose Jewish faith blossomed in the crucible of suffering was Etty Hillesum (1914-1943), a young woman from Holland who died in the concentration camp at Auschwitz. Working by procuring medicines for the prison camp, she did not want to escape the fate of the Jewish people. She believed she could do justice to life only if she used her strength to bring light into the life of others. Her diaries, written just months prior to her death, argue that Jewish suffering should give birth to a world of mutual dignity and solidarity so that no group of people should ever suffer again. Hillesum believes that the beauty of creation and the goodness of life exist side by side with overwhelming suffering and demonic brutality. She writes: "If you do not clear a decent shelter for your sorrow, and instead reserve most of the space inside you for hatred and thoughts of revenge—from which new sorrows will be born for others—then sorrow will never cease in this world and will multiply. And if you have given sorrow the space its gentle origins demand, then you may truly say: Life is beautiful and so rich. So beautiful and so rich it makes you want to believe in God."

Hillesum believes that solidarity within suffering can open the possibility of hope for a new age. Everything in her screams out in protest against the many sorrows and sad circumstances she knows and shares with the others in the prison camp. Yet she does not cling to these sorrows: They pass through her, like life itself, as a broad, eternal stream. As a result she preserves her strength and her familiarity with God. "There is only one way of preparing the new age: by living it even now in our hearts." The witness of her life is an uninterrupted dialogue with God. Her commitment, for which she gave her life, is faithfulness to the presence of God. She feels it is

clear that God is powerless to help the Jewish people, and they have
to help God to help them, by their commitment to their faith and by
their compassion tried through fire. In the concentration camp she
embodies the messianic spark through which a new Jewish life
might emerge.

Communities

Jews today still retain the notion of a "Jewish community" but without as much emphasis on the notion of the covenant or the presence
of God as in the past. There are three major religious groups in
America today: Reform, Orthodox, and Conservative. Though the
distinctions between them have blurred since World War II, Jews
are united only when there is a threat to Judaism, to fellow Jews, or
recently, to the State of Israel. Many American Jews do not attend
the synagogue (the gathering place for prayer and for study of the
Torah) or observe dietary laws, but they do want their children to
have some kind of Jewish education.

Reform. For Reform Jews the major idea is acculturation, the aban-
donment of all pretense of a separate nationality of Jews. There is no
need to be separate, for the covenant obligations of justice and mercy are really universal. Adapting itself to modern civilization, the
Reform movement teaches liberal interpretation of the Torah and
rejects much of the Talmud. Their tendency is to glorify progress
and abandon the past. In contrast to the other two movements, Reform Jews consider the rabbi as a guide rather than the final authority. In worship, they greatly reduce the prominence of the Hebrew
language and allow women to do what men do. They reject out-
moded forms of dress and regard dietary laws as obsolete.

Orthodox. Orthodox Jews still retain a life centered on the synagogue and traditional patterns of worship. Their hope is in fully following the Torah and Talmud, and in keeping the minute details of
dietary laws. They reject contemporary learning and scholarship.
Visibly projecting their hostility to modernity, the Hasidic groups of
Orthodox Jews live in Yiddish-speaking enclaves and retain Eastern
European habits of dress and personal manner. Because Orthodox
Jews see themselves as the guardians of the authentic tradition, they
do not find it easy to recognize the other forms of Judaism as legitimate, thus serving as a significantly divisive influence.

Conservative. The majority of Jews are Conservative, falling somewhere between Orthodox and Reform. They stress the study of Torah and Talmud and the holy character of Yiddish language. Though they recognize dietary laws, they do not keep kosher homes because they do not see the kosher laws (which were based on considerations of safe and healthy diet and on the avoidance of ancient idolatrous practices) as relevant today.

Some Conservative Jews are Reconstructionists, a group that stresses Jewish self-identification, more for the sake of memory of their parents than out of religious conviction. Their founder, Mordecai Kaplan (1881-1983), wanted to reconstruct Jewish folk life and other cultural forms and to make the Jewish community authoritative with regard to Jewish practice. For Jewish life to be meaningful, it has to reflect a democratic commitment to modernity. Group conformity in practical things, rather than conformity of belief to the laws of the covenant, is basic. They believe that only in the land of Israel can Judaism as a civilization be realized.

Twentieth Century

As the elected people of God, Jews experience the presence of God and hope for a messianic kingdom, yet their history has been replete with religious persecution and relentless discrimination. The domination by foreign conquerors that they experienced in slavery in Egypt and in the exile in Babylon was continued at Masada (the palace fortress near the Dead Sea where more than 900 Jews took their own lives rather than surrender to the Romans). In the Middle Ages, the Jews in Jerusalem were destroyed by Christian crusaders. The Jews were expelled from Spain; in Portugal, they were scourged and forcibly baptized; in Italy and Germany they were forced to live a ghetto life where they were isolated from outside influences and made to wear yellow badges and pointed hats. In the twentieth century, the perennial Jewish paradox of suffering in spite of (and because of) being God's chosen people has come to the fore as never before.

Anti-Semitism. The tragic Jewish suffering has reached extreme proportions in the last 150 years due to anti-Semitism. Anti-Semitism is the term given to the feelings of anger, alienation, and paranoia that Europeans projected on the Jews. Jews were blamed for the growth of industry, for poverty, suffering, and for everything wrong with the modern world. Forced in Eastern Europe to live in shtetls (villages) in the Pale of Settlement, many Jews were executed in pogroms (organized massacres). Only after the frustrations of confinement and prejudice in Europe had gone on for over a century were Jews allowed to move. Beginning in the 1890s many relocated to Palestine, where they began to forge out new lifestyles, mainly in kibbutzes (agricultural communes).

Zionism. In the 1890s, too, anti-Semitism reared its ugly head on the occasion of the Dreyfus trial, when a Jewish officer in the French army was falsely accused of spying and selling military secrets to Germany. This trial forced Theodor Herzl (1860-1904) to conclude that the "Jewish problem" could be solved only by complete assimilation into European culture or by complete evacuation. This was the beginning of Zionism, the movement to establish a Jewish state in Palestine. Masses of Jews in Eastern Europe wanted to settle at Zion hill in Jerusalem. They wanted a Jewish community in a Jewish homeland with Jewish self-determination.

Zionism was a crusade to liberate (non-American) Jews from persecution by acquiring a homeland and a land of refuge where the Jewish masses might find economic opportunity and political security. It aimed to create a genuinely Jewish culture that would express the Jewish people's spirit in an untrammeled way. The early Zionists were pioneers devoted to reclaiming the land. For them, the land was not simply the locale in which Judaism developed, but an essential component of their faith and hope—the very location of God's preeminent presence with humans.

Today Zionism secularizes the Jewish messianic symbols. The Jews are still the people chosen to lead the world, and they sustain their hope of returning to the homeland. The very heart of their messianic belief, its symbols and fantasies, is shaped by that hope. The Zionists take with utmost seriousness the history of the modern world, agreeing that the world is changing and moving toward a climax. Now, though, the messiah is identified with the dream of an age of individual liberty, national freedom, and economic and social justice. Zion is not off somewhere in heaven, but a specific earthly place.

The Holocaust. Many Jews became passionate, active nationalists and swung their support to Zionism after the Holocaust in World War II. The Holocaust was the systematic extermination of six million Jews between 1933 and 1945, after they were collected in con-

A memorial garden at Dachau recalls the atrocities of the Holocaust during World
War II: "Never again."

centration camps where they were subjected to inhuman and
unimaginable terrors. After the Holocaust, many Jews found it impossible to maintain their traditional beliefs in the presence of an
omnipotent and beneficent God. They could not preserve their ancestral conviction that catastrophes in Jewish history were God's
punishment of a sinful Israel. To do so, they would have to regard
Hitler and the death camps as instruments of God's will.

For other Jews, though, the Holocaust produced a new commandment to preserve the Jewish people and Jewish religion. The
atrocities made the surviving Jews more desirous for a homeland
and increased their solidarity around the world. The traditional
messianic hope was able to impart meaning to the Holocaust. Jews
found comfort in the story of disaster followed by salvation, of
darkness followed by light, of death followed by life. Their vision of
a new Jerusalem led eventually to the creation of the modern state
of Israel in 1948. Building the state of Israel has now become an essential aspect of belonging to the Jewish people, and making financial donations to the State of Israel a sacred act.

Messianic hope is still present in Israel, even symbolically in their
official flag. The Star of David has been part of the flag of Israel
since 1948. In medieval times this six-pointed star was a symbol of
magic power and in the seventeenth century it was identified with

the shield of the son of David, the hoped-for messiah. In the twentieth century it was officially adopted as the symbol of the newly formed Zionist movement. Though it suffered ignominy as a badge of shame for Jews under Nazi control, it is today a positive symbol of Judaism and serves to identify most Jewish houses of worship.

Human Rights. The memory of suffering and the sense of covenant responsibility make Jews sensitive to the plight of others in their midst. Jews make efforts to create social conditions that humanely and effectively address justice and suffering. Their record of philanthropic contributions to improve human welfare and their involvement in the helping professions (such as teaching, social work, and psychotherapy) is astonishing. They bring their belief in the absolute worth of human life to their concern for human rights and to their involvement in business, arts, medicine, and science.

Still, tensions between the Law and contemporary sensibilities are evident in the different Jewish communities today. This is especially true regarding the role of women. Reform Jews, appreciating pluralism and recognizing the importance of freedom of conscience and human rights, have several women rabbis. The Conservative Jews have recently given more equality to women in laws and ritual practices, and now count women as part of the quorum required for worship. The Orthodox, though, believing in sex-segregated duties and roles, refuse to grant women substantial legal equality. In the state of Israel, Reform Jews grant divorces, Conservative Jews have revived the ancient rabbinical privilege of retroactive annulment, and Orthodox Jews resort to legal measures in civil courts to force compliance with the Halakah.

Ritual: Passover and High Holy Days

Jews today still celebrate their community hopes and respond to the covenant with the ever-present Yahweh in their annual festivals. Each week they observe the Sabbath day as a day set aside from other days, not for work or worldly concerns, but to rejoice, restore their bodies, and concentrate on the presence of God. Symbolizing a state of perfect harmony with nature and among individuals, the Sabbath expresses the Jewish hope of the salvation and freedom of messianic time.

In the spring at the Pesach (Passover) festival, they retell the story of the Exodus from Egypt and celebrate their liberation from bondage in the elaborate Seder meal. By retelling the story of the Exodus, the reception of the Torah, and the wandering in the desert, Jews remind themselves that these are not historical moments of the past

After the rite of passage of the Bar Mitzvah, a Jewish boy becomes an adult and may now read the Torah at the Sabbath service.

that occurred to one specific generation, but the personal and immediate experience of every generation.

The struggle for freedom celebrated at Passover is also commemorated at Hanukkah and Purim. Hanukkah celebrates the courage of the Jewish people to fight for Judaism and to maintain its separateness from the world. At Hanukkah, Jews keep the menorah (light) burning proudly and proclaim their courage to remain a unique religious community in the face of tyrants. Purim is a joyful feast recalling the heroic resistance necessary, in the face of overwhelming anti-Semitic aggression, to ensure Jewish survival at any place and any time in the modern world.

The major services in the Fall festival are the ten High Holy Days, beginning with Rosh Hashanah (the Jewish New Year) and concluding with Yom Kippur, the Day of Atonement. A shofar (ram's horn) is blown, its sound assisting each person to be reconciled with God, the universal king. This is a time for restitution to one's neighbors, when Jews apologize for previous wrongs, and a time of introspection, when they reflect on what they have accomplished and where they are going. The oft-repeated phrase of Yom Kippur, "Remember us for life," announces a vision of hope and celebrates the passion and vitality of life. The Day of Atonement is a day of joyful hope that gives Jews the courage to dream and work for a new future.

The Stories Appropriated

The Jewish stories about Moses and David provide a context for meaning, not only for the lives of those within the Jewish tradition, but for those of us outside it. These stories present new ways for us to envision our own spiritual convictions. Reading about God's presence and hope for a new world challenges us to respond in a personal way to our own religion on the basis of transformed decisions.

Order from Chaos

The Exodus journey of Moses and the Jewish people through the chaos of the wilderness represents the journey we all have to take in order to find order amid chaos in our own search for a vision in life. A tale of transformation and possibility, it generates energy, courage, and action. Moses never did get wholehearted support from his people. What sustained him was the intimacy he experienced with God, ever since the encounter with the burning bush. It seems that now and then God has to do something extraordinary to get our attention, to make us look into ourselves. In our depths we can find God. When we do, we give our lives direction and can then move toward a meaningful goal. Our lives are founded on mystery; but what we achieve in them comes from ourselves. Our experience of mystery (the burning bush) is the knowledge of what is real, and the experience of the task (the commandments at Mount Sinai) is the knowledge of what we have to achieve. These two experiences are really one: Mystery and commandment both come from the one God, and our spirit experiences them as one.

The Exodus story, with its narratives of freedom and vision, is a fundamental event not just for individuals, but also for communities. In many unsettled and unsettling places in the world today, oppressed communities find strength in the story of God's justice and righteousness in leading the Jews out of slavery. Suffering people are creating worlds, authorizing actions, and nullifying other worlds. The Exodus story of the escape from oppression helps distressed people find a power and legitimacy to rebel in protest against an unjust world, to act and live in new ways.

God's Call

We tend to think of the experience of God's presence only in terms of special places of unusual power and prominence. We think that God is found only in extraordinary events, dramatic moments, sublime circumstances, and peak experiences. Yet by consigning this presence to remarkable signs and wonders or to special miracles, we empty vast regions of our lives of any possibility of encounter with the divine. We should not conclude, as we so easily do, that God is to be found only in mighty whirlwinds and burning bushes. Our call from God will probably not be a profound mystical encounter in anything dramatic, but rather in and through the common events of everyday life. In our search for spiritual wholeness we surely want to capture and recapture fleeting moments of religious ecstasy, but we should well understand that surely God is not limited to such moments.

God's call interrupts what has up till now seemed normal and important in our lives and sends us off in a completely new and perhaps disturbing direction. Like Moses, we see ourselves as unworthy; we are afraid other people will not believe that we are called; we lack confidence that our skills are adequate to the task. Even if God's call were as fascinating as a world suddenly afire, it would still not draw some people to action. The great enemies of our spiritual growth are sluggishness and indifference, not insecurity or ignorance. In our world of scintillating objects, ideas, and events jumping out from all directions and in all shapes and sizes, we find it very difficult to be truly and profoundly impressed.

Divine-Human Relationship

On the other hand, when the unfathomable and unthinkable enters into life, some of us react not with sluggishness, but with overconfidence. Our experience of intimacy with God pushes us further: We try to control God, telling God to come and go as we wish, to show the divine face. When this happens, when we desire something for ourselves, we experience the same tragic failure as Moses.

We all desire to share the joy of the presence of God and divine promises, yet we have to do it on God's terms, not ours. We cannot forget that Moses gradually came to recognize that life is framed by infinity and eternity, transcending all human knowledge and surpassing all that is natural. The divine-human relationship is a quite complex combination of God's majesty and our insignificance. If we recognize the holy in reverence and if we accept what is infinitely and eternally commanding into our lives, then this transcendent experience can have great impelling force to revitalize and support us. Further, if we try to lead others out of the slavery of social injustices, recognizing our human limitations and relying on God, then anything is possible. If we try to do everything alone, though, we surely fail.

Success and Failure

David's story poignantly demonstrates both the burden of having to keep the lofty covenant and the painful consequences of not keeping it. People who are successful in public life—not just politicians like David, but also movie and TV stars, sports figures, millionaires—may find David's story in their lives. Success in public life does not necessarily mean success in one's private life; indeed, there is a danger that success in one sphere may preclude it in the other. Even powerful leaders and public figures have personal and private desires that can, if unchecked, damage the public welfare they have a responsibility to maintain.

Most of us are not public figures, though, and we too undergo reversals in life. A general pattern of setback and renewal is familiar both in our human relationships and in our relationships with God. In our own little worlds, we can win the war and lose the battle. We all hate to lose: Losing is no fun, and we don't have to pretend that it is. What we don't recognize is that there are times when it is not possible to distinguish winners from losers. Though there is a complex relationship between success and failure, it is a delusion to divide the world into heroes and failures. In many circumstances, in fact, success and failure are interchangeable, with success often leading to failure, and failure pointing to new ventures. Awareness of this repeating cyclical pattern helps us get through very difficult situations.

New Life

All of us betray God many times and in many ways, like David did. Once we come to realize our sinfulness, we can throw ourselves on the mercy of God, undergo a true conversion, and rise to new life. When David hears the parable from Nathan, he undergoes a tremendous death and a tremendous conversion that issues in the humble and penitent cry: "I have sinned against the Lord." We can all utter these words.

Recognition of personal failure does not have to lead to disappointment. The Jewish messianic images of perfection and love, justice and harmony arise as the upbeat and confident result of suffering and consolation. Their hope for a messiah is their corrective for suffering. The messiah is Israel's answer to tragedy and the Jewish gift to humanity. We can all take on their powerful drive to liberate and renew life. This compulsion to create a new world derives from a strength beyond all strength, one that grows in those who know mystery, who are not afraid to speak out and contradict injustices. Messianic hope can provide us with hope that is certain and settled, with hope that strengthens our courage and vitality to create and anticipate a world that is beyond present visible reality.

Conclusion

The Jewish master story is the story of the presence of God in the midst of oppression. Through their history as the chosen people, the Jews have experienced both distressful suffering and powerful blessing. Their suffering comes to them independently of their wills, as their rabbis have taught them: "The best which God gives to Israel, God gives through suffering."

The story of the sublimity and tragedy of Moses is the story of the Jews in miniature. He experiences great success in leading the Jewish people on their Exodus through the wilderness and in receiving the covenant from God. Yet his success and his intimate experience of God's presence are also the source of his vulnerability: His achievements are shattered against thresholds that he cannot cross.

The story of David's public success and private failure are changed when the Jews retell them later in their Scriptures, for he represents the ideal king and their continuing hopes for a better future. Because of this enduring hope, Jews are free to live with passion and without compromise, to be optimistic as a people even though they have suffered so much in their history.

Discussion Questions

1. Why do you think the author chooses the Western Wall as a symbol of Jewish election and covenant?

2. Describe the Jewish God in terms of oneness and presence.

3. Summarize the Jewish belief in salvation in terms of oppression, obedience, and Messianic age.

4. Describe Moses as the symbol of both sublimity and tragedy.

5. Why do you think that David was so powerful in his public life, yet so helpless in his personal life?

6. Summarize the cause and effects of anti-Semitism in the last hundred years.

7. What can Christians appropriate today from the stories of the Exodus, Moses, and David?

8. Discussion Starter: One day a Gentile asked the rabbi Hillel: "Tell me the entire Torah while you are standing on one foot." Hillel quoted the Tanak (Leviticus 19:18): "You will love your fellow human being as yourself." Hillel then explained: "That is the entire Torah. All the rest is meant to explain that simple rule. Now go and learn."

9. Discussion Starter: "In the face of suffering, one has no right to turn away, not to see. In the face of injustice, one may not look the other way. When someone suffers, and it is not you, he comes first. His very suffering gives him priority....To watch over a man who grieves is a more urgent duty than to think of God." (Elie Wiesel)

10. Discussion Starter: "Give your sorrow all the space and shelter in yourself that is its due, for if all people bear their grief honestly and courageously, the sorrow that now fills the world will abate." (Etty Hillesum)

The cathedral at Chartres, with its two unique spires and great rose window, is one of Europe's most impressive Gothic monuments.

Chapter Four

CHRISTIANITY
Forgiveness and Freedom
Setting the Scene

Chartres

The spires of Chartres are visible from a great distance across the rich corn fields of France. Pilgrims who take the two- or three-day pilgrimage out of Paris spot the twin steeples from several miles away, and their gladness quickens with each stride. Joined by similar groups who have taken different routes, they all converge on the cathedral square to enter the church. They feel themselves deep in the heart of Christianity, united with the Christians of many centuries ago.

The cathedral at Chartres presents one of the grandest and most impressive of Europe's Gothic monuments. Not only is the church renowned for its early architectural use of flying buttresses, but its doors, statues, and windows are famous as medieval teaching tools. Because so few copies of the Christian Scriptures existed and because most of the people in medieval Europe were illiterate, the images on the doors, statues, and windows kept people in touch with their Christian story.

Chartres was a favorite church of the industrial classes, and its construction was a vast community endeavor. The portals proclaim the majesty of Christ in scenes of his birth, presentation in the temple with his virgin mother, and his passion. They tell the story of his ascension into heaven and proclaim the apocalyptic vision of his Second Coming. Blue light continues to stream through the prominent stained-glass windows, revealing the splendor of medieval art. These windows encouraged, helped, and instructed worshipers, directing them toward life rather than death. Images in the windows depict scenes from the lives of Jesus, Mary, and the saints. The portals and windows depict in miniature the beliefs of the Christian religion.

Jesus

Christianity is the largest religion in the world today, with about 1.8 billion members. Christians proclaim Jesus, called the Christ, as the savior of the world and the unique revelation of God in human history. At the very heart of this religion, underlying all the diversity of practices, organizations, doctrines, and ethics lies a master story, the story of Jesus of Nazareth. The God-man, the self-giving of God, and human receptivity are concentrated in a fashion never to be surpassed in Jesus of Nazareth. For Christians, the source of salvation is God, who out of compassion reaches out to humans through Jesus and empowers them to do what they cannot do on their own.

Jesus has been called variously a carpenter from Nazareth, an itinerant teacher, a wise storyteller, a proclaimer of the kingdom, a friend of outcasts, an example of love, a miracle worker, and an innocent victim. Most especially for Christians, though, he is crucified Lord and resurrected Savior. He is the human who is totally open, responsive, and obedient to the mystery of God, whom he addresses as Abba ("Daddy"). As the God-Man, Jesus is the incarnation of God, personally present to humans. He invites his listeners to share his experience of God who, while beyond any human manipulation and control, is breathtakingly present in every aspect of daily life. In his public life of miracles and preaching, he proclaims the kingdom of God and the parental love of God, and calls for radical moral behavior that requires a reversal of basic human tendencies.

Death and Resurrection

The story of Jesus' death and resurrection expresses the Good News that God, out of divine love, offers humans a share of divine life. By his death, Jesus completes a lifetime of surrendering himself totally and finally to doing the will of his Father. Christians believe that, in this unconditional act of self-sacrificing love, his cause for the kingdom is won and his teaching is authenticated. The Easter faith of the followers of Jesus proclaims that "Christ is risen; Christ is risen indeed." In a relatively brief time his frightened and confused group of dispirited disciples, who had fled into hiding in order to distance themselves from the brutal death, are filled with unshakable self-confidence. As they share their conviction with others, they gradually develop a larger understanding and more comprehensive message of the resurrection. Today Christians see God's action on Jesus' behalf—renewing his life and sending his spirit—as the center point of their faith. The resurrection confirms that Jesus comes from God, that he is, in fact, the Son of God, and that he lives on after his death and burial.

By his death, Jesus completes a lifetime of surrendering himself totally to doing the will of God.

The story of the death and resurrection of Jesus is God's supreme promise that the kingdom will be fulfilled for all Christians. In turn, it issues them a challenge to adopt Jesus' way of dealing with others so that they too may experience the resurrection. Jesus' passion and resurrection call for his followers today to see their lives essentially as gifts, enabling them to give just as graciously to others, neither expecting nor requiring anything in return. They are called to experience and express his spirit in a life of self-sacrificing love of God and others. Living as Jesus did, they are capable of healing divisions and reconciling people with each other and with God.

The Church

After the execution and resurrection of Jesus, his followers formed a community to continue his ministry and spread his teachings. They wished to carry on his service of healing the sick, feeding the hungry, and announcing the coming of the kingdom of God. This community of followers of Jesus is the church, the whole people of God, bonded together with a common set of beliefs and practices. They shape their lives according to their conviction that Christ is the savior and that access to God is through their faith and rituals. They are the community of those who follow Jesus, who is the way, the truth, and the life.

The church today is comprised of local communities where the word of God is preached and the ritual of the eucharist (or Lord's supper) is celebrated. At this banquet meal, a visible reminder of Jesus' continuing presence, Christians are in solidarity with the early followers of Jesus. They take seriously his essential call to love and forgive others as he did. Their community transcends various groupings to embrace all who accept Christ. They see truth not as the static possession of a single group, but as an unfolding gift of God.

Christians see themselves as a minority in the service of the majority, called to transform the earth and thus to prepare the way for the final reunion of all people with God. The community of the church reflects historical changes in social and cultural contexts, and comprises diverse policies, rituals, and practical codes. Still, the church community is united in the conviction that God, who calls them by name, always forgives them and empowers them to move toward greater and more encompassing charity, toward a disciplined growth in the likeness of Jesus.

Faith and God

At the core of Christian faith is a belief in God who uniquely reveals divine nature and divine love in Jesus Christ. This belief enlightens and directs how Christians view God, themselves, the world, and history. With their faith grounded in history, they perceive the past as sacred story, the present as the arena of God's continuing action, and the future as the time of hope for a new heaven and a new earth.

The Christian God is immanent, that is, active within the world. God is fully present and decisively revealed in the created realm. God has become incarnate in the world as a human named Jesus. God's definitive self-revelation is in Jesus, who is fully divine and fully human. God's power breaks into the world in the deeds of healing power that Jesus performs. Jesus reveals God as a loving parent, a God of respect and familiarity, full of forgiveness, tenderness, and care. This God offers to all people a share of the kingdom that is present—present in time, in place, and as a gift. This kingdom makes each individual person a singular and unrepeatable center of creativity and freedom. With the resurrection of Jesus, God's activity in the world is now manifested in new ways within the lives of Jesus' followers. Humans cannot adequately describe God's goodness or being. Nevertheless, adequate evidence of God's inexhaustible power, caring wisdom, and self-sacrificing love is present in the God-man Jesus, in the Christian community, and in the created world.

The Christian God is also transcendent, that is, beyond the created universe. It is a paradoxical mystery how God can be both present within the world and yet transcend it. To help experience and explain this mystery, Christians gradually evolved philosophical doctrines of the two natures of Christ (both human and divine) and of the Trinity (the teaching that there are three persons in God—the Father, the Son, and the Holy Spirit).

Human Salvation

The Problem: Sin

Humans are made in God's image: They reflect the divine creative freedom. With that freedom, they have the power either to open treasures locked deep within themselves or to turn against their created goodness. They can manifest the image of God in their lives or they can separate themselves from the source of all life, from their creative possibilities, and from fulfilling relationships with other humans. When they use their freedom to reject their full communion with God, they fall into slavery to Satan, to themselves, and to the world. This slavery is sin.

Sin causes humans to lose their freedom to be fully human and to be like God. When the image of God becomes unclear, the longing for wholeness becomes flawed and in need of healing. Sinners are filled with willful self-indulgence, having their way even if it means self-destruction. Sin is the distorted and tragic misuse of God-given human capacities and spiritual powers within the universe. Sin is primarily—"originally"—self-deification, the attempt to wrap all life, and all that lives, into one's own orbit. Sinners reduce all things to their own dominion and they exalt their individual selves above all else. This glorification is really enslavement, for sinners become servants to their own ultimacy. Sin is an affliction that originates from within, causing paralyzing guilt, alienating discouragement, and excessive fear. It leads to a sense of poor self-esteem, of ultimate meaninglessness and powerlessness.

Personal sin leads to social sin. Before sinners are consciously able to take precautions against it, the self-damaging alienation from God, from themselves, from fellow humans, and from the whole created universe spreads contagiously. By refusing to put the welfare of others ahead of limited selfish interests, it causes estrangement. Some persons, for example, commit aggressive crimes of violence or unkind deeds of social injustice that produce psychological suffering in their victims. They exploit others through racism, prejudice, or economic inequities, systematically despoiling them of their humanity.

The Strategy: Grace

The way for humans to overcome evil is to open themselves to God's activity—grace—in their lives. In the end, things manage to work out after all, not because of any human doings, but solely because of this grace. Part of the gospel story that Jesus proclaims is that nothing can deter God from saving humans, not even those humans themselves. Jesus breaks through into human consciousness and demands the overturning of prior values, closed options, and set judgments. Christians proclaim, too, that Jesus, by his birth, life, death, and resurrection, restores humans to their full freedom and original communion with God. Jesus provides salvation for all people: He supplies the way for all human beings to be reconciled with God. Jesus acts for God by taking the willful alienation and suffering of the created world into himself and overcoming it. This triumph comes through Jesus who, as John's Gospel proclaims it, reveals the knowledge that God loves humans and who, as Paul's letters express it, atones for sins by his death. The activity of God in Jesus is the ultimate strategy for overcoming evil. Christians can participate in this activity in different ways. They can experience it through their rituals (the sacraments). They can also rise from the death of self-destruction and from alienation to a new life of right relationship to God, self, and others through faith and repentance. They can also receive this new gift of life through conversion, the spiritual revolution of giving up their old way of life and putting aside the corrupted, selfish self.

The Solution: Kingdom of God

Jesus described salvation as the realization of the kingdom of God. Christians use different images for this solution to the problem of evil. Salvation is resurrection, or heaven, or paradise. Salvation is the ultimate realization of the beatific vision, a heavenly state of full and unqualified awareness of the presence of God, a state of spiritual perfection. These are all descriptions of the divine life that God offers to humans out of love.

Salvation is the ultimate consummation of the work of Christ in which a new heaven and new earth are established, the whole of creation and history reaches its fulfillment, and the entire human family is joined in solidarity. Salvation is the reign of mercy, justice, and peace—a gift from God that comes as a shocking surprise. Salvation is experienced only in community, a community of peace and tranquility that affirms the world as a whole. This community anticipates the kingdom and makes it present in the struggles that humans undergo to reshape their existence by reversing their basic tendencies to act selfishly. Christians who believe in the kingdom take the present seriously and integrate inevitable death into a meaningful life.

Christians are not sustained by a hope that is wholly otherworldly, for they believe that the kingdom of God is already here in their midst. Salvation is present now: It is available and at hand. Jesus states unequivocally in his parables that the kingdom has already arrived. The kingdom is accessible to everyone and does not have to be awaited or anticipated in some near or remote future. Christians believe that the goal of their lives through overcoming evil is not the prolongation of life's happier moments, but the fullness of the present moment. They know that no eyes have seen what has been prepared for those who love God. They know too that the end of life is not a total rift between this life and the next life, but the eternal (rather than everlasting) transformation and fulfillment of human destiny, where the total uniqueness of the human personality is preserved.

The Sacred Writings

Many Christians consider the Bible, both the Hebrew Scriptures and the New Testament, the chief source of their spiritual nourishment. They consult it daily for guidance in their everyday lives. The New Testament writings teach through imagination's forms: parables, paradoxes, visions, laws, history, dramas, hymns, gospels, letters, and more. They detail the stories of Jesus' ministry and death, Paul's missionary activity, and the faith of the early church. The chief writings of the twenty-seven books that make up the bulk of the New Testament (that is, "new covenant" with God) include the Gospels and the Epistles.

The Gospels

The Gospels, written more than forty years after the death of Jesus, depict the major events in his life. The master story is told in light of Christian belief in Jesus' resurrection after death. Some people who encounter Jesus are fascinated by him and decide to follow him. This encounter, together with the events that take place in Jesus' life and in connection with his death, gives their own existence new meaning. They experience a change, or conversion, in the direction of their lives. This change instills enthusiasm in them for the kingdom of God that Jesus preaches and a special compassion for others in a way that Jesus has already shown to them.

Jesus openly confronts the authority of the Jewish religious leaders, and he is willing to flout both social convention and sabbath law where he sees fit. He overturns the tables of the money changers in the temple and heals blind persons and cripples on the Sabbath. He extends the intimacy of table-fellowship to those who put themselves outside the covenant people of God, and he insists upon openness to the poor and the oppressed. Jesus teaches a prayer of filial intimacy to God as Abba. He portrays God as a friend of sinners, searching out and forgiving outcasts. Jesus also poses a political threat to the Roman occupational government, for groups acclaiming him as messiah could easily turn into a violent, nationalistic uprising. When still young and just inaugurating his mission on behalf of the kingdom, Jesus is arrested. Brought before a Jewish high priest and then Pilate, the Roman governor, Jesus refuses to answer their questions. He is flogged and handed over to soldiers to be crucified. Before he dies cruelly on a wooden cross, Jesus asks forgiveness for his tormentors.

This is not the end of the story. Not long after the death, his followers report that Jesus has been seen again. Raised from the dead, he appears to his disciples a number of times, on a mountain, along the road, and especially at the supper table. Before he finally leaves them, he gives them a commission to bring the good news of salvation and forgiveness to all people.

The Epistles

Of the many Epistles (letters) in the Christian sacred writings, the earliest and most important are written by Paul. His letters are documents of the moment, tailored to the specific concerns of the individual Christian congregations to whom he wrote. Many of his epistles are not actually pieces of correspondence or communication among geographically distant Christian groups, but ethical essays and theological treatises with fine distinctions, ranging from dazzling eloquence to thudding brutality. Sometimes he writes in an effort to help where there are serious problems in the community; at other times he wants to give general encouragement. In all cases he attempts to relate the life of Jesus to the specific or general needs of the people of the early Christian community.

There is some narrative material in the majority of the Epistles, but generally they provide Christians with Paul's understanding of salvation, of faith as acceptance, and of new life in Christ as freedom. His epistles contain much high drama—conflicted, paradoxical, and existential—in his response to his experience of Jesus.

Book of Revelation

Many Christians locate their master story not in the Gospels or the Epistles, nor in the story of the death and resurrection of Jesus, nor in the parables, but rather in the apocalyptic writing called the Book of Revelation. Written as Christians were being persecuted for their unpatriotic refusal to worship the Roman emperor, the Book of Revelation encourages them to strengthen their resistance against engaging in public rituals that honor the emperor's divinity. Using the device of a vision, it tells a story of Jesus as the Christ appearing amid a series of catastrophic events, the near success of an Antichrist who oppresses the faithful, and Christ's counterattack that culminates in the establishment of a new cosmic order.

The book represents the persecutions by Roman authority (the Antichrist) as the beginning of a spectacular struggle between the forces of good and evil. The forces of evil are described in vivid imagery: mountains dropping into the sea, stars falling from the sky like balls of fire, sulphurous lakes burning. Trenchant symbols also describe the forces of good: the new city of Jerusalem, its walls built of diamonds and rubies and its streets paved with gold, and Jesus riding on a white horse to inaugurate a reign for a thousand years. This universal war will end in Christ's slaughter of all enemies and in the kingdom's complete triumph. New heavens and a new earth will be created from which all pain and sorrow will be excluded. Those who are thirsty will drink from the well of life and all will share the wedding supper of the lamb.

The First Story: The Prodigal Son and Forgiveness

In the Gospel narratives, Jesus describes God's active presence in human hearts as manifested in deeds of compassionate, fraternal, and costly love for others. Jesus shows his fertile imagination in his parables (as does the early community, which embellished them through constant retelling). Immersed in the Jewish tradition, Jesus wrestles with efforts to create new images for the kingdom of God and for the role of humans in bringing it about. The terms, images, and symbols are those of the popular culture of his day (e.g., stories about shepherds, seeds and soil, bread and wine, farmers, widows, bridegrooms). The forgiveness that Jesus announces is good news concerning liberation from anything that makes human life less than life and less than human. It is freedom for a completely new start: The blind can see, the lame can walk, the deaf can hear.

Luke's Gospel presents Jesus as the merciful savior who preaches the universal compassion and forgiveness that God offers to those who recognize their need for it. This is especially apparent in the parable of the Prodigal Son, probably the best known of Jesus' stories. Sometimes referred to as the parable of the Prodigal's Father, it is the last in a trilogy of stories on forgiveness that all follow the same plot line: tragic loss, anxious searching, and, finally, joyful finding and rejoicing.

A father, Jesus tells us, has two sons. The younger son, unhappy at home, demands his inheritance so that he can leave home to move to a faraway country. He wants to be free from the parental yoke and to pursue his own pleasure. An extravagant squanderer, he quickly spends everything in a rapid and escalating decline. He wastes his inheritance through misconduct and is subject to destitution and famine. Not only does he spend all the family money, thus depriving his parents of the financial security they had for their old age, but he disgraces their name and reputation with his loose living.

When a time of famine arises, he finds work slopping hogs for a local farmer, an occupation no Jew would assume since the animals are considered religiously unclean. The reckless son does not find what he expected in leaving home. Instead of happiness, freedom, and joy, he experiences only sorrow, slavery, and misery. At this point he thinks of his parents and his home—just when he has used up all their money and could not possibly be of help to them. Having wasted his property, he returns home, repentant and asking for forgiveness. Aware of the depth of his sin and accepting personal responsibility for what he has done, he repents of his actions.

The father, seeing his son from afar, is filled with compassion and runs to embrace him. Far from the harsh censure and judgment that we would expect, the father wants to forgive his prodigal son and reinstate him into the family. With a flurry of orders the old man directs his servants to get the best clothes from the house and to put a special ring on the son's finger. To celebrate the son's return, the father orders his servants to slaughter a calf and prepare a sumptuous banquet. This extravagant party, with hired orchestra, singers, and dancers, seems a match even for his son's wastefulness and extravagance. But, the father exclaims, it is only right that they should rejoice, for his son was dead and has come to life, was lost and is found.

When the elder brother discovers what is occurring, he is angry and will not participate in the joyful celebration of his brother's homecoming. The older boy has served his parents faithfully during their lifetime and old age, and expects to receive his portion of the inheritance at the father's death. His father has never celebrated with this type of a feast for him, so how can he now do it for his disgraced brother? Indignant and embittered, he resents his father's leniency. Gasping at the music, dancing, and frivolity, he is miserable, while the others are having a wonderful time. His father tries to bring some life into this older son, affirming a bond of unity and acceptance with him: "Son, you are always with me, and all that is mine is yours. But we have to be merry and rejoice, for this your brother was dead and is alive, and was lost and is found." Indeed, the father is also forgiving the elder son for being selfish, judgmental, and unforgiving.

The Story Magnified

Christians savor this parable, for it shows how God manifests unceasing devotion to humans, and how humans in consequence ought to display such dedicated constancy themselves, both to God and to each other.

Breakthrough

Jesus presents more than moral lessons or elaborate allegories in his stories: They require his followers to imagine God as always active. Jesus' way of speaking has a powerful edge: The forgiveness and reconciliation he proclaims is demanded for everyone's life. Jesus' purpose in the parables is to create a breakthrough and conversion—Christians have to engage in making connections, in seeing the world in a new way. The parables clearly undermine the dominant social reality of his day, characterizing an alternative society that he calls the "kingdom of God." His stories do not offer blueprints or programs. Instead, they confront persons with a crucial moment of decision whether or not to turn their lives toward God. They are open-ended, requiring participation and transformation if persons are to perceive the depths of the message.

The Banquet

A banquet plays an important part in Luke's parable of the prodigal son. For Luke, this banquet is a sign of the eucharistic meal, a time of special discernment during which all participants are to see themselves engaged in a holy communion of gift sharing and joyful repentance. The eucharist, then, is not so much a memorial of the last supper as a feast in anticipation of the fulfillment of the kingdom. It is a joyous celebration of the future hope of the Christian community, where table-fellowship is not limited to the righteous, but to all those who accept God's offer of unlimited forgiveness.

Unconditional Love

The father of the prodigal son does not need any higher motivation: His love is so total and unconditional that he simply welcomes his son home. This is an encouraging thought for Christians. God does not require a pure heart before embracing them. Even if Christians return because they cannot make it on their own, God's love demands no explanations about why they are returning. God is glad to see them home and wants to give them all they desire, just for being home. The wisdom of the story is simple: If this can be the case with fathers and sons, how much more it is with God. Regardless of what awful and loathsome actions are in the past, humans can be welcomed by God whose love is limitless and whose forgiveness is total. There is brilliant irony and juxtaposition here. According to the ancient Jewish law in which Jesus was raised, parents had the right to put rebellious children to death, and yet, in the religious experience of a meal in the ancient world, guests were sacred—to invite them to a meal was to offer them the deepest fellowship.

Joyful Return

The younger son is a victim of his own immaturity and impatience and creates a world with himself as its center. He experiences his own misery and realizes his error in leaving the house of his father. He does not return because of renewed love, but simply to survive. He discovers that the way he has chosen is leading him to death, and that returning to his father is necessary for him to live. He realizes that he has sinned in turning away from his family, yet this realization occurs only because his rebellion has brought him close to death. The return to the father's house is a joyful experience. Life drifts away from God, Jesus tells his followers, and they have to return. Returning is a lifelong struggle, but with happy consequences.

Transformation

And the elder son? He cannot understand—indeed, he resents— mercy and love and forgiveness. The elder son is typical of those who think of religion only in terms of justice and obedience and commandments. Those who know only justice do not know the real meaning of God's love and mercy. Jesus is calling for a transformation in the consciousness of such persons: The shadow side of rigid obedience to the law, which is secretly resentful of the profligate behavior of sinners, cannot enjoy forgiveness without becoming conscious of how inappropriate it is in the present context. The kingdom that Jesus proclaims breaks abruptly into a person's consciousness and demands the overturning of prior values and established conclusions. The parable is not meant to imply that Christians have some set of obligations or regulated behavior that they owe to God. It suggests, rather, that the experiences they have of compassion, forgiveness, extra assistance, and the like, are meant to be directed outward.

Forgiveness

When Jesus speaks about forgiveness, he bases his most telling words and deeds squarely on selflessness. Before the prodigal gets even a word of confession out of his mouth, the father forgets all his own anguish, throws his arms around his son, and kisses him. Jesus takes care to point out that the gift of forgiveness proceeds solely out of God's love, prior to any qualifying action on the part of those who receive it. In other contexts Jesus refuses to set any limit to the number of times a person might be forgiven. Humans are not necessarily changed by experiences of forgiveness. Still, the story shows that failure to change is not right: It is an offense against the extraordinary compassion that has been manifested. Forgiveness surrounds Christians, beats upon them all our lives; they can only become aware of what they already have.

The Second Story: Paul and Freedom

The second story from the Christian tradition is the story of Paul's call, commonly referred to as his conversion experience. Paul's experience of liberation from Jewish law was certainly one of the most exciting events in the first generation of the followers of Jesus. It sets the scene for Paul's letters and his teachings on salvation in Christ, on reconciliation and freedom. Paul alludes only briefly in his letters to the story of his conversion. He even seems reluctant to talk about it, as if it would suggest overconfidence in his own religious experiences. Paul says that God revealed Jesus Christ to him as Son, that the risen Lord appeared to him, and that he saw the Lord. Paul spends much time in his letters explaining what his seminal experience means, but he never provides scintillating details of what actually happened. In his meager description of the event, there are no heavenly lights or voices, no attacks of blindness, no supporting visions from others, no falling to the ground, no scales dropping from the eyes.

Luke provides a much richer and fuller version of the story in the Acts of the Apostles. For Luke the story is so central to the theme of the gradual spread of the good news of salvation and forgiveness throughout the world that he tells it three different times. For Luke, God is actively at work in human history to achieve his purposes, and humans are endowed by God with the freedom, the power, to be the divine instruments to accomplish those purposes. Against this background, what Paul does against the church is entirely senseless, and to resist Christ now is equally senseless: Christ is stronger than he is.

Paul, Luke writes, is a Jew so zealous for the traditions of his ancestors that he violently breathes threats to slaughter the disciples of Jesus and tries to destroy their community. Paul's murderous actions are of a piece with those of his Jewish compatriots, mobilized to defend Judaism against this upstart Christian movement they find so offensive and threatening. On his way to Damascus to arrest these

Temporarily stricken blind by a heavenly light, Paul encounters
Jesus while on the road to Damascus to persecute Christians.

"followers of the Way," Paul is knocked to the ground, and a light
from heaven shines all around him. A sense of awe pervades the
scene. Paul hears a voice from heaven chastise him for his behavior
toward the Christians. Paul asks, "Who are you, Lord?" A voice
from heaven exclaims: "I am Jesus, whom you are persecuting. Saul,
Saul, why do you persecute me?" Thus does Paul encounter Jesus.

Paul is speechless and, temporarily stricken with blindness by
the heavenly light, has to be led by the hand. He eventually reaches
Damascus where a disciple named Ananias prays for him to recover
his sight and be filled with the Spirit. With Paul's sudden change of
heart, his sight is restored and he is baptized and instructed concerning his future mission as the chosen apostle to the Gentile (non-
Jewish) world. At his conversion Paul learns that he is being sent so
that the Gentiles "may turn from darkness to light and from the
power of Satan to God, that they may receive forgiveness of sins
and a place among those sanctified by faith in Jesus." In his dramatic religious reversal, Paul comes to champion the movement he
once persecuted. He begins preaching in Jewish synagogues that Jesus is the Son of God, and then he quickly turns his attention to
Gentile audiences.

The Story Magnified

Unmerited Gift

Luke's technique of repeating the Damascus story three times calls our attention to the importance of this event for subsequent history. Luke stresses the gratuity and unmerited quality of God's favor. God's lavish forgiveness, which Jesus develops in his parables and exercises in his earthly life, is now surprisingly extended to those not considered to be the primary recipients of the Jewish messianic promises—the Gentile world. Paul would never have undertaken his mission to the Gentiles on his own. It is the irresistible power of Christ alone that leads him to it. This good news of God's unmerited gift to all humanity calls for celebration, for it gives them a new power, a new freedom.

Paul's Heroic Call

Paul's experience on the road to Damascus is not a conversion in the sense that he becomes a member of another religious community. When Paul is knocked off his horse and blinded, he suffers absolute darkness, poverty, and emptiness. Then comes the light. What comes to him in that blinding light is a new conviction about the way he should fulfill his vocation as a Jew. His conversion is rather his sudden calling to be a prophet, a spokesman for God, not only to his own people but also to the Gentiles. His vocation, he believes, is to proclaim the good news of the enlargement of the covenant both to those who are already inside (the Jews) and those who were previously outside (the Gentiles). By now inviting Gentiles into the covenant, God is reconciling alienated peoples to each other.

Through his liberating experience, Paul writes in his Letter to the Philippians, he now knows he is "righteous before God." That is, he has been "redeemed" by the grace of Christ, not by keeping the Law. He is confident of his relationship with God, but not on the basis of any moral achievement or some kind of merit system. Christians are freed from the Law, Paul explains, for by the death and resurrection of Jesus, God is no longer interested in examining anybody's deeds ever again. All people are free to become children of God. The initiative is from God, whose action liberates and creates a new relationship, that of adoption. This new relationship empowers Christians with the freedom to address God with the same intimate term, Abba, which characterizes Jesus' prayer.

To fulfill his heroic calling, Paul has to express his new awareness to others. Paul knows that if the treasure he has found is only for himself, it is not enough. He realizes that God is intervening on behalf of all humans. Heroes who experience the divine call and proclaim it to others are indeed "masters of two worlds." They have been reborn. They are no longer confined or trapped by the values of the society they have rejected, even though they continue to live there. They participate in another world, another truth, and another set of values; they have a larger perspective. Paul is called to be a hero, and the goal of his heroic quest is to reconcile humans with God. In that reconciliation he finds a new "freedom to live." With his new dedication to Jesus Christ, Paul thus embarks on a career that includes success and failure, harmony and conflict, acceptance and rejection, tranquility and crises. He experiences Christ's sufferings and rejoices in the power of his resurrection.

Christ as Center

Central to the story is Paul's encounter with Jesus. Paul sees his own experience of the risen Jesus as similar to the apostles' encounter with Jesus after his death. The revelation of Jesus is an inward experience, rather than a vision encountered from without. It is no less real because it is internal: "Have I not seen Jesus our Lord?" he asks in his First Letter to the Corinthians. There can scarcely be a more forthright claim of an interior religious experience. Paul's life is turned in a new direction when God reveals Jesus Christ as Son to him. As a Pharisee, he cherished the Law, but now he lets go of it to embrace Jesus Christ as Lord, as the center of his relationship with God. His experience of the resurrected Christ convinces him that humans are destined to rise to immortality, if they open themselves to the divine spirit as Jesus did.

With this new center Paul freely relinquishes former values. In the past he saw works of the Law as personal achievements by which he earned and kept his relationship with God. Now he realizes that his relationship with God is a pure gift. Made aware of his own human weakness and his inability to save himself, he accepts Jesus Christ as the divine power who lives within him. In his Letter to the Galatians Paul indicates his really new self-image, his personal transformation and new self-understanding in terms of a participation in the Christ-self: "The life I now live in this body I live in faith; faith in the Son of God who loved me and sacrificed himself for my sake."

Freedom

Paul's experience of Christ is obviously a very liberating event. He now experiences a deeply positive relationship with God through his encounter with Christ. Paul uses a variety of images to describe this new relationship. His picture goes something like this: Human beings have been created for a close relationship with God, a relationship broken by human sinfulness that needs to be restored. Humans themselves can do nothing to restore it, though, for divine life can arise only as the free gift of God. Paul calls this gift justification, righteousness, redemption, and sanctification. God, on one side, freely restores the broken relationship; humans, on their side, merely have to accept God's grace, in faith. As humans embrace the grace of God in faith, they are granted new life, a life in Christ, by the power of the Holy Spirit.

Drawing on concrete images drawn from daily life (e.g., working, marrying, pottery-making, and dying courageously), Paul proclaims in his Letter to the Romans that a new life of freedom is possible. Everything humans try to do has been perfectly done, once and for all, by Jesus in his life, death, and resurrection. In accepting God's gift, humans find that their burdens of fear of death and guilt regarding failure are lifted. By opening themselves to God's activity in Jesus, Christians are freed from the confines of their suffocating egos, and can now live for others. Their world is changed. Indeed, creation and all of life are transformed to such a degree that humans are now free to respond to God as a close friend.

The Stories Exemplified

Other Stories

Stories have been popular throughout Christian history. They tell in various ways how Christians have imitated the master story of Jesus and incorporated the reality of forgiveness and freedom into their lives. Extensive collections of saints' legends grew increasingly elaborate and were compiled as a popular form of literature. These included both regional collections (e.g., that of Gregory of Tours in the sixth century), and classic encyclopedias of saints (e.g., the *Golden Legend*, assembled by Jacob of Voragine in the thirteenth century).

Miracles and wondrous stories of all kinds have been ascribed to popular religious heroes right down to the present day. The lives of Irish saints are particularly vivid models of expressing belief in the Christian story. Reading them, one is plunged into a magic world of mystery and wonder. More than other saints, the Irish held sway over the elements of nature (e.g., generating flames from their fingertips and surviving immersion for hours in ice water). In fact, Patrick, the patron saint of Ireland, melted snow by making the sign of the cross over it.

Human Witnesses

Francis of Assisi. Francis of Assisi (1182-1226) fully lived the Christian story. During the era of the Crusades, an infamous period when Christians embraced violence as an instrument of the kingdom of God, Francis came as a missionary of peace and justice with a radical new vision. As the result of a dream he freely gave up his great youthful ambition to fight as a knight with the papal armies. He renounced the army to become a "soldier of the cross." He heard his call not from a Christ who rules the universe, but from a Christ with

Francis of Assisi manifests his spirituality of suffering with Christ on the cross by bearing the imprint of Jesus' wounds on his body.

nails in his hands and feet and a lance wound in his side. Francis founded a religious community and led his companions, his friars, to seek a sharing in the sufferings of Jesus. In his writings he taught that life is a succession of vain deluding pleasures that is only countered by repentance and suffering. His personal identification with the Christian story focused on the sufferings of Jesus. He bore the imprint of Jesus' wounds: Nail marks appeared on his hands and feet and his right side was marked with a red wound from which blood often flowed.

Francis made the kingdom of God present in his life by inverting the values prevalent in his time with a vision filled with paradoxes. He saw poverty as true riches, weakness as strength, rejection as happiness. He confronted institutional Christian life with the challenge of living absolutely without possessions in the service of the gospel. Once, while visiting Rome, Francis struck up a deal with a beggar. Giving his fine clothes to the poor man and receiving rags in return, he proclaimed it a liberating and exhilarating experience. He spent the rest of his stay in Rome living among the outcasts of society, experiencing real poverty.

Francis manifested his spirituality of suffering with Christ especially by his identification with the poverty and humility of Jesus' birth. He saw the incarnation of the God-man Jesus as a window onto divine compassion. Francis introduced a new way of telling the story of the birth of Jesus: He was the first to present the nativity crib scene, with the manger, ox, and ass. By showing the humble circumstances into which Jesus was born and drawing attention to the simplicity and inconveniences of a stable, Francis proclaimed the joy of the incarnation with new directness. With his crib scene, he brought the story of Jesus to life again in the hearts of many who had forgotten him.

Penny Lernoux. One sterling Christian witness of the late twentieth century was Penny Lernoux. Until her death from cancer in 1989, she had spent nearly thirty years in Latin America as a very zealous reformer. Involved as a newspaper reporter and author, she won numerous awards for her journalism and books. Two contrasting visions of faith were at stake in her writings: the church of Caesar— powerful and materially rich, and the church of Christ—loving, poor, and spiritually rich. She wrote of the hope and freedom that an enlivened church of Christ could give to the impoverished masses of Latin America. The church of Christ she promoted was a force for democracy, justice, and peace, for empowerment of the poor, for the sanctuary movement.

Lernoux struggled to get the Roman Catholic bishops in Latin America to cease blessing the policies of the traditional ruling groups and to undertake dramatic gestures of solidarity with the poor and the oppressed. Her socially progressive message summoned people to change their hearts against the wave of savagery and religious persecution. She called for an end to the growing spiral of violence in Latin American culture. Whether writing of the impulses behind Castro's revolution in Cuba, or the Sandinistas in Nicaragua, or the assassination of El Salvador's Archbishop Romero, she was fully convinced that Christians had to commit themselves to political struggle in order to bring to it the light of the gospel and the salt of God's word.

Communities

Christian communities formed themselves around the proclamation that "Salvation is at hand," that "Christ has died, Christ is risen, Christ will come again." As these communities grew through the early centuries, Christianity gradually inherited the old Roman empire and its institutions. In its early days, it took on all that was good, true, and beautiful in the pagan world around it for its worship and practice. The church enriched its ritual year by accommodating the rhythms and cycles of nature and took over shrines and holy days dedicated to pagan gods. Easter, for example, was the name of a festival in honor of the Anglo-Saxon goddess of the dawn and of spring, and the fire and water rituals of the Easter Vigil echo Roman fertility rituals.

Christianity spread from its origins in the European and Mediterranean world and today is truly worldwide. Phenomenal growth continues to occur in Central and South America, and it is estimated that half the Christians in the world in the year 2000 will live in these two areas. Its growth in size made unity more and more difficult through the centuries, and today there are three major branches: Roman Catholic, Protestant, and Orthodox.

Orthodoxy. The Orthodox Christians were the first to break from the Roman church, splitting definitively in the eleventh century. Differences of wording in creeds, of the extent of teaching authority, and of collegiality all contributed to the split, as did language barriers, the Crusades, and the growing political power of the popes in Rome. Orthodoxy ("right worship") is more important than right teaching. "Don't ask what we believe," they say; "ask whom we worship." A sense of mystery, rather than law or judgment, pervades their understanding of God. They proclaim the liberating victory of Jesus' resurrection more than his redemptive suffering on

An icon of the angel Gabriel draws Orthodox Christians through the material world into communion with the mysterious world beyond.

the cross. "We died with Christ to be raised with Christ," they say. "If we knew the truth of it, every day is Easter."

The Orthodox stress theosis ("human deification"), that is, the restoration of God's image in humans through the incarnation of Christ. They believe that humans carry an image of God in themselves and are, indeed, icons ("images") of God. Icons are an insep6arable part of their tradition. When Christ's image is portrayed on an icon picture, his divinity flows through the icon and participates in their prayer life. Icons draw them through the material world into communion with the unspeakable world beyond. Icons are windows to heaven, representing God's mysterious coming to earth and the human passage into the spiritual world.

Christians in the Orthodox tradition are found mainly in the countries of Eastern Europe. Under communist domination, their story has been a tale of heavy censorship of official church information and religious services, of confiscation of church property, and of nationalization of the priesthood. Today church-state relations run the gamut from total oppression to relative freedom. In Russia, the Orthodox church, which has been excluded from the educational system and not allowed to own property, is in a state of flux in an era of glasnost. In Greece, the church is a state agency: In exchange for servicing the religious needs of the people, it enjoys economic support from the state.

Protestantism. As Christianity became the dominant religious and political institution in medieval Europe, reformers, especially Martin Luther (1483-1546) in Germany and John Calvin (1509-1564) in Switzerland, called Christians back to their original experience and purpose. Luther, for example, proclaimed that faith in Jesus' action on the cross, and this faith alone, is the essence of the Good News. Everything else is absolutely worthless for salvation. In Ninety-Five Theses he hit especially at papal claims to control the selling of indulgences (that is, remission of punishment due to sins), calling into question the whole structure of papal authority and the role of church as mediator.

The teachings of Luther and Calvin constitute the core of the classical Protestant tradition. The Bible, which can be interpreted by individuals, is the sole source of religious authority. Protestants testify for the sovereign place of God in human life: Clergy, tradition, and the pope have no claim to authority. Anything (dogmas, sacraments, church, the state, or human intellect) that commands absolute allegiance is diabolical. Humans, these reformers taught, have been given authority over the world of nature and are accountable for it. Because individuals have freedom they also have ultimate responsibility for the burden of their sins.

The Protestant traditions have played a crucial role in developing American institutions, and they provide a religious dimension for the whole fabric of American life, including the separation of church and state, religious pluralism, and freedom of conscience. There are more than 300 different churches in about a dozen main groupings in American Protestantism. While most come out of the Reformed tradition of Calvin and the Lutheran tradition, many belong to the Methodist tradition, started by John Wesley (1703-1791). His followers brought his revivalist methods and repertoire of hymns from England to America and fervently preached his message of personal conversion, cordial fellowship, and the warmth of God's love against the dominion of sin. The uplifting message that persons will never fall away or be damned once they are "born again" through personal conversion, has caused Pentecostals and Holiness groups to thrive. Many groups with distinct American roots have proliferated, among them Jehovah's Witnesses, Seventh Day Adventists, and Mormons. They flourish with their distinctive biblical beliefs, efficient social organization, and conviction that the end of the world is at hand.

Roman Catholicism. The Roman Catholic church is the largest of the Christian communities, with almost a billion members today. Characteristics stressed by Catholics include attachment to the pope, the sacramental (ritual) system, respect for the natural world and belief in natural law, devotion to Mary as the mother of Jesus, religious pilgrimages and processions, and the communion of saints.

When the Roman Catholic bishops gathered in Rome in the 1960s at the Second Vatican Council, they began to update their traditions and practices while retaining their vitality and commitment. In the Declaration on Religious Freedom, for example, the bishops openly recognize the inviolable value of personal conviction, that the individual conscience is infallible. They acknowledge that truth is to be found in the non-catholic Christian traditions and they spell out a theology of respect for other world religions. They underline the importance and role of lay people within the church. The pope, the sign of unity of the Catholic ("universal") church, is primarily servant, and his authority is to empower the people of the church. Priests are to be recognized for their pastoral presence rather than their administrative role in the church. The church is a pilgrim church, the people of God, moving toward human transformation.

Catholic immigrants came to the United States in large numbers in the middle of the nineteenth century, to escape famine or to find freedom of religious expression. Considered "unwashed, unlettered, and unfed" by the Protestant majority, many of these Catholics were illiterate, and very few had time or money for higher education. Meeting in Baltimore in 1884, the American Catholic bishops pulled their people back from the mainstream of American life by founding a separate, extensive private school system, and organizing Catholic neighborhoods and social units (parishes). This parochial separation characterized Roman Catholicism in America for a couple of generations. The separation has dissipated in recent years, however, and Catholics have become part of the mainstream of American social, economic, and political life.

Catholics in America today enjoy a healthy pluralism. Their newspapers are as diverse as *The National Catholic Reporter* (liberal in tone, urging the sanctuary movement and married priests, for example) and *The Wanderer* (arch-conservative). Groups are as distinct as the Catholics United for the Faith (right-wing) and the Women's Ordination Conference (which confronts the male hierarchical structure of the clergy and calls for full participation of women as ministers of the eucharist). Recently all American Catholics have been challenged in two letters from their bishops. In their letter *The Challenge of Peace: God's Promise and Our Response* (1983), the bishops came down hard against nuclear warfare and pressed for negotiation in any national conflicts. In 1986, in *Economic Justice for All*, they criticized the prevailing American capitalistic system and strongly stressed a "preferential option for the poor" in matters of social justice.

Twentieth Century

Ecumenical Movement. The Christian communities are discovering that they are not alone in confessing their faith or in their responsibilities of caring for the world around them. Through a flourishing ecumenical movement, both within and between the churches, they are showing great respect for each other and forgiveness for harsh polemics in the past. They promote better relations, mutual enrichment, and better knowledge of each other, especially through the organization of the World Council of Churches. They are forming bonds through dialogues on doctrines and church administration. They are working to provide for more creative and collaborative use of resources to achieve their common mission of proclaiming God's loving forgiveness and liberating the oppressed from social injustices. Success in discussions and interactions with each other has led them to begin similar creative enterprises with people in other world religions.

Fundamentalism. If there is an issue that divides Christians in America, it is the phenomenon of fundamentalism. Millions of Christian fundamentalists claim the Scriptures are infallible and without error, and they repudiate modern critical ways of interpreting the Bible as a work of human literature. They believe in a literalist interpretation of many Christian teachings, such as creation, sin, bodily resurrection, the second coming of Jesus, personal salvation through atonement, and miracles. They present a Jesus with little or no humanity: He was pre-existent, born of a virgin, claimed divinity, knew all things, and was in control of his destiny.

Fundamentalists are opposed to humanism, the idea that humans can solve their own problems (claiming that this reduces the power of God). They also oppose the theory of evolution (claiming it undercuts the authority of the Bible). They resist the rise of impersonal urban civilization (claiming city life is trivial, transient, vacuous, and detrimental to human values), and the modern liberal sexual revolution. Some Roman Catholics are also fundamentalists: They believe not only in the literalism of the Bible, but also in a literal and non-historical reading of papal pronouncements as a sure bulwark against the tides of relativism, the claims of science, and other inroads of modernity.

There are many ties between fundamentalists and the "electronic church," that is, the commercial religious networks and programs that proliferate on radio and television. These groups use modern technology and business strategies for political as well as religious purposes. Their preaching, worldview, and interpretation of American religion commonly include a message to keep America strong against communism, to fight against drug abuse, and to promote self-esteem as the healthy core of humanity-helping religion. They regularly include the revivalist stress of being "born again" and accepting Jesus as sole savior. Recently the electronic church has suffered a loss of popularity due to allegations of mismanagement of its considerable financial funds and the personal misconduct of some of its leaders.

Liberals. Far removed from the fundamentalists are those who are more liberal and modern in their approach to Christianity. They welcome scientific and humanistic discoveries. The liberals attempt to reconcile critical biblical scholarship with traditional thinking, seeing Scripture as a fallible but inspired guide for human lives. Recognizing the existence of individual charisms, they call for the collegial exercise of authority in institutional decision making. They raise sexual issues in the context of married love—of loving, caring, serving, and forgiving another human being—and not merely the usual questions about pornography, birth control, abortion, family planning, premarital sex, homosexuality, or test tube babies.

Liberals are involved in resistance movements against nuclear war and in struggles for minority rights. Archbishop Raymond Hunthausen of Seattle is a prophetic witness in this area, a peace-movement activist who has withheld part of his income tax to protest government spending on nuclear arms. Dorothy Day, founder of the Catholic Worker Movement in 1934, was also active in peace movements and opposed nuclear armaments. As part of her ministry to the poor, she fought against underemployment and cutbacks in social programs and operated a soup kitchen and shelter on the Bowery in New York City, for many years.

Human Rights. In America, many Christians, both fundamentalist and liberal, live out the Christian story through their involvement in issues of human rights. Forgiveness and freedom foster in them basic attitudes and ways of undertaking programs of action. Through their awareness of their relationship with God and their commitment to help fulfill the kingdom of God, they possess a certain strength and perspective in relation to other people. They exercise care and compassion in the struggle to liberate all human beings from hunger and poverty, from greed and consumerism, from technological threats to the environment. They acknowledge the tolerance necessary for effective political and religious action in a pluralistic society. Sensitive to the natural world and to other people, they struggle against the proliferation of nuclear weapons, the pollution of the environment, and the widening gap between rich and poor nations. They encourage women and women's organizations to develop self-affirmation, self-confidence, and self-worth.

The struggle for human rights is very real in rural areas and the peripheries of large cities in Brazil and other Latin American countries. Thousands of small groups of Christians band together in "base communities." Skirting problems with the church structure and a shortage of clergy, these groups use a grassroots approach to confront the causes of injustice wherever possible. They study and apply the Christian Scriptures to their experiences, linking up their religion with social transformation and striving to make visible the signs of the kingdom of liberation that Jesus preached.

Ritual: The Eucharist

Participation in the sacramental system is important both for individual Christians and the body of Christian believers. Christians set aside key moments each year and key moments in the human life cycle for ritual celebrations. Each year, they celebrate the birth of Jesus at the popular feast of Christmas and encounter their risen Lord Jesus at Easter, the culmination of the most profound Holy Week of the ritual calendar.

The eucharist (or Lord's Supper) is the central ritual for Christians. In it they remember the final wish of Jesus who, at his last supper, took bread and wine and gave thanks to the Father, thereby reenacting the master story of Jesus' life, death, and resurrection and commemorating God's gifts of forgiveness and freedom. Each time they celebrate the eucharist, and particularly on Sundays, Christians anticipate Jesus' return and the banquet of the kingdom of God.

In the ritual of the Eucharist, Christians remember the final gift of Jesus who took bread and wine and gave thanks to God.

The ritual of the eucharist is a communal sharing of the Christian story, a thanksgiving feast for God's generous love and gifts of forgiveness and freedom. Listening to the proclaimed word of the Scripture readings, Christians share a common faith in the deeds and sayings of Jesus' life and in the good news that Jesus is risen and present among them. In their prayers and hymns, they share their needs and hopes, their sorrows and joys. Christians ask for forgiveness, exchange a kiss of peace, and share the meal of bread and wine. Before they leave, they share a moment of silence, during which the Spirit strengthens them for their mission to be witnesses and instruments of the kingdom in their daily lives.

The Stories Appropriated

What can Christians learn from reading again the stories of the forgiveness of the prodigal son and the liberating conversion of Paul? These stories present new ways for us to envision our own spiritual convictions. Reading about forgiveness and freedom challenges us to respond in a personal way to our own religion on the basis of transformed decisions.

Compassion

The prodigal son "comes to himself" when he is forgiven by his father. Though he has wandered from the center of his tradition and family, the word of forgiveness is the social gesture that helps him overcome his estrangement. We do not know whether his older brother joins the banquet celebration or whether he chooses alienation over reconciliation. Christianity is at bottom a gift that can be accepted or rejected. It is a religion established on the word of forgiveness and the healing touch of Jesus. Still, this remains little understood and rarely taught. It is just so hard for us to accept that God is compassionate, like the prodigal's father, and loves us in spite of ourselves. So many of us remain convinced that the only way to keep God happy, our children safe, our psyches adjusted, and our neighbors reasonable is to always do what is expected by tradition, to be ready at every moment for God's accounting.

We find it difficult to recognize that in forgiveness there is a sense of giftedness, both fascinating and frightening, that comes over into our own lives and family relationships. We find it difficult to make forgiveness a zero-sum game in which all are winners, and in which no one person succeeds at the expense and sacrifice of others. In his many parables, Jesus teaches the way of compassion, the ability to be equal and interdependent, and to interact through and with each other. Persons can choose death by not forgiving; they can destroy themselves by not saying "yes" to justice, to celebration. Forgiveness is the great "yes" to life.

We forget that forgiveness is an act not necessarily of forgetting, but certainly of remission that allows life to go on. Persons who cannot forgive others—and perhaps more importantly, who do not know how to accept being forgiven—are blocked from wisdom and even from growth. They cling to the belief that revenge is the root of discipline, or the source of authority, or their only trustworthy security. Harboring resentment makes for stunted persons. The triumph of our human maturity and wisdom is the movement beyond such revenge to forgiveness.

Hospitality

Like the father who welcomes his alien son to his family table, Jesus receives marginal people, eating with tax collectors and sinners, calling all to share in God's great supper. He calls to our attention the presence of God in ordinary exchanges between human guests and hosts. As God's hospitality to us in person, Jesus gives himself in the most radical fashion to be the sustenance of life and hope for others, at the same time inviting his guests to do the same for each other.

Though there are risks inherent in hospitality, strangers received graciously will enlarge rather than diminish our total well-being. In the mutual giving and receiving of hospitality, both guest and host can reveal their most precious gifts and bring new life to each other. Hospitality means inviting the stranger into our private space, whether the space of our own home or of our personal awareness and concern. And when we do, some important transformations occur. Our private space is suddenly enlarged and illumined, no longer tight and cramped and restricted, but open and expansive and free. Hospitality to the stranger gives us a chance to see our own lives afresh, through different eyes. This reality has not been lost in the Christian tradition: The three major festivals of the Christian church, Christmas, Easter, and Pentecost, all have to do with the advent of a divine stranger. The child in the manger, the traveler on the road to Emmaus, and the mighty wind of the Spirit all encounter us as mysterious visitors, challenging our belief systems even as they welcome us to new worlds.

Reaching Out

To participate in the kingdom, our own actions have to be in tune with God's action. The prodigal son's father shows us what God's action is: reaching outward in love, reaching beyond the self to all that exists. This is not in any way self-destructive, for authentic self-love and authentic love of the other are necessarily mutually inclusive. The significance of Jesus lies in terms of the values he lived by, which are centered around the concrete needs of human beings. For Jesus, human welfare is an absolute value that is the basis of his ministry. Those who want to focus their lives on the story of Jesus have to try to carry generosity out into the world. They also have to try to manifest the kingdom in action, that is, a solidarity with fellow humans that includes those from other religions. They try, with God's grace, to cooperate with others to overcome fears and hatreds and to create a climate where people are enabled to live together in the solidarity of love as brothers and sisters.

Finding the Self

Paul is a model of how God can surprise even the most staunch and merciless persecutor of the church with a call to follow Jesus. His life exemplifies the search for the true self. In finding Jesus, Paul finds himself, or begins to find himself. He then sets out on a journey of self-realization that extends over the whole cycle of his life. Paul freely accepts the invitation: Knowing Christ Jesus as his Lord and addressing God as loving parent is a profound experience of liberation that turns his life upside down. He achieves a new life of wholeness. In our own maturing process we are involved in a group enterprise, using our particular gifts to help "build up the body of Christ," not just a personal journey. Because our lives are measured against "the stature of the fullness of Christ," they have to develop in such a way that the good of the whole and, indeed, the good of the universe, take priority over individual development.

Born Again

Just as Paul's conversion is a transformation, inaugurated by faith in Jesus, so are we called to follow Christ by seeking God's glory and by showing compassion to others. Conversion is a turning away from a life characterized by sin and alienation from God to a new life of meaning and purpose through God's love and forgiveness in Jesus Christ. When we experience conversion, we begin to develop a personality that is not self-centered, but centered on the transcendent and on other persons. We then become witnesses to God's activity in us through our joy. We cease trying to bring about our own wholeness and instead surrender our will to a higher power. This final leap of faith is surprisingly met by a sudden surge of confidence, peace, and freedom, in the conviction that the kingdom of God is being established.

Conversion is the transition from painful self-consciousness and competing desires to a new sense of unity and its accompanying feelings of assurance, comfort, and freedom. This means letting Christ's word reshape our thoughts, letting his example refashion our conduct, and letting his love completely transform us. Conversion is a therapeutic act of reinterpreting the past in a spirit of forgiveness and gratitude, a deep inner feeling of balance in relation to the rest of the world. Finally, conversion is answering the call to transform the world, for it is addressed not only to a change of heart, not merely to a change of the cultural structures of human existence, but to the well-being of the entire planet.

Conclusion

The Christian story is the story of the death and resurrection of

Jesus. Through Jesus, God gives humans the gift of a share of the kingdom, indeed of God's own eternal life. Humans can participate in this kingdom in many of their own experiences, but especially in their experiences of forgiveness and freedom.

Christians treasure the story that Jesus tells in the parable of the prodigal son, for it portrays the universal compassion and forgiveness that God offers to all humans. In consequence, they are called to display such dedicated constancy themselves, both to God and to each other.

The story of Paul's conversion experience is the story of freedom. It tells how Christianity is not a religion based on observance of the Law, but on God's free gift. By recognizing that they are saved by God's activity in Christ, Christians are free to live with passion and without compromise, knowing they are cooperating in bringing about God's kingdom.

Discussion Questions

1. Why do you think the author chooses the cathedral at Chartres to introduce Jesus and the church?

2. Describe the Christian God in terms of unity, incarnation, immanence, and transcendence.

3. Summarize the Christian belief in salvation in terms of sin, grace, and kingdom of God.

4. Describe the differences in character between the prodigal son, his brother, and his father.

5. Explain Paul's language of grace and righteousness in referring to his call.

6. Summarize the differences between the fundamentalist and the liberal approaches to Christianity.

7. What can Christians reappropriate today from the stories of the prodigal son and the conversion of Paul?

8. Discussion Starter: "If you have a house of your own, you are poor; if you have the house of God, you are rich. In your own house you will fear thieves; in God's house God himself is the wall. Blessed, then, are they who dwell in God's house. They possess the heavenly Jerusalem, without distress, without pressure, without diverse and divided boundaries. All possess it; and each singly possesses the whole." (Augustine)

9. Discussion Starter: "Often our trust is not full. We are not certain that God hears us because we consider ourselves worthless and as nothing. This is ridiculous and the very cause of our weakness." (Julian of Norwich)

10. Discussion Starter: "Christian people should commit themselves to political struggle in order to bring to it the light of the gospel and the salt of God's word....Let my death, if it is accepted by God, be for my people's liberation and as a witness of hope in the future." (Oscar Romero)

The encircling movement of the pilgrims around the Kaaba at Mecca in Saudi Arabia helps them concentrate their attention continually on Allah.

Chapter Five

ISLAM
Submission and Martyrdom

Setting the Scene

Mecca

In Saudi Arabia, a great boundary stone marks the beginning of the sacred territory of Mecca, prohibited to those who are not Muslims. Mecca is a sacred space, a zone of special sanctuary and consecration. In the heart of Mecca, surrounded by the splendid Great Mosque of nineteen arched gateways, is the Kaaba. A simple cube of masonry housing a Black Stone, probably a meteorite, in one corner, and traditionally decked with black cloth with gold arabesques, the Kaaba is the sacred house of Allah (God), the center of the earth.

The Kaaba, or place of prostration, symbolizes the seat of the divine presence. It is the magnetic center toward which the mithrab (the prayer niche) in every mosque of the Muslim world is directed. It is the center to which all Muslims bow five times every day in their prayers. Believers throughout the Muslim world face in the direction of the Kaaba at Mecca with open hands, palms forward at head height and recite "Allahu Akbar" ("God is most great"). Then they recite verses from their sacred writings, the Qur'an (or Koran), with more bows and prostrations. Every year the Hajj (the great pilgrimage) brings millions of Arabs together to Mecca. The encircling

123

movement of the pilgrims around the Kaaba during the Hajj recalls the movement of thoughts or meditations turning perpetually around Allah, the Lord of this House, who provides them with food in their hunger and safety in their fear.

With more than 925 million members throughout the world, Islam cuts across many cultures and encompasses a wide variety of social and ethnic groups. Expanding from its roots in the Arabian peninsula in the 7th century C.E., Dar al-Islam, the "house of Islam," today stretches from Morocco to Indonesia. There are more than forty independent nations where Muslims are the majority of the people. The most populous Muslim nation in the world is Indonesia, and the largest grouping is found on the subcontinent of India (including Pakistan, India, and Bangladesh). Muslims today live in a variety of political structures, from Islamic states like Pakistan and Iran to secular states like Turkey. Though concentrated for the most part on the continents of Asia and Africa, Islam is still growing rapidly in Africa, America, and the Soviet Union.

Islam permeates the self-perception of people in Muslim countries and provides a common pattern for religious and social life. A sense of Islamic unity is reflected in the art, architecture, and urban life of major Muslim centers all over the world. The overarching power of Islam across nearly all of the Middle East has made it a formidable political force to be reckoned with in the modern world.

Surrender

Muslim and Islam both mean "surrender" (to God's law). The Muslim religion is primarily voluntary submission in trust and faith to Allah. To be a Muslim is to fight the jihad ("holy war") within the self against anything that would take away the sovereignty of the one God, Allah. It is a religion whose community is wider than that of tribes, or even nations, with a special concern and care for the poor, the orphans, and the weaker members of society. All Muslims belong to the ummah, the ideal human society, in which they submit their lives totally in accordance with God's will as revealed through the prophet Muhammad. The ummah is universal and worldwide, but it takes on concrete form in various Islamic nations and also in the communities of Muslims grouped together for mosque assemblies. The Muslim ummah is characterized precisely by the organic relationship between the realms of religion and politics. Muslim fellowship does not rest on ties of blood, class, education, or politics, but on a common covenant, a mutual submission to

Allah, loyalty to one another, and recognition of Muhammad as the messenger who transmitted God's revelation and founded the Muslim community.

Shariah

The fundamental religious attitude of Islam is to maintain wholeness and proper order by accepting God's law. Perhaps more than any other world religion, Islam is a religion of laws. The rules, duties, and obligations of correct practice legislated by God for the ummah are contained in the Shariah, the sacred law for Muslims. The Shariah is the divinely guided way of life, the "road that leads to God." Derived from the revelation (Qur'an) and the example (sunnah and hadith) of Muhammad, the Shariah represents God's total design for the proper order of all human activities. At the political level, the Shariah defines the nature of the Muslim state, the duties and responsibilities of leaders, and the organization of institutions that assure the security and well-being of the community.

At the social and personal level, the Shariah elaborates exact standards for conduct. It guides and regulates Muslim lives, and it shows them the best way to fulfill their highest potential. In addition to providing rules for social, economic, and family life, the Shariah defines in detail the specific religious duties incumbent on Muslims. In today's complex world, when all countries depend to some extent on an international economic, political, and military order, the Shariah is increasingly subjected to some reforms or even supplanted by other legal systems. Theoretically, the Shariah rules all of Muslim life; in reality, many Muslims have never heard of it. In only a few countries (Saudi Arabia, Iran, and Pakistan, for example) does the Shariah court exercise jurisdiction in all spheres of life.

Faith and Allah

In Islam, every aspect of human life, every thought and every action, is shaped and evaluated in the light of the Shahadah, their basic article of faith: "I testify that there is no God but God; I testify that Muhammad is the Messenger of God." The other basic constituents of Muslim faith—belief in angels, in revealed books, in God's messengers, and in the Last Day—all revolve around the central Muslim belief that God alone is great.

Islam is a religion of surrender to God's universal sovereignty. It is a sober, almost fated acceptance of whatever life brings. The will of Allah dominates the Muslim psyche: Allah utterly controls the world, and even poverty and illness are accepted "as Allah wills." All the world and all human affairs belong only to Allah. There are no great rituals, symbols, or priesthood in Islam, for Allah can be worshiped anywhere by anyone in simple forms prescribed by the Qur'an and by tradition. Witness to the divine oneness includes consequences in everyday life. It has encouraged national resistance movements and been the war cry of Muslim armies.

Though the transcendent God of creation, Allah is not remote from the world. Allah is near to humans, "nearer than the jugular vein," and unceasingly calls humans to draw near. Whatever exists in space and time depends utterly on God. Allah is the all-knowing and all powerful arbiter of good and evil, the final judge of all humans. Allah is slow to anger and quick to forgive. The greatest prayer in Islam is the Fatiha (the first chapter of the Qur'an): "In the name of God, the compassionate, the merciful: Praise be to Allah, Lord of the creation, the compassionate, the merciful, king of the last judgment! You alone we worship, and to you alone we pray for help. Guide us to the straight path, the path of those whom you have favored, not of those who have incurred your wrath, nor of those who have gone astray."

The essence of Islamic spirituality is nothing other than the awareness of and resignation to tawhid (the oneness or unity of Allah). Allah is the source of all human life: Everything comes from Allah and returns to Allah, in this life and beyond. Allah is the first and the last, the manifest and the hidden, the outward and the inward. Nothing escapes the power, intentions, guidance, or divine favor of Allah. Recognition of the oneness of God means that everything exists in relation to God. As the great Muslim scholar and mystic Al-Ghazali (1058-1111) expressed it: "God is like a mirror: those who look at God see themselves reflected there in all their many parts, yet the mirror is one." Still, the divine nature is inaccessible to humans. To deny the sovereignty and oneness of Allah—to pay blind obedience to a dictator, or to a religious leader, or to one's own whims and desires, for example—is the greatest offense in Islam.

Human Salvation

The Problem: Neglect
Though humans are impotent little things (brothers and sisters to the ant) who walk briefly on the earth, Islam also recognizes them

as the caliphs of God, created by God to reflect the divine names and qualities in the world. Humans are created to serve as divine "managers" of the world. They are gifted with intelligence, alone capable of knowing the Reality of which they are a manifestation, alone able to rise above their own earthly and qualified selfhood. All humans have the possibility of realizing the fullness of their nature.

In spite of their gifts, humans are limited and imperfect and find many obstacles in the way of using their intelligence and wills in submission to God's law. Humans are inherently inattentive, not paying attention to their own true nature. They are preoccupied, allowing the guidance given by religious models in the past to slip gradually out of their memories. With their tendency to live in a dream world, they are unaware of who they are and what they should be doing in this world. This neglect, or lack of vision, or forgetfulness of their real nature is the deficiency that lies at the base of human sin and evil.

Humans deny the truth about themselves and the dignity that Allah has given them. This is another form of what Muslims call shirk. Shirk is the human refusal to acknowledge God as sovereign, or the human insistence on associating someone or something with God. Shirk is the most heinous and unforgivable sin. Giving in to their lower selves and to their greedy and vain feelings of self-sufficiency, humans act to cut themselves off from God. By focusing on something other than God, they deny the divine foundation within themselves. The basic human problem, then, is the disorder that springs from insufficient submission to God. This weakness, or flaw, in human nature is due to Iblis, the devil, the ultimate agent behind this misguidance. Iblis tempts humans to set up a society in which they stand themselves up against heaven and regard themselves as the unconditional masters rather than members of the natural world.

The Strategy: The Five Pillars

The good Muslim strives to offer the self in humble submission to God's divine will, to be content with what happens, especially in the face of tribulations, illness, and death. The Islamic religion is primarily a voluntary surrender to divine providence, a belief that everything has been decided by God, that all comes from God. Besides submission, though, the Muslims believe in high standards of justice and the proper exercise of political power. They believe that humans have the ability to transcend their pettiness (such as greed, fraud, holding back from spending for the poor) and to treat all people with compassion. The right and duty to use human faculties, powers, and resources in such a way as to fulfill genuine needs and desires, to achieve success and happiness, are perfectly permissible. Humans must do this, however, without jeopardizing the interests of other people or causing them any harm. Muslims achieve mutual assistance and cooperation by following the Shariah and, in particular, by carrying out the Five Pillars.

The Five Pillars include not only the previously mentioned profession of faith, but also the rites of daily prayers, fasting, pilgrimage, and the paying of a religious tax. Reminders of Muslim commitment to God's covenant, the Five Pillars are calls for social justice. Besides the spiritual benefits the observance of the Five Pillars bestows on individuals, it contributes enormously toward producing that cohesiveness and spirit of solidarity that is a palpable characteristic of the Muslim community to this day.

The first pillar, of course, is the profession of *faith*, the Shahadah: "There is no God but God, and Muhammad is his prophet." The purpose of the pillar of *prayer* is to awaken people from their dreams of forgetfulness so as to remember God always. Muslims are to pray five times a day, facing toward Mecca, thus orienting their entire life to God. By taking time from ordinary events, they bring their whole lives into the context of God and God's word. The purpose of the pillar of *fasting* is to die to the passionate self and be born in purity. During the month of Ramadan, Muslims neither eat nor drink from dawn to dusk. This binds them together in an awareness of their common goals: During their fast they accent exercise of obedience to God, thanksgiving for the gift of the Qur'an, the nearness of God, awareness of the poor, and spiritual purification.

The pillar of *almsgiving* implies spiritual generosity and nobility in the ethical and social dimension. Muslims pay a zakat, a kind of charitable tax meant to support the poor. Today this tax has lapsed except in such very traditionalist countries as Saudi Arabia, and it has been replaced by a state taxation that allows the financing of public enterprises, such as new roads and bridges. The pillar of the *pilgrimage* to Mecca (the Hajj) introduces Muslims to the significant events of the life of Muhammad and gives them a foretaste of the ultimate pilgrimage to the Gardens of Allah. Though all are obliged to make the pilgrimage once in their lifetime, most never go, since it is physically and numerically impossible.

The Solution: Paradise

The success that Muslims hope for in this world runs the gamut from ordinary physical and emotional well-being to serene joy and faith in adversity. They have intelligent regard for the wondrous gifts of this life. Muslims regard success or salvation as their final religious goal and essential destiny. Salvation means not so much that the soul can rest eternally with God but that a human community is willing and able to implement—on earth—God's will and guidelines for human societies.

Regarding the afterlife, Muslims believe that there are rewards for the righteous and punishments for the infidels, beginning immediately after death. The righteous will easily proceed across the bridge of judgment and return to God "whose hand controls everything." The righteous are those who feed the needy and beggars, care for orphans, free slaves, and are generous and God-fearing. The infidels will fall from the bridge of judgment into the pits of hell. The infidels are those who do not feed the needy, devour their inheritance, love wealth, pray without care, and make big displays but are not generous.

The success of the life to come is eternal and beyond human description. The Qur'an speaks continuously and joyously of praising God amid heavenly gardens, shelters of plenteous shade, and pure brooks and rivers. In picturesque language it describes heaven where goblets of wine will flow without headaches or addled wits. There the righteous shall have the flesh of fowl as they desire. Music will be provided for those who like it, horses for those who wish to ride, and beautiful serving maidens. Thoughtful Muslims of all periods have discerned deeper symbolic levels in the vivid Qur'anic depictions of paradise that ultimately transcend worldly physical description and the life of the senses.

The Sacred Writings

The Qur'an

For the Muslims, the primary sacred text is, of course, the *Qur'an*, a faithful recording ("recitation") of God's special revelations to the prophet Muhammad through the angel Gabriel. As Muhammad grew older he took seasonal retreats in a cave in a mountain outside Mecca. One night Gabriel came to Muhammad while he was alone in meditation and commanded him to "recite." This experience continued periodically for twenty-two years. Muhammad reports that the inspiration that came to him was often accompanied by strange sounds, like the clanging of a bell. The early revelations are poetic and passionate. The later ones, dating from the years that Muhammad spent in Medina, are more political and military. They specify instructions and regulations for the ordering of every detail for the community he is constructing. The revelations are eventually put down in writing in 114 surahs, or chapters.

Most chapters deal with several different subjects, often in a repetitious way. In addition to its many oracles, the Qur'an also contains stories, poetry, laws, exhortations, moral principles, and apocalyptic warnings, with little in the way of narrative historical matter. Muhammad offers encouragement, assurance of the reality of his inspiration, and advice on how to act. He employs concrete images (e.g., ants, ladders, earthquakes) and metaphors. Those who imagine other gods besides Allah, for example, are like the spider weaving its own frail house; their works are like ashes blown away by the wind; their prayers are only the whistling and clapping of hands.

The Qur'an depends greatly upon the Hebrew Scriptures. A prominent story is the account of Abraham's willingness to sacrifice his son, Isaac, to God. Muslims recite many episodes from the life of Moses—his deliverance of the children of Israel and the giving of the Law, for example. They read Nathan's parable to David and the stories of Solomon as a great builder and lover of horses.

Muhammad also shows some, though not intimate, knowledge of the Christian Scriptures. Drawing from the narrative material of the Gospels, he lays particular stress on the virgin birth and the miracles of Jesus. Muhammad includes the parable of the wise and foolish virgins, the judgment scene, and the institution of the eucharist. He denies the divinity of Jesus and he rejects the crucifixion as a fable. Muhammad is never simply a borrower of these two traditions. He molds the stories by his reflections and he uses them for his own purposes of spiritual instruction.

Hadiths

Certain collections of *Hadiths* ("reports") have as much influence as the Qur'an in shaping Muslim religious consciousness. They are authoritative compilations of stories about the Prophet's sayings and deeds. Many of them are related by one of Muhammad's trustworthy companions to someone else in the period after his death. His companions take great pleasure in describing him, recounting what he said and did, and telling of their experiences in his company. The

Hadiths are short, unconnected texts, ranging in content and character from simple declarations of Muhammad's view and judgments on a variety of subjects to exalted theological discourses and proclamations of his virtues and achievements. Hadiths include prayers, festivals, bankruptcy matters, wills and testaments, tricks, and dreams. They also deal extensively with livelihood for individual families, as well as social, economic, and political affairs concerning society as a whole. The Hadiths consider ritual problems and the inner life, discuss details of faith and doctrine, tell about the punishment in the next world, and simply describe the prophet's behavior while eating, sleeping, or giving advice.

The most trustworthy Hadiths were put together in large collections in the middle of the ninth century by a series of scholars. The work of Bukhari, containing some seven thousand traditions, is the best known. When authenticated by tracing them back to those who actually knew Muhammad, they possess authority almost equal to the Qur'an itself. On the basis of the Qur'an and the Hadiths, Muslim religious scholars have set forth in detail what submission to God means in daily life.

Muhammad

Many of the details of Muhammad's life (570-632 C.E.) come from the Hadiths rather than the Qur'an. As a young orphan, Muhammad is entrusted to his uncle Abu Talib. He later marries Khadijah, a wealthy widow, and they have four daughters from this marriage. Muhammad works with Khadijah in the camel trade, operating out of Mecca. Impressed by his honesty and sincerity, she is Muhammad's greatest support when his life suddenly changes. Muhammad, pensive and searching for something higher and purer than the traditional religious forms he knows in the Arabian desert, has his first revelation at age forty.

Miraj ("Heavenly Journey"). The miraj is a significant experience only briefly alluded to in the Qur'an, but elaborated and expanded in detail in the Hadiths. This is the visionary flight of Muhammad from Mecca to Jerusalem and his ascent to the Divine Presence. It is an ecstatic experience where Muhammad has an immediate vision of the divine essence. He is awakened by angels near the Kaaba in Mecca who split open his body, take out his heart, and purify it. He is then placed on Burak, a fabulous winged horse with a woman's face, a mule's body, and a peacock's tail. Able to cover distances as far as the eye can see in a single leap, Burak carries the prophet in "the twinkling of an eye" to the temple in Jerusalem. Then, gradually ascending up through the seven heavens, Muhammad is welcomed by the prophets of the Hebrew Scriptures, whom he leads in prayer. As he proceeds, Muhammad encounters falsehood in the form of a stone, jealousy as a scorpion, and greed as a mouse. He is allowed to witness infidels suffering in hell.

Muhammad ascends to the Divine Presence accompanied by angels and transported by Burak, his fabulous winged horse.

Muhammad and the angel Gabriel climb a ladder to heaven and gain entry only after Gabriel vouches that Muhammad has been given a special divine mission. At the gate of Paradise, Muhammad has a flash encounter with Allah, then a debate with Moses. Finally, the veil is lifted, and Allah, seated on the divine throne, draws Muhammad near. This journey, in which Muhammad enjoys intimate, direct, and personal contact with God, has proven for most Muslims his role as the chosen prophet, the authenticity of his predictions, and the reality of the future Paradise.

Hijra ("Flight"). Muhammad, a strong-willed person who feels himself fully consumed by a godly calling and exclusively appointed to his task, accepts the call to preach what he has heard and seen. Like the Hebrew prophets, he speaks to a religious and social crisis with passionate piety and revolutionary spirit. His preaching requires both unwavering faith and high courage, since it brings him scorn, ridicule, and mistrust.

Early in his career, he suffers the tragic deaths of his wife, his main support, and his uncle, the head of the clan. His followers are subjected to physical abuse—garbage is delivered on their doorsteps—and social ostracism. He explores the possibility of moving to another town and finally, forced to flee, he chooses the oasis of Yathrib, a couple hundred miles to the north. Legend tells how he and his followers seek shelter along the way in a cave over which a spider spins its web and pigeons hurriedly build their nests. Because the Meccans in pursuit cannot imagine that anyone can be hiding in this musty cave, Muhammad makes good his escape. His flight to Medina in 622 C.E. is the Hijra, the great migration that begins a new age and marks the beginning of the Muslim calendar.

Success. The city of Yathrib soon becomes known as Medina, the City of the Prophet. Medina is a city-state dedicated to the worship of the One God. There the citizens are impressed by Muhammad's wisdom and fairness: He seems to be an ideal arbitrator of their social and political problems. The emphasis in Muhammad's personal career shifts in Medina from prophecy to statecraft and community organization. He takes on all sorts of functions—judging disputes about fair prices for land ownership, effecting marriages and divorces, making diplomatic decisions, and punishing people for crimes.

During the final ten years of his life, Muhammad organizes several military campaigns. He gains considerable prowess as a warrior, and his power increases immensely. Beginning the campaigns that soon after his death will send Islamic armies on a far-reaching conquest, he wins back Mecca. Most of his earlier opponents embrace Islam and are generously rewarded. Muhammad dies in 632, shortly after returning to Mecca on a farewell pilgrimage. In the confusion that ensues after his sudden death, his father-in-law, Abu Bakr, makes the poignant remark to a mourning Muslim community that "If someone has worshiped Muhammad, Muhammad is dead. If someone has worshiped God, God is alive and never dies."

The First Story: The Seven Sleepers and Surrender

Stories are more difficult to find in the Qur'an than in the sacred writings of other world religions. Even when narrative does predominate, the story is hardly ever told in a straightforward fashion, but tends to fall into a series of short word pictures. The stories that Muhammad recites in the Qur'an are given for teaching purposes, not for their narrative or entertainment value. They deal with the sovereignty, providence, and protection of Allah, and the beauty of paradise reserved for those who are faithful to Allah. The stories show precisely how Allah manifests unceasing dedication to human beings and how humans, in consequence, ought to display such fidelity themselves, both to Allah and to each other.

In surah 18 ("The Cave") Muhammad tells us the story of the seven sleepers. Seven young men refuse to offer sacrifices to idols, believing that Allah will extend divine mercy and give them all they need. They distribute all their possessions to the poor, and retreat to the cave, where they fall sleep for over 300 years. Finally brought out of their sleep, they question each other on how long they have been there. One goes into town with some silver coins to look for food. He proceeds discreetly, still fearing that people will stone him or force him into their religion.

In the Christian version of this story that Muhammad has been following so far, when the youth tries to buy some bread, he attempts to pay with ancient coins and is immediately accused by the vendors of having stolen the ancient imperial treasures. Slowly the truth is uncovered and a miracle is declared. Both religious and imperial authorities come to the cave and express their wonder before the youths pass into a final sleep. Here Muhammad breaks off from his source, though, to extol the youths as models for those who have faith in their Lord and courage in their hearts. He exhorts Muslims to follow the example of these youths who surrendered totally to Allah and now await a heavenly reward.

"There is no refuge except in the Lord," continues Muhammad. "Do not let your eyes be diverted from Allah in search of the gaudy things of this lower world. For those who are bent on doing evil, a fire has been readied that will envelop them like an awning on every side. Should they ask for water, water like molten metal will be theirs to scald their faces. As for those who have faith and do good works, they shall not lose their reward. In the gardens of Eden where rivers flow, they will recline upon soft couches, arrayed with golden bracelets and robed in garments of silk and satin. How excellent a reward, how delightsome a haven in which to lie." Muhammad then amplifies the story of the seven sleepers with a long description of the struggle against idolatry and two more parables.

The Story Magnified

Jihad

The seven sleepers are loyal souls who struggle against idolatry with courage in their hearts, calling on no other God besides Allah. A night or a day that a person spends on holy war has more value than the bounty of the earth, Muhammad teaches. A place in paradise the size of an eyelash is better than this world and all that is in it.

The jihad that Muhammad calls for has, on occasion, meant fighting against the enemies of the faith and of the good, and it has involved spreading the Islamic religion by force. The story is told of a ruler from the Abbasid dynasty (leaders in Baghdad during the Golden Age of Islamic scholarship and of the *Tales of the Arabian Nights*) who attempts to kill all challengers to his power from the Umayyad family (the rival dynasty, centered at Damascus). On one occasion this ruler in Baghdad deviously pretends to relent and invites the Umayyad heirs to a banquet as a token of forgiveness. While the guests are enjoying their meal, they are attacked savagely and unexpectedly by the servants. A carpet is quickly spread over their dead and dying bodies, and the banquet continues in the same room to the sound of their groans. Whether or not there is any factual basis for this and similar brutal tales, it has led many to conclude, mistakenly, that Islam is a religion of the sword, of violence.

Interpretations of jihad pass from an external war against the enemy to an internal moral struggle according to circumstances and personalities. Muslims have justified outward war to recover their citizenship and their goods or to protect themselves when they are threatened. Certain politically radical Muslims resort to acts of terrorism and proclaim holy war against evil and Islam's enemies, whether Western countries or fellow Muslims with whom they disagree. The extremist "Islamic Jihad" movement in Lebanon and the invasion of Kuwait by Iraq's Saddam Hussein are examples of this.

Yet wars for land, resources, power, and wealth are all prohibited in the Qur'an. Muslim religious scholars have repeatedly condemned this use of the language of jihad as illicit and obscene. They also claim that the term has been used too freely to lend a sense of legitimacy to military operations, easing consciences otherwise pained by taking lives. In its essence, though, jihad carries no connotation that violence should be employed. As the Qur'an states it: "Fight in the way of Allah against those who fight against you, but be not aggressive. Surely Allah loves not the aggressive."

Those who are fighting the internal jihad attempt to carry out God's laws about equality and justice for all. They recognize their task, confront it through resourceful action, often in obedience to a higher voice. They do not look to gain immediate rewards but to put their meager strength and few talents in Allah's service. In the internal jihad Muslims exert much effort to learn their role in the created universe and in the theater of their brief experience of worldly life. The unsung heroes of the jihad are those who care for the elderly and ill with reliable kindness and who pass up opportunities to be angry. They create hospitals for the poor, give to others in innumerable ways with unstudied blindness to their own comfort, and dedicate themselves to a life of serving and charity on all levels. They know they cannot be idle and that they must rectify not only what is amiss in the world around them, but also within themselves.

Two Vineyards

Muhammad explains his story of the seven sleepers with a parable about two men who own vineyards. This story defines further the centrality of submissive faith in Allah and the necessity of expressing it in the spiritual jihad. The first vineyard owner, Muhammad explains, brags that he is richer than the other, that his crops are more abundant and give their yield in unstinted supply, and that his clan is mightier. The second is poorer than the first and blessed with fewer children, but he has faith in Allah. Playing false with his own soul, the first goes into his garden and says: "I can't think that this will ever come to perish: I can't imagine the Last Hour happening. But if it does and I am ushered before my Lord I will surely have something better in its place."

The second man upbraids him for denying the sovereignty of Allah. "When you went into your garden, you should have said: 'What God's will may be—there is no power except in God.' As you see, I am inferior to you in respect to property and family. Yet maybe my Lord will give me something better than your garden. He may well let loose a thunderbolt from heaven and your garden will become a barren stretch of dust, or by morning its water may recede so far down into the ground that you will never be able to reach it."

It comes as no surprise that the vineyards of the first man are completely destroyed, while those of the second are spared. The first wrings his hands in grief: "Would that I had not let anything take the place of my Lord." He has nothing to turn to for help, and he is in no shape to help himself. Muhammad drives his point home: It is only in God, the God of truth, that we have any sure reliance. While wealth and children may grace this present life, deeds of righteousness provide hope for a better reward on the day when Allah agitates the mountains and destroys the earth.

Al-Khidr

Muhammad continues surah 18 with further elaboration of his story of the seven youths in the cave. He tells of the meeting of Moses and the wandering saint al-Khidr, Allah's servant. Muhammad relates that when Moses asks to follow al-Khidr on the understanding that al-Khidr will teach him what is right, al-Khidr replies: "You will never be able to bear patiently with me." When Moses insists, though, and promises to be patient, al-Khidr relents. He commands Moses not to question him about anything until he brings it up. As we expect, when al-Khidr makes a hole in a boat, Moses anxiously asks him if he did it to drown the people on board. Again, when they encounter a youth and al-Khidr kills him, Moses impatiently asks him why he has taken an innocent life. Finally, when they find a wall that is on the point of falling down and the Lord's servant rebuilds it, Moses restlessly tells him that he could have earned money doing this.

Only then does al-Khidr interpret for Moses the things he has had no patience for. As for the boat, it belonged to some innocent poor men, and al-Khidr wanted to make it unseaworthy because a king was hot on their trail, forcibly seizing all boats for the chase. As for the youth, his parents were believers, and the servant of Allah feared that the youth would afflict them by his wickedness and unbelief. And, as for the wall, it belonged to two orphan boys in town. Beneath it lay a treasure. Their father had been a godly man, and Allah wanted the children to come to full age and take out that treasure. In all three instances, al-Khidr was obediently acting on the orders of Allah, and not doing his own will.

Surrender

Muhammad thus exhorts Muslims to follow the example of the sev-

en youths who surrendered totally to Allah and now await a heavenly reward. He amplifies his counsel with two more stories, one
about the two vineyard owners, and one about the wandering saint
al-Khidr. The Muslim who surrenders to Allah, Muhammad con-
cludes, has to strive on the road to God, struggling continually
against all God's enemies, chiefly unbelievers and evildoers. Even
more important, though, Muslims should not do what may be reasonable, but rather what Allah wants, for God's purposes are not
known to humans. Those who struggle continuously, who constantly repent, study, and who pray to establish God's design in the
world through resourceful action, Muhammad recites, will gain not
only immediate rewards but everlasting happiness.

The Second Story: Husain and Martyrdom

In the Sunni tradition, the Hadiths are limited to the sayings and
deeds of Muhammad. The other major group in Islam, the Shiite
community, includes many more stories in their Hadiths. The

The Shiite hero Husain, accompanied by his grandfather Muhammad,
his father Ali, and his brother Hassan, is ferried across the ocean of life.

Shiites also incorporate the sayings and deeds of their Imams, that is, the twelve rulers whom they hold to be the legitimate successors of Muhammad. The Shiite collections, such as that of al-Kulayni (tenth century), transmitted from and about the twelve Imams, are considered the continuation of the prophetic light of Muhammad. Undoubtedly the most consequential of these stories is the account of the martyrdom of Husain, the third Imam. Grandson of Muhammad and son of Ali, Husain was killed at Karbala in 680 in a cruel massacre that is considered to be the main reason for the present-day division between Sunni and Shiite Muslims.

Husain draws up his little band in battle order on the plain of Karbala in Iraq, facing 4000 troops of Yazid (a caliph in the Umayyad dynasty). Husain feels it is necessary to go into battle against him to protest the injustices that are being carried out in the name of Islam. Husain's troops are hopelessly outnumbered. Aware of the inevitable outcome of the battle, Husain makes the decision to fight anyway, for he believes that his imminent death will demonstrate to all Muslims the godlessness of his opponents. Also, he is convinced that his martyrdom will set an example for all ages, calling Muslims to rise up and fight against tyranny and godlessness.

When Yazid demands unconditional surrender, Husain and his troops demonstrate uncommon courage and resolve to die. To display his bravery and refusal to retreat, Husain commands his soldiers to hobble his horse. After a suicidal charge, Yazid's troops drive a spear into Husain's back and cut off his head. His body, already torn by numerous wounds, is trampled underfoot by horses. His tents are burned and looted; helpless women and children are shamelessly paraded through the streets and treated to humiliation as captives. Yazid's soldiers carry the heads of Husain and his fellow martyrs on spears and hang them around the necks of their horses.

The Story Magnified

Good vs. Evil

Because Husain actively chose to face death and worldly defeat in order to manifest his surrender to Allah, he has become an eternal witness for all Shiites. Husain's tragic attempt to establish Muhammad's succession through the family line is the supreme sacrifice for the faith. Persian literature devotes hundreds of heart-rending poems and dramatic representations to commemorate it. Shiites believe that weeping for Husain opens the gates to Paradise. Their ritual wailing also causes Husain's mother Fatima ("the Radiant") to intercede for them: Daughter of Muhammad and wife of her father's cousin Ali, Fatima's life of dedication, compassion, and suffering for the forces of good makes her a powerful servant before Allah.

Husain's struggle represents the eternal human struggle between good and evil, the dialectic between political expediency and moral idealism. In death, he becomes a symbol for all generations of the uncompromising struggle against external forces of tyranny. The Shiites consider Husain the defender of the faith, the possessor of inner purity and strength, and the great martyr in the name of truth. Yazid and his henchmen, by contrast, become the supreme symbols of corruption. They are not only murderers, they also represent false doctrine, imposed from without. The sufferings of those in Husain's family who survived the slaughter of their patriarch are blamed on Yazid as are, by extension, the sufferings of later Shiite leaders. To this day, a cruel, corrupt individual who brings ruin to others is labeled "Yazid."

Karbala

Husain is buried at Karbala in Iraq. Karbala (karb means "grief" and bala means "misfortune") is an area of legendary heroism and a site of divine blessings for those who make pilgrimages to it today. The day of his martyrdom (Ashura) has become the most solemn day of the Shiite calendar, marked by processions and fervent mourning. Through an expressive ritual dramatization, the Shiites reenact the story of innocent suffering and the mystery of vicarious merit. Each year, for ten days around the date of Husain's death, women wail chants of lamentation. Thousands of penitent men march through the streets of Iran and Iraq with their bodies dyed red or black, whipping themselves with chains and branches, pulling out their hair, inflicting sword wounds upon themselves, dragging chains behind them, and performing wild dances. Fights break out with Sunnis, resulting in casualties and even deaths. The grief has universal significance: the Shiites weep and wail not only for the death of their gallant, doomed warrior, but also for a world in which such things can happen, in which the good are put down while the wicked prosper.

Martyrdom

Martyrdom is the highest degree of self-sacrifice for the sake of religious principles. In recent years, captured Shiite soldiers have proudly showed off the dog tags that were issued to them when they enlisted. They call these identification pieces their "keys to heaven": They are still fighting the battle of Husain. Tens of thousands of young people have been ready to die—and have died—because of Husain's heroic death. In doing so they hope, consciously or not, to defend the faith and irrigate Islam with their blood. Martyrdom offers them a chance to imitate their sainted hero and to express their feelings for human sufferings and their compassion for the downtrodden.

The Stories Exemplified

Other Stories

Among the most famous stories that have appeared in the history of the Islamic tradition are those of Jalal al-Din Rumi (1207-1273), known as Mawlana ("our master"), a member of the Sufi Order of Whirling Dervishes. His hundreds of tales and parables, especially in the *Mathnavi*, are an important commentary on the Qur'an and provide a storehouse of Sufi stories of religious experience. The focus of his musical writing is always surrender: the surrender of love and detachment, not sterile surrender to the law. His melody is invariably love, the moving power of life. The true mystery of love is to die before dying, i.e., to sacrifice the self to acquire new life, to suffer and die for the sake of transformation. He intones the lamentation of the soul and the nostalgia it suffers in longing for its true home with Allah.

The Sufis make use of stories and parables to implant religious concepts and to describe their preference for a life of asceticism over riches. They represent the flowering of Islamic spirituality. Ever since the scholar al-Ghazali created a respectable place for their spirituality in the orthodox fold, they have represented the mystical wing of Islam. They seek to know Allah intimately through purification of their souls. They continue to survive, even thrive, in many parts of the Middle East. Their stories describe the tariqa ("the way"), the specific methods of thought and feeling activity by which they attain ecstasy and union with God. Their rituals, devotional prayers, music, breathing exercises, dancing, and even exotic practices such as fire-walking and eating of snakes, all aspire to deepen the inner life of the heart. They rehearse their attempts to experience the reality of Allah under the guidance of a shaykh, a type of guru known for self-abnegation.

Human Witnesses

Rabia. One woman who well represents the living out of the Islamic story is Rabia al-Adawiyya (713-801). She was a Sufi woman known for her surrender to God out of pure love. One story about Rabia relates that when she visited Mecca on pilgrimage, it moved forward to greet her. Again, one day when she went into the streets with a jug of water in one hand and a flaming torch in the other, she was asked where she was going. Rabia replied: "I am going to quench hell and set fire to paradise so that God may be adored and loved for himself and not for any rewards."

Another time Rabia went into her room and bowed her head in meditation. Her maidservant called her: "Mistress, come outside and see the marvelous works of God." She replied, "No, come in, so that you can contemplate their creator; contemplation of the creator prevents me from contemplating what he has created." In her writings, Rabia incessantly stresses that humans should strive for detachment from all that is not God and for attachment to religious experiences that can radiate the love of God in their lives.

Al-Hallaj. Another Islamic hero is al-Hallaj (857-922), an excellent example of one who fought and won the interior jihad. Al-Hallaj was a Sufi mystic who preached in Baghdad so eloquently that the crowds wept in the streets. He pictures true surrender to Allah in terms of the relation of the moth to a candle. The moth that sees the light, feels the heat, and finally immolates itself in the flame, never to return to its peers, is the model for the lover who has found Allah. Al-Hallaj tried to awaken a sense of personal relationship between believers and God, and his whole life was devoted to the realization of the deepest truth of Islam, complete surrender to the one God.

Pronouncing that he was the Truth and the Light of the World, titles reserved for Allah, al-Hallaj was condemned to death. The eminent religious jurists of Baghdad had him led out to be executed for claiming that he was God himself: They could not understand that he was speaking mystically or metaphorically. Seeing the scaffold on which he would die, al-Hallaj danced in the streets and laughed and prayed for the grace to be truly thankful for the opportunity that God had granted him to suffer and witness to the jihad. He endured several hundred lashes from the whip and was left to hang all night. Before he was decapitated the next morning, his last words were: "All who have known ecstasy long for this moment, to be alone with the Alone." Al-Hallaj died because his burning love of

God, expressed in his stories, aroused the anger of others who denied the possibility of real love between humans and Allah.

Communities

There are two major religious groupings in Islam today, the Sunnis and the Shiites. They are united in their acceptance of the Oneness of God, the prophetic role of Muhammad, and the idea of the Last Judgment, as well as their reverence for the Qur'an. They emphasize different aspects of Islamic spirituality, however, and have their own doctrinal and practical formulations concerning the theological, philosophical, and social teachings of Islam.

The Sunnis. More than 80 percent of Muslims belong to the Sunni community. The Sunni tradition began with the leadership of the Rightly Guided Caliphs, the immediate successors of Muhammad. These caliphs gave central place to the law. Derived from the Prophet's teaching and conduct and the exemplary teaching of his earliest disciples, the sunnah (law) became the norm of behavior in the Muslim community. For the Sunnis, Islamic law regulates all of human behavior, including intentions. They hold that the four sources of law are the Qur'an, Hadiths, Ijtihad (analogical reasoning of individual religious jurists), and Ijma (consensus, either of the religious lawyers or the entire community).

The Shiites. While only a minority in the Muslim tradition, the Shiites constitute a major substantial presence in Iran, Iraq, and a few other Muslim nations. They are the descendants of those Muslims who, after Muhammad's death, initially supported the claims of the Prophet's son-in-law Ali and his sons to the headship of the Muslim community. They favored Ali because they believed that charismatic knowledge of the ways of Muhammad, and hence of God's will, was retained in a fuller and purer form in Ali's family than elsewhere. Several other groups were each pushing their own candidates, especially the Umayyads who, as leaders of Muhammad's tribe, also claimed the right to be the caliphs, or successors, of Muhammad. While the Sunnis favored the Umayyads, who did in fact rule Islam for the first century after Muhammad's death, the Shiites insisted on Ali as Islamic leader. Even after Ali was quickly assassinated, the Shiites continued to support his descendants as the Imam, that is, the legitimate successor of Muhammad and intermediary between Allah and humans.

Arabic calligraphy shows the lion as symbol of the strength of Ali:
"In the name of the Lion of God, the face of God, the victorious Ali."

The Shiites have a strong belief in a future cosmic battle of good and evil. This catastrophic battle will terminate in an apocalyptic reversal through the Mahdi. The Mahdi is a messianic figure, a descendant of the twelfth Imam, the "Rightly-Guided One." The Mahdi went into hiding in the tenth century and will one day re-emerge to restore the purity of the faith. He will effect the final victory of faithful Muslims through Allah's decisive intervention in human history. He will bring true and uncorrupted guidance to all people, and create a just social order and a world free from tyranny and wickedness.

On the whole, Shiite piety is much more colorful than the general Sunni orientation. Their religious fervor and special devotion to Husain has more of an emotional tone, with an atmosphere of sorrow and suffering, and a sense of persecution. Whereas Sunnis tend to stress submission to God's will, the Shiites emphasize surrender to the divine inner nature and intelligence. Marked political consequences flow from this difference in spiritual and emotional climate.

Twentieth Century

The Challenge of Modernity. The greatest challenge confronting the Muslim world in the twentieth century has been the problem of how to react to modernity. There is a great concern to assert the force of the Islamic ethic and presence in the face of modern science and economic development. How can Muslims preserve the distinctive values and traditional teachings of their heritage while accepting the technology that has allowed the scientific and industrial rise of Western Europe and America?

Many Muslims, more properly called revivalists than fundamentalists, refuse to accept modernization at all. They accuse the Western nations of cheating humanity of its basic values with their technology, exploitation of colonial territories, economic savagery, and destruction of the family as an institution, all in the name of progress. They claim that attempts to emulate the West have been corruptive. As a result, they refuse to accept modernization, reassert Islamic identity strongly, and emphasize the perfection and self-sufficiency of Islam. They want effective organizations that will implement a clearly Islamic system of government and law through political action. They promote communities of the faithful, trained religiously and militarily, and governed by Islamic law. This Islamic revival is marked by increased religious observance (mosque attendance, prayer, fasting), more emphasis upon Islamic dress and values, and an expansion of religious programming in the media.

Iran. While Egypt, Sudan, Libya, Saudi Arabia, Pakistan, and Indonesia have all shown a revivalist or fundamentalist resurgence, the West has felt the most repercussions from Iran. In the 1970s, with the strong support of the United States and assisted by Western-trained elites and advisers, the Shah of Iran attempted to modernize the country. Led by the mullahs, or religious leaders, the people rebelled against this autocratic leader and fomented the revolution of the Ayatollah Khomeini in 1979. Khomeini, one of several ayatollahs ("signs of God") in Iran—rulers who gain their power not by election but by recognition of their followers—claimed that their life had lost its spiritual core. It had become poisoned, obsessed with materialism and the acquisition of money and consumer goods. He blamed this spiritual corruption on the imperial power of the United States and assigned it the symbolic image of the Great Satan.

Khomeini proceeded to declare an Islamic republic in Iran. He proclaimed that he was leading a struggle against the economic oppression within his own country and against the political persecution and deprivation of rights suffered by the people at the hands of the Shah. He proclaimed war against the intrusions of a secular lifestyle that corrupted traditional Islamic values. He thus politicized religion, theocratized the state, and mobilized all Iranians as holy warriors.

Turkey. Other Muslim leaders have tried to bridge the gap between their religious heritage and modernity. They assert that Islam is a dynamic, creative, and progressive religion, and offer a rationale for modern political, legal, and social change in Islam. They seek to utilize the best of Western technology and learning in order to revitalize the Muslim community and inspire movements for educational and social reform. Exposure to Western ideas can provide brilliant solutions to problems of Islamic society. Of all the Islamic nations, Turkey has done the most to attempt westernization on all levels.

The most radical reforms in Turkey were those of Mustafa Kemal (known as Ataturk, "father of the Turks") in the 1920s. Ataturk seized control of what was left of the old Ottoman Empire, forcefully transforming Muslim Turkey into a nationalistic secular state. He outlawed men's fezzes, widespread fasting, and the Arabic alphabet. In his new republic, Ataturk helped establish new legal codes, replacing religious laws with secular codes. The Turkish people were free to accept or reject Islam. The religion of the Qur'an was not rejected (for this could still meet the spiritual needs of modern people) but the religious lawyers were denounced. They were censured for their inability to understand the dynamics of modern history. Legal equality for women was installed on the basis of European, not Islamic, law. As part of a program to emancipate women from the religious constraints of Islam, polygamy was abolished, veils were banned, and women were granted the right to vote and hold office.

Human Rights. In some Islamic countries, there is strong resistance to male-female equality, for the equality of women is often seen as part of a Western cultural offensive against Islam. The liberation of women from their customary roles is viewed by many Muslims as a grave threat to the integrity of the Islamic way of life.

In other Islamic nations, however, positive steps have been taken toward women's equality, including access to public jobs, legal reforms, and expansion of women's education. The Muslim custom of covering a woman's head with a veil is a practice enforced by social custom, not by law, and in many countries Muslim women can choose when, where, and even whether they wish to follow it. The veil has almost disappeared in Egypt and the Near East, but is still seen in parts of Northern Africa, India, and Pakistan, and it is strictly worn in Saudi Arabia.

Of the four million Muslims in the United States, many are African-

Americans converted because of Islam's social protest against white supremacy. Their spiritual struggle has been a battle against drugs, family breakdowns, and other social ills. Also active in the United States for human rights are the Baha'is, a group that split off from the Shiites in Iran in the mid-nineteenth century. They condemn all types of prejudice and advocate the equality of women and men. They are pacifists, dedicated to seeking universal world peace.

Ritual: The Hajj

The Hajj, the pilgrimage to Mecca, is the most visible of the Muslim rituals, the one that best draws Muslims together into a single community. One of the Five Pillars, it is properly made in the last month

In a plaintive cry, a muezzin calls the faithful to prayer five times each day from the minaret (tower) attached to every Muslim mosque.

of the Muslim lunar calendar, the month when, traditionally, Muhammad began to receive the Qur'an. It can, however, also be made at other times. Pilgrims arrive in Saudi Arabia by land, sea, and air from every corner of the Muslim world. During the sacred days of the pilgrimage, they separate themselves from their ordinary lives and submit themselves in utter availability to the call of Allah. Their prayers are prayers of invocation and appeals for intercession by the Prophet, great penitential acts that secure remission of all their former sins.

Each one in this immense multitude of more than a million people wears a special white, seamless garment, symbolizing the common search for purity, the renunciation of worldly pleasure, and the unity and absolute equality of all. The pilgrims constantly proclaim their response to Allah's call: "Here I am Lord, doubly at thy service, oh God." When the pilgrims first arrive in Mecca, they circle the Kaaba seven times. They then run back and forth between two low hills, symbolizing their desperate human needs and God's ready response. The central act of the Hajj is the standing at Arafat, held the next day some miles east of Mecca, on the Mount of Mercy. Men and women stand shoulder to shoulder as equals. The vast throng continues to stand in silence from noon to just before sunset, signifying their awareness of the divine presence and their unity with all other believers, but most of all their submission to Allah.

As they return to Mecca the next day they stop at the outskirts of town to throw seven stones at the pillars of the "Great Devil," signifying their communal repudiation of evil. Sheep and goats are sacrificed, and a portion of the animals is shared with those less fortunate. It is a day of joy and feasting throughout the Muslim world, and a celebration is held by Muslim households everywhere in solidarity with the pilgrims. On this day the entire Muslim world is united in proclaiming their common witness to the sovereignty of Allah.

The Stories Appropriated

The Muslim stories of the seven sleepers' submission and Husain's martyrdom provide a context for meaning, not only for the lives of those within the Muslim tradition, but for those of us outside it, presenting new ways for us to envision our own spiritual convictions. Reading about submission and martyrdom challenges us to respond in a personal way to our own religion on the basis of transformed decisions.

Spiritual Struggle

The Qur'an asks: "Did you think you would enter the Garden without God having determined who was willing to struggle in jihad and endure with patience?" The seven sleepers were willing to hide in a cave at the cost of their lives rather than deny their faith. Their jihad was not a question of fighting battles for Allah, but rather struggling in their faith, cultivating an inner life in search of divine love and knowledge. Their intimacy with God earns them straight passage to the garden. Their story grips our imagination, prompting us to wonder and speculate about our own jihad, our struggles and questions about our nature and our destiny.

Jihad is a spiritual struggle to establish God's design in the world. It entails striving to conquer all that opposes God's will, starting with one's own sins and unbelief. We too fight a "holy war" for the sake of all-embracing peace. Peace belongs to those who are inwardly at peace with the will of God and outwardly at war with the forces of disruption and disequilibrium. Jihad sets our reason and judgment on an even keel: Now the whole of our existence embodies truth, for in all spheres of life, we voluntarily obey the laws of the Lord of the Universe. In this war, we are at peace with the whole universe.

Caliphs
Caliphs are the human representatives of God, with a preeminent status and role to exercise dominion over the rest of creation. As caliphs, our proper relation to God is servant to master, and thus we need guidance, similar to the guidance the Muslims find in the Shariah. In striving for religious wholeness, we can shape our lives into harmony with God's will and achieve peace with the creator by following the laws established by our own religious traditions. An inward spirit is indispensable for us as God's caliphs, but it cannot entirely displace outer laws and teachings. Even if we experience the truth directly and personally, we should not imagine ourselves exempt from the common human obligations of our tradition's sacred laws. The road or path of submission requires striving, repenting, studying, and praying. The encounter with God and the authority of the holy community are both indispensable.

Sovereignty of God
The seven sleepers put their lives on the line to profess that Allah is the one responsible for everything that has being and breath. They make their own the words of the last surah: "I take refuge with the Lord of all things human, our king, our God. He is my refuge from the evil of Satan who whispers insinuations in the human heart. He is my refuge from evil spirits and evil people." The seven sleepers

tell us that God's will is the only thing that matters. To put anything in the place of God violates the uniqueness of God and mars the divine perfection. God is transcendent and has almighty power, but God is also with us all along, guiding us from within. "To God belong the East and the West; wherever you turn, there is the face of God."

In our daily prayers, we also give glory to God, the Exalted, the most High. We also express our submission to God by proclaiming all worldly things (e.g., the joys of marriage, food, paradise itself) as divine gifts to be accepted and enjoyed in gratitude. We too profess that all power, blessings, and wealth come from God. This makes it possible for us to treat other creatures fairly, to have a humble and modest attitude, and to strive in everything to keep God's power and authority above all. Just as the Muslims at Mecca express sheer devotion and attempt to identify with the mind of God, so we can undertake a pilgrimage, internal or external, in the attempt to identify with the mind of God. Prayer and pilgrimage purify much of the egotism that easily lingers in a heart that considers itself pure.

Sacrificial Action

From the story of Al-Husain's martyrdom we can all learn of the virtue of readiness to die for one's beliefs and of the power of innocent suffering. His martyrdom points out the impermanence of the world of human experience and shows how anything valued in the visible world must be valued primarily, if not solely, for its capability to move one forward on one's journey to the Absolute Reality.

Martyrdom makes clear the meaning of life on earth: True human existence consists in holding a belief and being prepared to fight and die for it. The closeness and finality of martyrdom wonderfully concentrate the mind and pare the goals of religious experience down to its essentials. Martyrs are not afraid to weep for a world where the good are put down while the wicked prosper. Martyrs confirm that all human history is a continuous struggle between the forces of evil and the forces of good. Martyrs regard death as a journey from one form of life to another: They come closer to God and they also remove the obstacles that exist between God and humans.

Building a worldview on the example of Husain's martyrdom, we gain a sense of personal worth. Giving the self in witness for our beliefs makes it impossible to view ourselves as helpless, powerless, and dependent. No longer placing primary importance on our own worldly troubles or material advantages, we can concentrate on spiritual progress. Ready to give up everything, selflessness replaces selfishness. Moreover, we increase our respect for others whom we view as partners in the spiritual struggle. Their self-sacrifice makes them worthy of our esteem and emulation.

Becoming a martyr is not a passive act, as if one stood somewhere and waited to be killed. It is an active commitment. Individual initiatives and efforts do have an effect, and personal decisions and actions can make a difference. While few of us would be inclined to stand up before a firing squad to witness to our faith, the notion of martyrdom is deeply challenging. Today, martyrdom is more subtle: It means being willing to be a witness for those who are poor or oppressed, for those who cannot take the basic necessities of life for granted. The emphasis on sacrificial action leads us to take seriously the plight of those devastated by war, famine, or natural disasters. For would-be martyrs today, compassion has to be the first and last word.

Martyrs make a courageous statement about the world by their lives. They are not escapist; in fact, their involvement is so strong that it stimulates other individuals of religious sensitivity to exercise moral responsibility. The will to ask what needs to be done and to do it, the will to confront an adversary, the will to upset the status quo and pursue change—these aspects of moral courage depend on a prior assurance that accompanies the martyr's vision. Such a vision bestows eternal significance on the particulars of history.

Conclusion

The Muslim story is a story of jihad and martyrdom, the story of submission and witness to the sovereignty of God. Muslims are called to display the committed fidelity, both to God and to each other, that they find in the witness of Muhammad in the Qur'an and the Hadiths.

The story of the seven sleepers portrays the sovereignty, providence, and protection of Allah and the beauty of paradise reserved for those who are faithful to Allah. It shows how Allah manifests unceasing dedication to human beings and how humans in consequence ought to display such fidelity themselves, both to Allah and to each other.

The story of Husain's martyrdom invokes passionate commitment, not only for the Shiites, but for all Muslims. Husain's struggle represents the eternal human conflict between good and evil, even to death. Muslims strive to balance the inner purity and strength that accompany total surrender with the intense dedication that martyrdom evokes.

Discussion Questions

1. Why do you think the author chooses Mecca and the Kaaba as a symbol of Islamic submission?

2. Describe the Muslim God in terms of oneness and sovereignty.

3. Summarize the Muslim belief in salvation in terms of neglect, the Five Pillars, and Paradise.

4. Describe the seven sleepers as the symbol of both faith in Allah and the interior jihad.

5. Why do you think that Husain has been such a powerful model of martyrdom over the centuries?

6. Summarize the various ways that Muslims have reacted to the process of modernization in the past hundred years.

7. What can Christians appropriate today from the stories of the Muhammad, the seven sleepers, and Husain?

8. Discussion Starter: "The number of roads to God is equal to the number of human souls." (Muhammad)

9. Discussion Starter: "At the Hajj, we were all displaying a spirit of unity and brotherhood that my experiences in America had led me to believe never could exist between the white and the non-white. America needs to understand Islam, because this is the one religion that erases from its society the race problem." (Malcolm X)

10. Discussion Starter: "I examined my motive in my work of teaching, and realized that it was not a pure desire for the things of God, but that the impulse moving me was the desire for an influential position and public recognition....Worldly desires were striving to keep me by their chains just where I was, while the voice of faith was calling, 'To the road! To the road!'" (al-Ghazali)

Steps descend to the Ganges, the holy river where Hindus come to worship, offer prayers, and sit for hours on the banks.

Chapter Six

HINDUISM
Detachment and Initiation

Setting the Scene

The Ganges
Devout Hindus yearn to make a pilgrimage at least once in a lifetime to the Ganges river, especially at Banaras, a holy city with thousands of temples. They pray "to live a virtuous life and die beside the Ganges," for to die there is to be transported immediately to paradise at Lord Shiva's side. All along the river, from the Himalayas to the Bay of Bengal, there is a constant state of festivity. Marriages and births are regularly celebrated along its banks. Descending the ghats, the steep steps that cascade to the holy river, pilgrims immerse themselves in the soupy water. Gathered along the water's edge in brightly colored clothes, women and men come to worship the river, offering prayers and sitting for hours on the banks. When they are ready to return home to their families, they fill brass pots with the river's waters, confident that the river goddess will purify everything.

Along the Ganges we see both the essence and the incredible diversity of Hinduism. The Hindu religion is in reality a wide variety of religious traditions, rituals, folk customs, contradictory meta-

physical theories, and ascetic practices. Hinduism is a collage of ideas and spiritual aspirations, subsisting side by side on the subcontinent of India. Hinduism is a religion of an ethnic character, the faith
of a single cultural unit. Hinduism is the religion of the great majority of the people of India, and over 90 percent of the world's 700
million Hindus live in India.

Karma

The cornerstone of Hindu religious practice is karma, the law that
human actions in the past converge in the present and shape future
lives. It is the principle that one's thoughts, words, and deeds have
consequences for future existences, whether relatively happy or
miserable. Karma is associated with the teaching of transmigration,
the idea that human existence goes in cycles, lifetime after lifetime.
Human beings are reborn again and again to lives of varied fortune
on earth. The circumstances of each life, up or down the scale of existence, in suffering or happiness, are determined directly by the
moral quality of each person's actions (karma) in a previous existence. Accumulated karma for those who have led a good moral
life, for example, might effect well-merited freedom from disease, a
virtuous disposition, a sharp mind, or good looks.

Karma should not be understood as the equivalent of impersonal
fate nor should it be associated with forces beyond human control.
It is not some kind of negative or restrictive determinism that calls
for resignation. Karma is really an incentive to better the self, to
strive to create action in a purposeful fashion. Karma is a key to
freedom, calling for human initiative and action. Within the realm
of karma, human actions may not create anything new, but they do
recreate out of a common source of energy. Human effort, not blind
luck, can achieve liberation in the midst of this life. When karma is
properly understood, action becomes a joy, rather than a fetter.

Dharma

The actions for good karma are required or prohibited by the law,
or truth, of dharma. Dharma provides a pattern for the total order
of the natural world and for the social order of human civilization.
Dharma is the order of cosmic justice, a system of universal values
into which each person is born with particular social and ritual duties to fulfill. Living by the law of dharma, humans harmonize individualistic proclivities with the pattern of life and society, so that all
activity in the world becomes part of a great cosmic dance. Humans

support the world and sustain the work of creation through upholding the great cosmic-social order, no matter what their stage of life or aim of life is. The religious duty of dharma is an expression of true personal participation in maintaining cosmic order. At the same time it is a means of release from bondage to the world.

Caste System

With their beliefs in karma and dharma, Hindus organize life through well-defined castes or social classes. In the pattern of Hindu society, the castes constitute a fixed ranking system for social and economic organization. All Hindus are born somewhere in the structure of fixed castes and economic occupation, according to their long personal history of good and evil deeds done in former lives. The particular grade of freedom and responsibility offered by their present caste and sex is recognized as not only just, but also as their best opportunity for personal betterment. The actual caste system is very complex, with innumerable subcastes. Individual rights are safeguarded within the castes: There is equality, opportunity, and social insurance; there is a sense of security, protection, and identity.

Hindus are obliged to accept their caste position and all its obligations, privileges, limitations, and deprivations. Dutiful participation in this religiously sanctioned and organized society is appropriate and advantageous. To attempt to take on the duties of another social station would be dangerous as well as unjust, since it would lead to poor performance and even more restricted rebirths in the future. Hindus believe that, as a result of a virtuous life, they can move up the ladder of castes in the next rebirth.

Faith and Gods

The Hindus manifest their faith in many different ways, and their focus of worship changes from village to village. Devotees of the different Hindu gods strive to encounter their gods and to experience Darshana, that is, a sighting or a showing of their god, usually in a temple where the deity takes form in an image. Hindus express their faith in many different religious festivals associated with the various aspects of their lives. Individual Hindus may reverence one god, or a few, or many, or none at all. They may also believe in one god and in several gods as manifestations of that one god. The traditional number of 330 million visible gods (a number to startle the intellect) includes all living things reflecting the universal god: They are different manifestations of the one Absolute Reality.

The Absolute Reality

An old Hindu story tells of a holy man who tried to count the gods. Although he was the son of a brahmin priest and could have enjoyed a life of wealth and ease, he decided at the age of 20 to travel across India for a year or two to ask people which gods and goddesses they worshiped. In great cities and humble villages he wrote down the name of every god in a large book. When he filled one book, he started another. From the furthest Himalayas to the burning plains of the south he saw magnificent temples filled with beautiful statues, as well as crude stone idols. He discovered thousands upon thousands of different deities and finally, at the age of 93, he began adding up all the names he had written. The task alone took another seven years, and finally, on his deathbed the holy man wrote on the last page of the last book the grand total of all the gods in India. He wrote: "One."

The one god is the Absolute Reality. It is depicted with an impersonal and a personal side. This Absolute Reality irradiates all situations and all activities: It is both transcendent and immanent, present in everything and everywhere, even to the tips of the fingernails. From the higher, impersonal standpoint, this divine power that circulates in the universe, pervading all things as their essence and making them live and function, is Satchitananda. It is Sat (being or truth), Chit (consciousness or awareness), and Ananda (bliss or joy).

The Hindu Trinity

This divine power, pictured in personal form in its relationship to the world, is the trinity of Brahma, Vishnu, and Shiva.

Brahma. Hindus identify Brahma with the genesis of the world: He is the creator of the grand illusion. Known as Prajapati ("the greatest god") and as Brahman ("cosmic energy"), Brahma is the source and ground of all existence. Today Brahma does not have a great following, and is almost forgotten.

Vishnu. Vishnu, a masculine, dominating god, representing order and righteousness, is a prominent personal manifestation of the One Absolute Reality. Vishnu is frequently depicted sitting on a lotus throne with his consort Lakshmi, the goddess of wealth and abundance. He is primarily preserver of the universe, descending to the world in his avatars (incarnations) as Rama and Krishna. Rama, epitomizing the divine attributes of beauty, loyalty, and morality, is a model for human suffering and sacrifice, for truthfulness, love, and goodness. Krishna, representing Vishnu's concern for human beings, is gracious and receptive. People lay their hopes and troubles before Krishna.

Shiva. Shiva, fierce and stern in holiness, holds the powers of destruction that are considered a necessary part of the ongoing pulsation of creation and annihilation by which the Hindu universe runs. In charge of preserving the balance of the universe, Shiva is the

Shiva and Parvati destroy the universe when it is beyond repair and revitalize it again in a never-ending process.

destroyer when the world is beyond repair. Shiva is Lord of Dancers, simultaneously destroying and vitalizing the universe in a never-ending process. The beat of Shiva's eternal dance is transformed into the rhythms of the whole universe. Shiva is the embodiment of both male and female gods, and is often pictured with both male and female parts. Sometimes Shiva dances with serpents in his hair, six arms, veiling and unveiling the Ultimate Reality to his devotees. Sometimes Shiva stands on a lotus base (the flower of wisdom) crushing a dwarf (the symbol of selfishness and ignorance).

Shiva encompasses all dualities: male and female, good and evil, creation and destruction. The dualities are represented in his shaktis, his female powers with the capacity to bring forth life. These shaktis of Shiva are worshiped under more than a thousand names. The most important are Parvati (passionate, erotic), Umma (wife and mother, nourishing and protecting), Durga (unpredictable in her vengeance), and Kali (terrifying and terrible). Parvati is the goddess of refuge and savior, able to destroy the afflictions of the world. Kali is the destructive goddess whose face is usually blackened because she announces the future we cannot see. With her bloodied sword and necklace of skulls, Kali stands upright, her mouth filled with the flesh of her victims (the snares and illusions of the world). Because she devours these illusions, she is worshiped as the generous and loving mother who comforts her trusting children.

Human Salvation

The Problem: Illusion and Samsara

Humans are deceived by the power of Maya ("illusion") to believe in the reality or value of the world of ordinary experience. The real essence of life is not this passing world, though, but what connects humans with the sacred. Humans commonly view the world as full of separate and individual realities, persons, and things. They do not know that their true selves are really eternal and identical with Brahman, the cosmic life force.

Because of this illusion, or ignorance, or selfishness, humans fail to realize their place as they should within the order of things. Because life is not what it should be, there is suffering in the world. This is Samsara: Humans are tied to a wheel of suffering and repeated death. Samsara is a trap of existence, the rebirth cycle with no beginning or end. At death, the Atman ("human soul") does not pass into some permanent state in another world; instead, it is trapped in an endless chain of deaths and rebirths. Humans are caught in a vicious circle: What they do now, out of ignorance and illusion, creates conditions for karmic rebirth in their next existence where they will continue to act in ignorance and illusion.

The Strategy: Yoga

How can humans discipline themselves to withdraw their attachment to this passing world and thus block up the causes that bring about future existences? How can they achieve liberation or release from Maya and Samsara? Liberation cannot be reached merely by improving human conduct or reforming human character; it can only be attained by transforming human consciousness.

Transformation comes by following a path or discipline ("yoga") to inward liberation. There are four main types of yoga that help humans see the sacred within and that join Atman, the individual human soul, with Brahman, the cosmic force of the universe. They are based on the different types of temperament: intellectual, psychological, active, and emotional.

One yoga is the way of knowledge, the search for a living experience of truth about life. This discipline seeks release from the bondage of illusion through direct knowledge of the human situation. The truth that sets one free is not mere intellectual knowledge, but the direct experience of the Absolute Reality. A second yoga is the way of practical discipline or the meditation technique of withdrawal. This path seeks moral, physical, and mental restraint, leading to samadhi, a state in which all mental activity ceases and, with it, all consciousness of the phenomenal world. The discipline or training to achieve this state may be ethical (leading to detachment from pain or pleasure, joy or sorrow); physical (using postures and breath control); or mental (withdrawing from sense stimuli to achieve an altered state of consciousness).

A third yoga is the way of action in the world, without concern for the fruits of the action. This path seeks liberation even while living an ordinary life. The action is unattached or detached, building karma that creates the conditions for a higher rebirth. The fourth yoga is the way of faith, of devotion to a god. This path seeks union through bhakti ("devotional love") with Vishnu or Shiva, or one of Vishnu's avatars or Shiva's shaktis. The unreserved loyalty and willingness to serve the gods require no special education, training, or caste. This path is open to all, male and female. Its practitioners use image worship, temple ceremonies, pilgrimages, and festivals to express their faith that the gods will use their beneficent and tender grace to help humans on the way to release.

The Solution: Release

The goal of these Hindu religious practices is to break through the illusion of an independent self and to bring Moksha ("release") from the round of birth, death, and rebirth. This release involves voluntarily losing the self, the individual atman, in order to find its true nature as the universal Brahman. This goal is liberation from the turmoil and troubles of the present life. Moksha is the realization of oneness with infinite being, infinite awareness, and infinite joy. It is the endless and unlimited resolution of frustration, futility, and boredom. Moksha is the fulfillment of the ultimate unity of the universe, beyond time and space. It requires great spiritual knowledge and perfection; it is many lifetimes away at best for most people.

Moksha should not be perceived as a perpetual life in the highest caste or an unending state in some heaven. When Moksha is achieved, there is a final and unconditioned release from the bondage of karma, samsara, and caste. The atman is no longer reincarnated. If a person realizes that the true self is indeed Brahman, and that Brahman is the life force of the entire universe, then there is nothing left to desire, for the self is already all. Since this awareness destroys all desires, it destroys all karma, so there will be no more rebirths once this knowledge is fully and completely realized.

When Hindus speak of heaven, it is not a vision of ultimate fulfillment or destiny, but an intermittent state in the cycle of deaths and rebirths. Traditional Hindu cosmology supplements heaven, earth, and netherworld with seven additional heavens above the earth and human world. Those who have entered the heavens, in between death and rebirth, preserve their personal identity. They enjoy the pleasures and delights they have known on earth in communion with the gods, but greatly enhanced and without the limitations known before death. The picture of these pleasant celestial realms is elaborated with endless detail, but with little consistency or authority.

The Sacred Writings

The voluminous Hindu sacred writings were gradually written down over several centuries. Most ancient are the Vedas, anthologies of religious poetry containing thousands of hymns, devotional prayers, and rhythmic chants for use at ritual sacrifices. These form the shruti ("revelations" that have truth and power when spoken and heard) along with the *Brahmanas* (lengthy, complex, and highly technical ritual instructions) and the *Upanishads*. The Upanishads (literally, "sitting near") are philosophical dialogues on the nature of existence and ultimate wisdom for those who sit near the sages. They first introduce the master phrase "You are that"—the joyful truth that a person's ultimate self at the roots of being and consciousness is, like all beings, the Infinite Reality.

Other writings are smriti (sacred writings that are "remembered"). These are not as authoritative, but are still considered sacred. The *Laws of Manu* define the duties and privileges of the various classes of humans according to their level of birth and stage of life. They indicate the specific forms of rebirth for specific transgressions: If persons steal silk, for example, they become partridges; if they steal cotton cloth, they become cranes; if they steal linen, they become frogs. The *Puranas* are myths, extraordinarily rich in symbol and essentially devotional, that narrate inspiring feats of gods and sages and their effects on human affairs. There are also Sutras ("clipped prose sentences"), such as the *Kamasutra*, a handbook of the specifics of erotic pleasures.

The most popular Hindu classics are the *Ramayana* and the *Mahabharata*, two epic stories of love and war that stress the value of popular devotion to the gods, to human duty, and to human nature. Today storytellers recite them publicly to enliven festivals and pilgrimages. The Ramayana narrates the trials and victorious struggle of the hero Rama, an incarnation of the god Vishnu to regain his beloved wife Sita from Ravana, the many-headed lord of the demons. The Mahabharata is a joyful and tender, often funny, yet sometimes terrifying story of warring families, a glorious archetypal tale of good and evil. It asks the questions: What are destiny and choice? What causes jealousy and hate? What is duty? Its exploits and events unfold in a way that has an impact on every aspect of human behavior. As Vyasa, the arranger-narrator of the Mahabharata, says: "If you listen carefully, at the end, you'll be someone else."

The First Story: Arjuna and Detachment

The *Bhagavad-Gita* ("The Song of the Lord") forms part of the Mahabharata. It teaches that satisfying peace and joy come from breaking through illusion and finding the path to inward liberation. It is the story of Arjuna, a soldier who has doubts concerning war and killing, and Krishna, an avatar of Vishnu, who tells him that it is his duty to fight in a detached way, that is, without seeking the consequences of his actions. There is no question here of doing evil that good may come: The Bhagavad-Gita does not countenance such opportunism. Indeed, as Gandhi has noted, the story is an epic against war, not for it: It describes the utter futility of a pyrrhic victory in which both victors and vanquished lose everything.

Arjuna is one of five Pandava brothers who are forced to go to war with their cousins, the Kaurava clan, who claim they have won

Krishna explains to Arjuna that the warrior's detachment in the midst of battle is superior to action: victory and defeat are the same.

the right to rule the kingdom. One of Arjuna's brothers has gambled away the family's kingdom and vast wealth in a crooked dice game that he is too proud to quit. Arjuna is a despondent warrior because he is bound by caste-duty to fight against his relatives and respected teachers who are in the ranks of the opponents. As the time for the decisive battle draws near, Arjuna is horrified by the vision of the coming slaughter and seized with fear at having to shed blood. He is fearful before battle, but not because he is afraid to die. Arjuna cannot bring himself to slay his own relatives, not even for all the worlds, much less a kingdom.

Arjuna's failure of nerve at the point of battle triggers the most arresting scene in the story. He questions Krishna, who has taken on the friendly form of his chariot-companion. Actually, Krishna is a mentor for both sides: He gives military weapons to the Kauravas and spiritual advice to the Pandavas. Arjuna argues with Krishna that he has no desire for victory, kingdom, or pleasures. His mouth parched, his body trembling, his hair standing on end, Arjuna flings away his bows and arrows and sinks down in his chariot. He is overcome by grief.

Krishna's response deals not only with Arjuna's immediate personal problem but with the nature of action, the meaning of life, and the aims for which humans must struggle here on earth. His distinctive message about war is that victory and defeat, pleasure and pain are all the same. Krishna argues that Arjuna must fight because it is his class duty as a warrior: It is a violation of dharma to abandon his duty by not fighting in the battle. Arjuna must act, but not reflect on the fruits of his act: "Forget desire; seek detachment; you must rise up free from hope and throw yourself into battle." Krishna tells Arjuna that he has no choice between war and peace, that he can only choose between war and war. Giving him the chance to rally his strength before making his choice, Krishna pours his wisdom into the anguished hero.

Krishna explains that liberation from the world is to be achieved by abandoning all attachment to it: "You must learn to see with the same eye a mound of earth and a heap of gold, a cow and a sage, a dog and the man who eats the dog." Humans excel when they engage their body with detachment and with their senses under the full control of their minds. They must do their allotted task as a form of sacrifice to the gods without thought of reward. "The soul is neither born nor does it die," Krishna declares; "weapons cannot cut it; fire cannot burn it; water cannot wet it; wind cannot dry it. Nothing can kill the soul." Thus Krishna encourages Arjuna to fight with mind devoid of excitement and with no anticipation of reward.

More perplexed than ever, Arjuna asks Krishna why, if detachment is superior to action, the Lord wishes him to engage in this dreadful battle. Krishna reminds him that the warrior's dharma is to fight for a righteous cause, to view pleasure and pain, honor and dishonor, gain and loss as the same. If people fail to do their dharma, there will be chaos in society. In the end, Arjuna has no questions left: "My delusion has fled," he tells the Lord. "By your grace, O changeless one, the light has dawned. My doubts are gone, and I stand before you ready to do your will." Arjuna finally resolves to fight and takes up arms. After eighteen days of fierce battles and bloody attacks, death and destruction are everywhere, and the pretensions of the Kauravas to rule the kingdom are annihilated.

The Story Magnified

Multiple Paths

Prior to the Bhagavad-Gita most Hindus had been taught that liberation consisted in withdrawing from the world. Those in the householder stage of life, that is, in that period of life when their duties centered around their family, their finances, and their politics, had little chance of realizing the truth of the ultimate Reality. The Bhagavad-Gita carried a unique message for them in teaching that there are many paths to the release from the cycle of birth and death, all of them legitimate. All the paths—participating in rituals and worldly action, withdrawing in knowledge and asceticism—are subsumed in a higher path and are equally beneficial. It is better, then, to have personal confidence in one's own insight and strengths and to die in one's own path than to attempt the path of another. It is better to do one's own dharma poorly than to do another's well. Humans are what they are at any given moment in time; they have to accept the consequences of being themselves.

Krishna disclosed to Arjuna, "Action in the world is in itself righteous if pursued selflessly." Thus it is possible to achieve union with ultimate Reality in the world of everyday affairs, apart from an ascetical way of life. Each person can achieve self-realization in this life by social action and by self-control in everyday living. Krishna is saying, therefore, that Hindus should act according to the laws of cosmic development and carry out those duties required at each stage of their human development. When they do, their activity is performed in a spirit of service to all and has a place in the great process toward universal oneness.

Devotion

Part of the popularity of the Bhagavad-Gita is due to the ultimate revelations, where Arjuna (and all Krishna's faithful devotees) is assured that Krishna truly loves him. In the full spectrum of Hindu teachings, such love is extraordinary. Though Krishna's word to Arjuna urges adherence to the institutes of dharma, it emphasizes even more that persons may obtain liberation by simple devotion to Krishna. Liberation is accessible to all those who, having purified action by the renunciation of desire and illuminated their minds with knowledge, suffuse their action with love of Krishna.

Krishna accepts simple offerings of a leaf, a flower, fruit, or water given in love and surrender. Krishna reveals that unreserved loyalty and willingness to serve out of bhakti requires no special education, training, caste, or sexual dispositions. Selfless love can take anyone to the highest union with ultimate reality. Indeed, those who express their faith in Krishna are loving Vishnu, the Mighty One, whose true unveiled reality and splendor are like the radiance of a thousand suns bursting into the sky. Krishna symbolizes the fullest powers of divinity, the blinding light by which the universe hangs together, and those who express faithful love for him are not so much expressing devotion to a god separate from the self as they are recognizing the self as divine. Atman and Brahman are one.

Detachment

Krishna tells Arjuna that humans may select the battleground, though they cannot avoid the battle. Arjuna is bound to act, but he is still free to make his choice between two different ways of performing the action. People generally act with attachment, that is, with desire and fear—desire for a certain result and fear that this result will not be obtained. Attached action binds persons to the world of appearances, to continually performing more action. However, there is another way of performing action and participating in the world without fear and without desire. This is the way of holy indifference or non-attachment, where persons offer everything they do as a symbol of devotion to duty.

Because persons acting this way remain indifferent only toward the results of their work—whether success or failure, praise or blame—all their work becomes equally and vitally important. When action is done in this spirit, Krishna teaches, it will lead to the ultimate Reality. Selflessness leads to calmness in the midst of strife: "Those who in the midst of intense activity find themselves in the greatest calmness, and in the greatest peace find intense activity, they are the greatest Yogis as well as the wisest persons." It follows that every action, under certain circumstances, may be a stepping stone to spiritual growth, if done in the spirit of non-attachment.

The Second Story: Ganesha and Initiation

Ganesha is the most popular and universally honored deity in the

Hindu pantheon. Ganesha is an unmistakable figure with his colossal elephant belly and his wide, flapping ears, recognized everywhere and, unlike some of the other divinities, everywhere welcome. Today Hindus generally regard Ganesha as benign and helpful, bringing success and assuring worldly well-being. He is happy and good-humored, a grantor of boons and prosperity, commonly worshiped as the Lord of Success and Prosperity. This elephant-headed god is venerated in temples and the privacy of homes. Shopkeepers and civic groups erect painted or sculpted tableaux of his doings at street corners as a way of voicing their concerns and demands for social and political justice.

Hindus depict the corpulent elephant dancing or riding a mouse, enormous as he is. In his arms he sometimes carries a hatchet to cut away illusion, or a lotus bud to bring creativity and beneficence. He may hold a pole like that used by an elephant trainer to whack away illusion, or a noose to restrain passions and desires. Sometimes he carries a radish or his missing tusk in one hand, gesturing fearlessness and reassurance; in the other hand he holds some candy for which he has an irrepressible fondness.

This elephant-faced lord makes his dramatic debut in the Puranas. The pivotal story of his birth, beheading, and restoration into the "holy family" of Lord Shiva and his wife Parvati is told many times. The story begins even before Ganesha arrives, with the tension and quarrels between the wife and husband over the question of children. Parvati fervently longs to have a child, to "feel the kiss of a son's face," as she tells Shiva pleadingly, but he resists. To protect her privacy, Parvati wants to keep Shiva and all other potential intruders away from her bath. She desires her own gana ("bodyguard") to protect the sanctity of her inner chamber. One day while she is alone she rubs her own body and brings forth a being in the shape of a young man. There is a playful intimacy and warmth between the mother and her newly created son, an intimacy enjoyed while the father remains away. Her son, Ganesha, takes over as her guard.

The great lord Shiva returns home and demands entrance to Parvati's room, but the loyal Ganesha will not let him in. Ganesha strikes the great lord with an axe. Shiva, not knowing that this is Parvati's creation, raises his trident in quick temper and strikes off Ganesha's head. When Ganesha collapses on the ground a great lamentation emanates throughout the whole world. When Parvati sees what stroke of ill fortune has befallen her, she threatens to de-

The elephant-headed Ganesha is worshipped by Hindus as the Lord of Success and Prosperity, the Lord of Obstacles and the Threshold.

stroy the universe in her inconsolable rage. She gathers together her army of shaktis (goddesses), determined to destroy all the gods and other creatures in retaliation.

Shiva has to go through the most strenuous efforts to propitiate the bereaved Parvati. He manages to cool her wrath only after he promises that he will restore Ganesha's severed head and appoint him as the chief over his ganas, the henchmen who act as guardians to scare away demons and evil spirits.

Shiva tells the ganas (who wield clubs, display fanglike teeth, and ride a ferocious dog as a vehicle) to bring back the head of the first creature they see. When a single-tusked elephant crosses their path, the ganas kill it and fit its head to the lifeless shoulders of the fallen Ganesha, thereby restoring the young boy to life. So it is that Ganesha has the head of an elephant. When Parvati sees that Ganesha has been restored, she promises that her son shall receive the worship of all people and remove all obstacles on their paths to liberation.

The Story Magnified

Lord of Obstacles

This unnatural origin for Ganesha is not particularly strange in itself, as many Hindu gods and goddesses are born in an unusual manner and sometimes unexpectedly, whether out of the cosmic ocean, sacrificial fire, spilling of seed, dropping of blood, or by some other means. Ganesha's origin shows karma at work: Ganesha is reborn to a higher existence, as the very Lord of Obstacles. No longer stuck at his mother's door, Ganesha's divine role now is to take the initiative both in placing obstacles and in removing them for all humans. Ganesha may put up barriers against people or he may help them overcome those barriers. Ganesha's capacity to remove and create hurdles stems from his adoption by Shiva and his initiation as leader of Shiva's circle of ganas. As the Lord of Obstacles, he may open doors or close them. Standing at the threshold, Ganesha plays a crucial role: Like the keeper of the locks on a river, he serves to regulate the flow of power according to the needs of the cosmos as a whole. He is the one who actually redresses the balance of the world by his expert placement and removal of barriers.

Placing and removing, as it turns out, are two sides of the same operation. Giving to one means taking from another. Half animal and half god, broken and joined together, half wild and half tame, son of the lord and lady of the universe—Ganesha does not reconcile these oppositions, but holds them together in dynamic tension. While standing as a reminder of the precariousness of all human adventures, Ganesha provides fearlessness and reassurance. He reveals and conceals himself and his actions as he sees fit within the terrain of obstacles. He places (and also removes) obstacles to gods, demons, and humans. Ganesha spends his energy defending the balance of the universe.

Lord of the Threshold

Ganesha is Lord of the Threshold of space and time. He is honored at the doorways of temples and homes, straddling the two orders of profane and sacred space. Because he provides access to other gods and goddesses, he is honored elaborately before life-cycle rites and ceremonies, at the beginning of weddings and pilgrimages. Ganesha makes new undertakings run smoothly. Because he holds the key to the success of any venture, his devotees ask for his graceful supervision of their undertakings, seeking his blessing at the start of any personally significant and possibly vulnerable undertaking. Ganesha is propitiated before commencing courses of study, opening new businesses, or simply beginning daily routines. The anxieties that humans inevitably feel in taking up new endeavors in an uncertain world find relief when they are laid, along with offerings of food, flowers, and sacred speech, at Ganesha's feet.

Initiation

The myth of Ganesha's formation, mutilation, and restoration also expresses a fundamental paradigm in the Hindu tradition, that of initiation. Ganesha undergoes a difficult passage beginning with a separation from his mother, followed by a liminal period in which he suffers a wound and loss of identity, and finally a restoration, with a new head and new identity as adopted son of Shiva and lord of the ganas. Through this process of creation, sacrifice and restoration, the story recalls the fundamental rhythm of the universe itself. By his crisis, struggle, and return Ganesha comes to know his cosmic work of regulating success and failure. Ganesha is both victim and victor: He loses his head, but by karmic law he gains a new head and more important status by virtue of his humiliation. His new power and authority over ganas, obstacles, and beginnings come from his being at once broken and whole. His beheading is inevitable and necessary, for only when he receives his new head can his full identity and power emerge.

Ganesha's story recalls the ritual of upanayana, the ceremony that confers twice-born status on young high-caste males. In this ceremony they begin their period of study and apprenticeship to a teacher, receive their sacred thread, vow to remain chaste, and learn their mantra (the epitome of all sacred speech). They are beginning the process of self-renunciation. The sacrificial violence that Ganesha undergoes is a reminder to them that the loss of self they are undertaking is not the tragic conclusion, but the necessary beginning of a passage into a new order. Renouncing the self transforms the self into an offering to the gods and induces them to give it a new life. Ganesha is a model for all Hindus as they pass through the various thresholds of life's demands and challenges. Ganesha knows their sorrows and desires: he is their best hope.

The Stories Exemplified

Other Stories

The ninth-century C.E. *Bhagavata Purana*, dedicated to Vishnu, fosters the selfless dedication of devotees to Vishnu's avatar Krishna. The *Gitagovinda* ("Song of the Cowherd") of Jayadeva, a twelfth-century court poet, is a medieval collection of devotional writing in honor of Krishna, extolling his love-play with Radha, his female-consort. These two stories take up the theme of devotional religion and detachment as a way of life. Through many touching details, they celebrate Krishna, the symbol of divine love and beauty with inner light and supernatural charm. The stories stir the emotions of motherly love for the baby Krishna and erotic love for the youthful, boisterous, and frivolous Krishna. The Krishna in these stories is a far cry from the Krishna of the Bhagavad-Gita.

Krishna, the thief of the heart, is the matchless lover of women and girls. For him, life is a karmic celebration, not a duty; life does not grind along but scampers in dance and rejoices in song. Krishna plays in the dirt, steals butter, and dances with cowherd girls who are enchanted by his haunting flute. Devotion to Krishna as the incarnation of Vishnu fosters a life free from jealousy, falsehood, envy, and injury. In such a life of devotion, birth and caste have no significance for salvation. This helps explain why Krishna is worshiped in homes and temples throughout India and is the devotional focus of the Hare Krishna movement ISKCON (the International Society for Krishna Consciousness) beyond India.

Human Witnesses

Ramakrishna. Ramakrishna Paramahamsa (1836-1886) is a Hindu model of detachment from the world through the way of loving devotion. In the spiritual experience of Ramakrishna, the Absolute Reality was manifested as the divine mother. His faith was intimate devotion to the mother goddess Kali. Because of his sense of her presence everywhere, a radiant joy permeated all his life. He spent most of his life at a large temple dedicated to Kali, just outside Calcutta. His relationship to her was so deep and all-consuming that he could not express it in the traditional rituals and hymns of the temple. He sought intimacy with her in various bizarre and unpredictable ways. One day he grabbed a sword hanging in the sanctuary in order to kill himself so that he could see if he could reach his divine

Mother by death. Mother Kali crossed the distance between them in order to give him the direct experience he sought.

Ramakrishna's attachment to Kali brought him to realize the divinity of all humans and the harmonious relationship between all religions. He expressed his detachment from any specific form of religion in a short tale: "A man woke up at midnight and desired to smoke. He wanted a light, so he went to a neighbor's house and knocked at the door. Someone opened the door and asked what he wanted. The man said: 'I wish to smoke; can you give me a light?' The neighbor replied: 'Bah, what is the matter with you? You have taken so much trouble to come and awaken us at this hour, when in your hand you have a lighted lantern.' What humans want is already within them; but they still wander here and there in search of it." Ramakrishna's example inspired Vivekananda, his greatest disciple, to bring the message of Hinduism to the World Parliament of Religions in Chicago in 1893. Today the followers of Ramakrishna maintain hospitals, schools, and ashrams (religious communities) all over the world.

Gandhi. Mohandas Gandhi (1869-1948), the father of modern India, is the Hindu apostle of nonviolence. One of the towering figures of the twentieth century, his political acts were at the same time spiritual and religious ones in fulfillment of Hindu dharma. He had the ability to combine vigorous and decisive political action with an ascetic and spiritual discipline in his own life. Gandhi taught Satyagraha ("truth force"), Ahimsa ("nonviolence"), and the equality of all men and women.

Satyagraha was a form of law-changing in which people challenged the conscience of the governing bodies by deliberately breaking laws and accepting the penalties. Gandhi wanted Hindus to be faithful to their consciences. This was much more than civil disobedience, noncooperation, and nonviolence, although it encompassed all of these. Satyagraha had to do with something more subtle and fundamental: the search for truth, for some way of decency in human encounters. It was a practical alternative to oppression, violence, and war. By promoting this force, Gandhi hoped eventually to liberate the political oppressors themselves from their blind and hopeless attachment to a system that enslaved everybody both spiritually and materially.

For Gandhi, Ahimsa was (and is) the chief glory of Hinduism. Though it was the chief vow in his own ashram, he held that it was meant for everyone. Ahimsa is the way of life, the way of non-injury, the way of joyful living, that India has to show to the world. Ahimsa stresses the inestimable value of life. Living by Ahimsa, humans attempt to avoid all violence that is intentional (e.g., through selfish motivation, pleasure, wantonness, or avoidable negligence). They avoid occupations that involve taking life and they refuse to make a profit from the slaughter of living things.

Representing the entire subhuman world, the cow is universally revered by Hindus because it is symbolic of the oneness and sacredness of life.

The oneness of all life was another of Gandhi's basic principles. In his treatise on "How to Serve the Cow," he suggested that the cow is sacred for Hindus not so much because it is the source of milk and new bovine life, but because it is symbolic of the oneness and sacredness of life. The cow represents the entire subhuman world and, in honoring it, humans indicate their oneness with all that lives.

His respect for the oneness of all life made it impossible for him to accept the traditional system of India where women were second-class citizens according to laws formulated and introduced by men. Gandhi argued that women required different qualities from men in order to fulfill the obligations of motherhood. In his view, the duties involved in maintaining moral standards and running a good home in the midst of bad social influences required as much sacrifice, courage, and fortitude as the duties involved in defending one's country against an aggressor. The energy that Gandhi spent in his writing, speeches, fasting, and nonviolent resistance for the cause of equality for women was also exercised for the Harijan (the untouchables) and for Indian independence.

Communities

Shaivites. The Shaivites and the Vaishnavites form the two principal religious currents of Hinduism. They distinguish themselves over and against each other by their bodily markings, forms of yoga discipline, and, in particular, their choice of supreme deity, either Shiva or Vishnu. They generally participate in wider Hindu activities such as pilgrimages, festivals, and temple worship, and draw upon fundamental Hindu belief structures.

The Shaivites teach that all that is required for liberation is to attune the mind to Shiva and be intent on his love and service. Inward and spiritual worship of Shiva is the essence of religion: Without it, external rituals and knowledge from the sacred writings are of no avail for liberating the soul from delusion.

Vaishnavites. Vaishnavism elicits a form of participation in the life of God, usually by self-surrender to the power of Vishnu or one of his avatars, especially Krishna. It has a strong emotional component and is replete with vivid imagery and quasi-erotic symbolism.

Caitanya (1486-1533) was one Vaishnavite revivalist and mystic who enthusiastically propagated devotion to Krishna in Bengal and East India. Rather than endlessly pondering and puzzling over religion, Caitanya interjected an emotional and exuberant dimension, proclaiming that liberation from karma is overcome by the power of divine love. He introduced a new mode of worship, with choral singing of the name and deeds of Krishna, accompanied by drums, cymbals, and rhythmic bodily movements. This worship led to an experience of ecstasy, that is, a selfless sense of timelessness and union with everything in the universe.

The Sikhs. The Sikhs ("disciples") are a strong community in India, especially in the northern Punjab region where their famous Golden Temple at Amritsar is located. The Sikhs are an offshoot of the devotional Vaishnavites. They developed in the sixteenth century, at a time when Islamic spiritual influence was also strong. Guru Nanak (1469-1538), the founder of Sikhism, proclaimed: "There is no Hindu; there is no Muslim." He taunted both Hindus and Muslims for what he considered the futility of their meaningless rituals and ascetic practices.

In one story about Nanak, Hindu pilgrims threw handfuls of water to the rising sun as an offering to their ancestors in heaven. Nanak countered by throwing the water in the opposite direction. When questioned, he answered simply: "If you can send water to your dead ancestors in heaven, surely I can send it to my fields in the Punjab." In another story, he fell asleep with his feet pointing toward the Kaaba at Mecca. An enraged mullah rudely woke him and told him of the indignity he had committed by having his feet toward the house of Allah. Nanak answered: "Then turn my feet in some other direction where God doesn't exist."

For the Sikhs, the best way to find God and his will is through discipleship to a spiritual mentor known as a guru. The pivot of their religious system, the guru is a teacher to be consulted and respected. Only with a guru as a guide can humans attain Moksha. Nanak believed humans have a basic fund of goodness that, like the pearl in the oyster, only awaits the opening of the shell to emerge and enrich them. The guru's chief task is to make humans aware of this treasure, help them unlock the jewel box, and teach them a pattern of living to unite themselves with their God.

Most Sikhs today are militant, though some have kept a pacifist stance and stress contemplation and scholarship. They have undergone much persecution in their history; and, in areas where they eventually came to power, they later took vengeance on their former oppressors. Religious hatred boiled over in 1947 when India achieved independence. The Sikhs were devastated by the partition of the Punjab, their homeland, between India and the newly created Muslim state of Pakistan. When many Sikhs were left under Muslim rule in Pakistan and many more had to move as refugees across the new border to India, leaving behind their rich farms and sacred places, they resorted to large-scale massacres and violence.

Jains. The Jains are another group that has made a substantial contribution to life and culture throughout India. Though their religion is much more ancient than Mahavira, Jains derive their name ("followers of the victor") from Vardhamana Mahavira, a sixth-century B.C.E. reformer also known as Jina ("victor"). Mahavira (the "Great Hero") is the twenty-fourth in a series of Tirthankaras ("those who conquer liberation from wheel of existence, who show the way across the ocean of suffering").

The Jains incorporate rituals, offerings, and mantras from the Brahmanic traditions in the Vedas. They do not believe in a creator god or supreme being: The universe, which was never created nor will ever cease to exist, operates according to its own laws, going through alternations of development and deterioration. The Jains believe that all human existence is suffering and that karma controls the process of an unending series of sorrowful rebirths. The way to release, which few ever attain, is through ascetic practices. By wandering on foot, receiving food offerings, penance, self-discipline, and meditation, for example, Jains hope to attain absolute control over the senses and desires. In this way karmic matter is removed, and the soul is freed from suffering and ignorance and thus realizes its true pure and omniscient nature.

The Jain shrine of Gomatesvara at Sravana-Belgola, the largest granite monolith in the world, exalts victory and liberation from the wheel of existence.

The major teaching of the Jains is reverence for life. They exercise the virtue of Ahimsa, resolutely refusing to inflict suffering on any sentient creature. To harm any living being is to hinder its evolution and take away its happiness. Jain monks carry whiskbrooms to dust the path in front of them as they walk (to avoid stepping on living things), and some Jains place a cloth over their mouths (to avoid swallowing any small insect accidentally). The Jains also apply their principle of the inestimable value of life to their eating patterns. They are vegetarians and will not eat meat even if someone else has killed the animal. They take the vow of satya ("truthfulness") and enjoy a high reputation for honesty and integrity in their business matters and personal lives. An influential and comparatively prosperous community, they make significant financial contributions to public welfare (e.g., hospitals and schools).

Twentieth Century

Modernization. Prior to independence from British colonial rule in 1947, many Indians rejected Western influences and called for a return to the early Vedas as the supreme religious truth. Researching into India's bright ancient heritage, they called on young people to identify with the happier times of the past. The West might be a worldly civilization, they said, but India was a spiritual culture destined to teach the world the art of lofty living. They saw other religions and other types of religious experience as valid but incomplete. Many called for unity of land, race, religion, culture, and language. The object of their devotion became "Mother India," and the liberation of India from all Muslim, British, and other foreign influences became the goal of final blessedness.

India did become a sovereign nation in 1947, and today it is the world's largest democracy. Indian independence was not won by the revivalist nationalists, however, but by Gandhi. His combination of decisive political action and spiritual discipline won him a following. His insistence on nonviolent civil disobedience and on the Bhagavad-Gita's teaching of outer involvement with inner detachment gave the Indian people a way of maintaining their distinct identity without closing themselves off from the modern world.

Two centuries of British rule made the struggle both to modernize and to cope with the impact of modernization inevitable. True, sacred cows still jam urban traffic and rivers still serve as washing machines. True, the vast majority of Hindus still live in villages, hardly touched by the encounter of Hinduism with Western religions. They keep to their caste dharma and they believe in karma and transmigration. In the cities and towns, however, there is restlessness, impatience, and violence. Political, educational, and economic movements push for a more joyous, more humane, and more just life. Worldwide commercial networks, industrial techniques

and organizations, and an educational system that inculcates Western values and culture are all well established today. Hospitals and
agricultural training institutes, mostly set up by Christian missionaries, have brought social optimism.

Human Rights. Resources for dealing with issues of social justice
are limited in traditional Hinduism, yet Hindu leaders now have to
deal with issues of human rights. Their challenge is to provide education, health care, and job opportunities to the poor and overcome
the inequities of Hinduism's traditional class system. Many of the
rights in India's Constitution (1950) directly challenge the unequal
privileges that are so fundamental to the traditional Hindu system.
The Constitution provides for equality before the law without regard to religion, caste, or sex, and forbids discrimination in public
life. It stands in clear opposition to ancient Hindu law books and
Hindu organization of society.

Women have constitutional guarantees of equality of status and
opportunity. It is now against the law, for example, to force (or
allow) a widow to burn herself alive at the time of her husband's
funeral fire. Still, women are often trapped as second-class citizens
and pressured to act contrary to the law because of traditions rooted
in their religion. Each linguistic group and cultural minority is guaranteed access to all educational institutions receiving state funds
and the right to establish and administer educational institutions of
their choice. The Constitution assumes human natures to be equal
and presupposes equality of opportunity and function in society.
Yet it also proclaims the freedom for each religion to live in accordance with its own beliefs. Thus, there is a clash between the inequality presupposed by the traditional view of karma-samsara and
the Constitution's statements regarding equality in the nature and
value of human life.

Caste System. The sacred caste system still remains today, though it
is often inefficient and destructive. There is much crossing of lines
between the castes and breaking down of the system in many occupations today, usually due to technological changes. Caste exclu-
siveness is still entrenched in the social and economic sectors: who
can cook food for whom, who can eat with whom, who can marry
whom, or who can come near whom without pollution. Yet money
and self-gratification are increasingly defining status for Hindus today, giving rise to a middle class that cuts across caste and region.

Restrictions of caste compatibility are giving way to financial considerations. People now often share food with persons of other castes, realizing that the system has no place in modern Hinduism.

Life Stages. Another major force of Hindu life that has come under attack by the pressures of modernization is the traditional organization of life into the four stages of student, householder, retirement, and sannyasin ("ascetic"). In the past, length of studies under a guru depended on caste, but education today is much more universal. The traditional householder stage (when Hindus were obligated to marry and set up their own household where they would burn the sacred fire and raise their children) conflicts with liberal divorce laws in the Constitution. In modern society it is more difficult to enjoy the traditional retirement stage (which comes with gray hair and grandchildren) by withdrawing to a secluded and peaceful place to practice contemplation in austere simplicity. Those who would join the sannyasin stage are meeting more and more family resistance to carry out their family obligations in modern society. Instead of voluntarily renouncing the comforts of the world and subsisting on the simplest of food and provisions, the sannyasis today engage in relief work at times of famine and flood and participate in hospital and clinical work. In this way they attempt to satisfy their yearning for that intense religious experience that will detach them from the plane where injustice and sorrow operate.

Ritual: Puja

While the individual and family approach to distant gods was traditionally performed through sacrificial fire offerings, the central religious ceremony of most Hindus today is a joyful, emotional, and exciting event called puja, a form of ritual worship paid to a god or goddess, usually in the presence of an image of the divine. Devotion to personal heavenly gods, if properly expresssed, can induce the gods to adopt earthly residences and thus become more permanently available to their worshipers. Some Hindus perform puja to seek earthly favors (e.g., health, wealth, safety) through the gods' good will. Others seek to accumulate good karma from their worship to attain a more fortunate rebirth on earth or in the blessed realms above after death.

Pujas are most commonly held at family shrines and festivals, but they are also held at holy temples or the shrines of local village deities. They are freely structured, consisting of little more than individual gestures of reverence and minimal offerings. At the family shrine, most Hindus maintain a daily routine of pujas to one or more divinities honored within the household. The shrine usually consists of a picture of a god set up on a table or low platform, or housed in a wooden cabinet, with the doors opened only during services. The traditional attendances at the family shrine begin with a purification and invocation of the presence of the god. The god is given personal care: The feet are washed, and water is offered for sipping, drinking, and bathing. Other respectful offerings may include perfumes, flowers, clothing, incense, and foods (e.g., rice, sugar). Songs may be sung and auspicious music played, then there is a prostration and dismissal of the god.

At the festival pujas the deities are mounted on large multi-storied carts and pulled through the town on a processional path. Devotees toss flowers and sprinkle the image with water as the cart progresses and they receive the opportunity for darshana, the "sight" of the god or goddess. This darshana is accompanied with intense feelings and emotions as the worshipers feel united with divine power and energy.

The Stories Appropriated

The Hindu stories of Krishna's advice to Arjuna and Ganesha's beheading and new life provide a context for meaning, not only for the lives of those within the Hindu tradition, but for those of us outside it. These stories present new ways for us to envision our own spiritual convictions. Learning about detachment and initiation challenges us to respond in a personal way to our own religion on the basis of transformed decisions.

Detachment

The events that befall Arjuna on the eve of battle are reflections of our inner lives. That is why the horrors and joys, the tragedies and wonders of the Bhagavad-Gita can grasp our attention so intently. Many of us feel that personal happiness comes through enthusiastic concentration and undivided focus of our whole life and mind on what we are doing. We find that when we risk everything on our efforts, though, there is great unhappiness when the results fail: The mind is divided between the memory of past hopes and the present evidence of failure. Defeat does seem to create unhappiness, unless some way can be found to pursue definite ends by combining an unlimited attachment with an unlimited detachment. What we can learn from the counsel of Krishna to Arjuna, not to seek the fruits of action, is this: By remaining open to an infinite number of unexpected possibilities, which transcend our own imagination and capacity to plan, we really can fulfill our need for freedom.

Detachment means many different things. Detachment may mean making our aim the pursuit of the goal rather than the reaching of the goal. In this case, the process of getting there has priority over the actual arrival: The focus is on the pursuit, and there is absence of an absolute end. This can lead to a kind of Stoic detachment and a refusal to attempt any moral achievements in the world, for fear of futility or illusion. Detachment may mean a kind of game spirit wherein we compete and try to win; in the case of failure we leave bitterness behind and make the next attempt to win with renewed enthusiasm. This is similar to the experimental scientists who have to be both attached and detached to results. They proceed in their experiments with hopes of success; if they fail, they recast the experiment with renewed hopes for later success. Detachment may also mean altruism or vicarious happiness: We look for success in the results, but that success need not be our own individual success. Like a patriot, we may not succeed in our own high moral aims, yet we can find happiness in knowing that history as a whole will succeed. There is a resignation to the ongoing process of history which we can only trust will prove successful in the end.

Somehow these types of detachment take the zest away from life to some extent or move the focus from this world to a realm beyond it. These kinds of detachment somehow keep us passive or never let us taste the quality of genuine happiness. Still, there need not be conflict between our desire for individual involvement and Krishna's message of detachment. In our own tradition we assert that each individual strives to have a sense of power in action, not ruthless power, but power that asserts the individual's own freedom and capacity to shape particular events toward good ends. From Krishna's perspective of detachment, nothing—no activity, no human psychological event—can be separated from the vast texture of which it is a part. When we balance our traditional need for a sense of power with Krishna's message of detachment we perceive that there is a connection between what we are doing as individuals and the whole cosmic flow of destiny.

War

Because war is Arjuna's duty as a prince and warrior, Krishna exhorts him to go to war against his enemies, who are also his own relatives. The Bhagavad-Gita appears to accept and to justify war and the use of violence. Yet the story is not a justification of war, at least as we know it, for here war is subject to all sorts of cultural limitations. Arjuna has a distinct repugnance for war and wants to avoid the cancerous nature of battle joy. That is the chief reason why war is chosen as the example of the most repellent kind of duty. What the story tells us is that we can act with pure intentions and with detachment, and thus be guided by divine awareness, even in what appears to be the most "unspiritual." This consciousness imposes strict limitations on our use of violence, then, because it is not directed by our selfish interests, and still less by cruelty, sadism, and blood-lust.

Arjuna ponders the puzzle of whether what he is doing will lead to good karma. Is what he is doing in true relationship with his personal dharma and with the great dharma of the entire universe? Why can't Krishna impel him to say: "Let's get rid of all of this; only one thing matters to humanity—that there be no more war." War marks for life the men and women who are caught up in it. It visits them in the hour before sleeping; it comes to them, unexpectedly, bringing grief, pride, shame. It never goes away. Though Krishna's response to Arjuna's troubles is aimed at allaying his and our fears about killing, he plunges us into a view of how to live that has much wider applications than the battle situation.

We have arrived at the essential question of our human destiny: To know and become our true selves in all activities, including battle, is the hardest task of all, requiring all our energy. Krishna knows the outcome, yet he will not relent in his efforts. Each person has to face choice after choice, until the point is reached where there are no more choices left and we are what he is: This is the union of the human and the divine. Our duty as humans, Krishna says, is not to change the world, but to change our perception of the world and to become part of the One, the eternal.

Work

What shield is there, then, against the self? What can free us from the self, our final enemy? Arjuna found freedom in fulfilling his duty to fight. Perhaps we too can find freedom in our work, in committing ourselves daily to a task that demands from us the full and strenuous exercise of our strongest selves. There is a considerable difference between our work and our job. A job is something we do because we get paid for it and make a living out of it. A job for most of us is neither the most elated and noble nor the most depressing and deadening thing we do. Our jobs are usually somewhere in between, usually just ordinary, repetitive, and basically tolerable. We often entertain high hopes for our jobs, but soon enough they derail into routine.

All of us may have jobs, but not all of us work. To work is to bring meaning and purpose to a job. To work is to take the trouble to discover and master and commit ourselves to some job that is rewarding. To make work out of our jobs, we have to blend our order-creating minds with our miraculously complex physical competence in order to liberate us from the chaos in our lives. A job helps free us from physical want, hunger, and disease; work helps liberate us from prolonged dependence on other persons and, occasionally, from our selves. Work frees us for the attempt to understand, if not control, the disorder in ourselves, in our world, and in our relationships with others. Work can even free us at times to participate in the most dangerous mystery of all—the love of other human beings.

We are really fortunate when we can make a living out of work, and work out of a job. Arjuna's job is to be a warrior, and Krishna is educating him to make work out of it. Education is the process that helps us discover, as early as possible in life, that work is simultaneously fulfilling, pleasurable, joyful, and nurturing. Work is what we can't help doing in order to express whatever drive there is in us to produce and to create. Our jobs engage us to produce something; our work, though, engages our whole person in the passion to find meaning in our lives.

Play

If the story of Arjuna brings insights to work, then the story of Ganesha brings a message about play and humor. There is a playful intimacy and warmth between Ganesha and his mother. Indeed, Ganesha is always playful: Dancing or riding a mouse, he is happy, good-humored, and welcome everywhere. Ganesha draws out the child in all of us adults who would play in the universe. This corpulent elephant reminds us of the Absolute Reality, the Supreme Player whose lila ("play") is manifested in the inexhaustible richness of the world. Ganesha invites us to play with him in spontaneous, amusing, and purposeless activity. Ganesha invites us to dance with the cosmic Dancer, with Absolute Reality. If we do, his story tells us, then we experience a new life and move to a higher level of consciousness by attuning ourselves with divine reality. Our lives then attain their true dimension, and we have found the key to the meaning of life.

To live without this illuminated consciousness is to live as a beast of burden, carrying our lives with tragic seriousness as a huge, incomprehensible weight. To live with the true consciousness of life centered on the Absolute Reality is to lose our self-important seriousness. If we take the Absolute seriously, we find joy and happiness in everything, for everything is then gift and grace. If we live selfishly, we bear an intolerable burden; if we live selflessly, we recreate our selves and celebrate our joyful reunion with the cosmic Player.

Obstacles

The beheading of Ganesha is not the tragic conclusion of his life, but the necessary beginning of a passage to a new order, to restoration to divine intimacy. It is as if his karma comes to fulfillment when personal attachments give way to acceptance of the divine order. With his revival and new life, Ganesha's role in the divine scheme is to be the Lord at the threshold. Once broken and now restored, he is the dweller on the boundary where all beings are vulnerable.

We are all vulnerable as we pass through different stages of life in moving from childhood to adulthood. We all face obstacles in our major decisions regarding family and career. Standing at the threshold of our undertakings, Ganesha helps us with our crises. Ganesha not only reminds us of the precariousness of all human adventures, he also assists us with his shrewd support and advice. With his feet planted firmly on the ground, available at the door, Ganesha rules the concrete world of action and its fruits, success and failure, triumph and pain. Ganesha offers us practical wisdom—clever, humorous, and playful—that can help us navigate successfully through the perilous waters of the ocean of Samsara.

Ganesha is a particularly clever character, making use of tricks and mischievous surprises. Ganesha is so valuable to us because there is precious little said about laughter and humor either in our images of the gods or in our religious situation before the divine. The wisdom Ganesha brings us is a reminder that the ability to see humor in things is among the most profound and imaginative of human achievements. Humor is a healthy response to the absurdities of life, and laughter gives the strength to bear the tragedies of human existence. A comic perception, no matter how brief the glimmer, helps us liberate our selves from the prison house of the self and its opinions and situations. We are free to laugh, and in that freedom, our lives open up to a different light and larger perspective.

Ganesha makes us smile with his elephant belly and flappy ears. How can an elephant riding a mouse fail to generate humor? What a gift Ganesha brings to us humans! Humor is indeed a grace that comes, not by inner tension, but by an inner harmony. Humor reflects resolution more than conflict, obstacles overcome more than the obstacles themselves. Humor proceeds from a position of strength, not from a position of weakness and turmoil. Humor helps us share in a common human nature and the common predicaments, embarrassments, and temptations of life. It helps us laugh with, rather than at, people. Humor curbs pride and keeps us honest. The ability to laugh at ourselves keeps us sane, healthy, and in balance. It leaves us feeling adaptable and lighter in spirit. Flexibility is the characteristic of life; rigidity the sign of death.

Conclusion

For Hindus, karma and dharma are powerful forces in human lives. Dharma, by giving a sense of duty in life, provides an order of cosmic justice in nature and civilization. Karma, by showing that thoughts and actions have consequences for the future, provides the incentive to exercise human initiative to better the self.

Krishna brings advice regarding detachment from dharma and reveals that unreserved loyalty and willingness to serve out of faithful and devotional love are possible for all. He challenges Hindus to view pleasure and pain, honor and dishonor, gain and loss as the same in their relationship to the universe and to each other.

The story of Ganesha's beheading and restoration is the story of growth through dying and rising. Good karma, it tells Hindus, comes from a life of sacrifice. A reminder of the precariousness of all human adventures, Ganesha provides Hindus with fearlessness and reassurance, inviting them to cooperate in the cosmic divine play.

Discussion Questions

1. Why do you think the author chooses the river Ganges at Banaras as a symbol of Hindu karma and dharma?

2. Show how Vishnu and his avatars as well as Shiva and his shaktis are all manifestations of the Absolute Reality.

3. Summarize the Hindu belief in salvation in terms of illusion, yoga, and release.

4. Describe Krishna's advice to Arjuna regarding action and non-attachment.

5. Why do you think that Ganesha is the Lord of Obstacles and Thresholds?

6. Summarize the role of the Jains and Sikhs in the overall religious tradition of India.

7. What can Christians appropriate today from the stories of Krishna and Arjuna and Ganesha's sacrificial beheading? Why do you think that humor and play seem so out of place in the religious life of most people?

8. Discussion Starter: "To call woman the weaker sex is a libel; it is man's injustice to woman. If by strength is meant brute strength, then indeed is woman less brute than man. If by strength is meant moral power, then woman is immeasurably man's superior. Has she not greater intuition, is she not more self-sacrificing, has she not greater powers of endurance, has she not greater courage? Without her man could not be. If nonviolence is the law of our being, the future is with women." (Gandhi)

9. Discussion Starter: "A man after fourteen years of hard asceticism in a lonely forest obtained at last the power of walking over the waters. Overjoyed at this acquisition, he went to his guru and told him of the great feat. At this the master replied: 'My poor boy, what you have accomplished after fourteen years' arduous labor, ordinary people do by paying a penny to the boatman,'" (Ramakrishna)

10. Discussion Starter: "Sankara was going to the temple after a bath in the Ganges. A candala (untouchable) followed by dogs and with a pot of liquor in his hand came near him. When Sankara asked him to get out of the way, the candala responded: 'Which should go away, the body or the self? As for the body, it is the same in composition in the case of every person. As for the self, it is one and all pervading.' Sankara realized at once that this was Lord Shiva in the guise of an untouchable. Prostrating himself, Sankara sang a hymn to Shiva declaring that anyone who realizes the oneness of life is his master."

The longest fortification in the world, the Great Wall symbolically unites the immense diversity of cultures and history of the Chinese people.

Chapter Seven

CONFUCIANISM AND TAOISM
Humaneness and Naturalness

Setting the Scene

The Great Wall

The Great Wall gambols over the hills of China, rising to the loftiest summits and plunging into the deepest ravines. Starting at the Yellow Sea and rising at one point over 10,000 feet above sea level, it travels 1500 miles into central Asia, toward the mountains of Tibet. Constructed during the third century B.C.E., it is the supreme monument to the engineering courage of ancient China. The longest fortification in the world, it is wide enough to allow five or six horses to gallop abreast along its top. It is the only man-made object on the earth that was seen from the moon.

Without doubt the Great Wall is the most magnificent monument ever created to mark the unification of a nation. Ch'in Shih Huang Ti (259-210 B.C.E.), the first emperor, completed this prodigious effort not only to protect northern China's frontier against the inroads of invaders, but to unite the country politically. Consolidation and unification of the people remained the goal of succeeding Chinese dynasties, who saw in the Great Wall a valuable symbol to bring together the immense diversity of culture, history, and geography of China. The Great Wall has symbolically joined together several separate cultures within China. In fact, the various cultures have blended so harmoniously that the vast majority of the 1.2 billion Chinese today share the same view of nature, humans, and social practices that their ancestors had thousands of years ago. It is such a precious symbol of unity that they have extensively repaired it from time to time, especially during the Ming dynasty (1368-1644).

A defensive barrier against the intrusion of the nomadic Huns of the Mongolian steppe, the Great Wall symbolized the might of the newly united empire it protected. Just as the Chinese believed that they lived in the "Middle Kingdom" and that they occupied the central place on the earth's surface, so the Great Wall has been the barrier separating them from the rest of the world. A heroic effort to perfect China's almost complete natural isolation, the Wall never permanently kept political or military invaders out. Still, the Chinese have maintained such a thorough cultural separation that, historically, the religion of Buddhism has been the only outside force to influence Chinese unity. Buddhism, in turn, was profoundly modified in its accommodation to Chinese ways.

Multiple Religious Systems

Chinese religion is an amalgam of several separate strains, not only popular religion, but also Confucianism, Taoism, and Buddhism. Here too there is a striking unity in diversity. The Chinese people have an overriding sense of the centrality of the family and thus a universal sense of their vast group of peoples as one national family. They focus their energy in their popular religion on practical, immediate human concerns, such as perpetuating the family, protecting property, sharing health and long life, expelling evil spirits, obtaining favor from the gods, and bringing peace to their homes and ancestors. The Chinese believe that together with the realms of sacred forces, nature, and society, they are all a part of this one world and that the highest good comes in maintaining harmony between these realms.

In addition to their universal loyalty to their popular or folk religion, the Chinese traditionally honor the teaching of Kung Fu (Confucius, 551-479 B.C.E.) and strive to attain his ideal of Jen ("humaneness"), which characterizes the Chun-tzu ("superior person"). They also respect the teaching on harmony with nature attributed to Lao Tzu (sixth century B.C.E.). The Chinese are Confucian and Taoist by turns, depending upon which system is appropriate to their particular activities or phase of life. In this way they contrive, with considerable success, to enjoy the best of two superb spiritual philosophies.

When Buddhism was imported to China 2000 years ago, the Chinese were able to digest its difficult philosophical system through the guidance of visiting masters from northwest India. They subsequently developed their own form of Buddhism, which was destined to become the third major religion of China, along with Confucianism and Taoism. Through centuries of growth and revitalization, Buddhism has contributed much to the popular religion of most of the Chinese people. We will look at the Buddhist tradition in the next chapter.

Harmony

Confucianism and Taoism are not bodies of ideas to which unbelievers can be converted, but ways of life which can be practiced only within traditional Chinese society. The Chinese ability to perpetuate the core values of both religions and adapt them to ever changing circumstances has led to long periods of stability and creative achievement. The religions are very different and yet very complementary. Both religions view the world as an organism of interrelated parts: When the function of one of the parts is disrupted, the harmony of the whole is impaired. The Confucian and Taoist traditions show a particular interest in affirming something about the world, one through society, the other through nature. Confucianism teaches that harmony with nature will come about by preserving harmony in society through humaneness. Taoism teaches that harmony in society will come about by submitting to nature.

While the Confucian tradition stresses the construction and maintenance of a viable harmonious, ordered, and just society, Taoism stresses experience that is both more individualistic and more cosmic in scope. Confucianism pushes for strong government, with a definite structure and hierarchy; Taoism counters with little or no government, giving more weight to life outside the office and outside bureaucracy.

Confucianism, in asking "What should I do?" emphasizes specific actions that will help a person be in harmony with the "decree of heaven." Taoism, in asking "What should I be?" underscores that being like the Tao or uniting the self with the Tao helps persons act in harmony with reality. Confucianism often stresses sacrificial rituals as a means of expressing reverence for ancestors; for Taoism, rituals most often concern healing or a way for obtaining immortality. Confucianism's concern for social propriety and ritual is supplemented with Taoism's nature-bound investment in leisure, retirement, solitude, and art. Along with Buddhism, these different aspects of religion exist in interplay in China, exercising a complementary influence.

Faith and Chinese Gods

Gods in Popular Religion

The Chinese do not sharply distinguish between gods and humans. Humans are potentially divine, and the many gods of popular religion often take human form. There is just this one unified world, with no separate transcendent god or eternal world outside this sacred cosmos. Local gods are seldom pitted against each other. The deities have special abilities and limited powers, but when linked together with other gods they are believed to be able to do just

The Chinese have intense devotion to the female bodhisattva Kuan-yin, the goddess of mercy who hears the distress of all suffering beings.

about anything a single, supreme god could, from helping an army win a battle to healing a sore on a child's neck. The Chinese call on their gods to adjust the order of nature (e.g., rain against drought); to deliver peace and harmony in family life (e.g., home protection and good health); to effect success in their struggles for livelihood (e.g., fertility, crafts, wealth); and to bring about a favorable rebirth (e.g., reincarnation into a wealthy family).

Earth deities are the T'u-ti kung, guardians of the local community in all its fortunes and misfortunes, associated with civic virtues and the fertility of the soil. One goddess who commands special affection is Ma Tsu, the protectress of seafarers. Not only does she use her special powers to communicate with and help fishermen, but she provides help in childbirth and for healthy children and happy marriages. From the Buddhist tradition, the Chinese have special affection for Kuan-yin. She is a goddess of mercy who saves people from danger and suffering and is also appealed to for other kinds of aid, especially to make barren women fruitful. All interactions between humans and gods are ruled by the principle of reciprocity: Gods have to come through with beneficial power; if they are not efficacious, the people will terminate their worship.

The Absolute Reality

In historic Chinese religion, the supreme spiritual presence, the greatest moral power, was T'ien ("Heaven"). Not only was T'ien the place where gods and souls of ancestors resided in the sky above, it was also Nature, which controlled the moral direction of the world. T'ien was sometimes personalized as Shang Ti ("Ruler Above") or as the Jade Emperor. Shang Ti was not an unlimited divine ruler, but a force for harmony and balance that governed the organic whole. The Jade Emperor was the supreme arbitrator over life, who could be approached only by the ruler, while the common people made offerings to their ancestors.

Gods are not a central focus in Confucianism. This has led many to question whether it is really a religion. For Confucius, it was a question of priorities: How could humans serve spiritual beings if they were not yet able to serve each other? How could they know about death if they did not yet know about life? Still, the Confucian system is a religion insofar as it certainly has a system of beliefs and practices suffused with a sense of the sacred. The sacred centers on the social and moral order of this world, rather than on some transcendent being. Confucians emphasize the oneness between the self and the universe rather than faith in personal gods. Their gods are humans deified over time by increasing recognition of their efficacy and status.

In medieval Confucian thought, the Absolute is T'ai Chi ("Universal Principle"). T'ai Chi is the Ultimate Cause, the Eternal, the Never-Changing. Nothing lies outside it; there is nothing that does not contain all of it. All things come from it; all things return to it. This is similar to, but not identical with, the Tao in the Taoist tradition.

The Tao ("The Way") is the source and origin of everything and also the power that maintains harmony and balance in the world. The Tao is the inexpressible, eternal Mother of the Universe. In greatness, the Tao produces; in producing, it expands; in expanding, it regenerates. The Tao is a deep, mysterious reality that cannot be grasped by word or concept. It operates simply as the innermost universal way of nature, not through power or coercion, not through commands or absolute structures. The Tao profoundly affects human existence, and humans must adjust to it in order to achieve a sense of peace and tranquility. Paradoxically, the Tao is everywhere, yet only the most sensitive and subtle mind can know it. If the Tao were ever to be followed everywhere, then heaven, humans, and earth would merge into a single, harmonious unit, cooperating toward universal well-being in every part.

The Tao is the Way the universe runs, the proper Way to Go, the Way to Be. The Tao generates change, based on the interaction of its complementary aspects, Yin and Yang. Yin and Yang are the two opposing but interrelated active forces that blend together in varying proportions to constitute all things in the world. The Yang force is positive, assertive, bright, and dry, and is an attribute of the sun and males (reflecting the dominant position of males in Chinese society). The Yin force is negative, receptive, dim, and wet, and is an attribute of the moon and females. Each is defined in relation to the other, and each contains within itself the generating source of the other. They are symbolized by a pair of interlocked comma shapes with a dot of the opposite color in the head of each. In balance, they complement each other and effect the harmonious and meaningful functioning of society.

Human Salvation

The Confucian Problem: Ignorance

Confucius teaches that human problems, especially corrupt social practices, are due to a refusal to seek the good of others, a refusal that stems from ignorance of the oneness between the self and the universe. As Confucius's chief disciple, Mencius (372-289 B.C.E.), expresses it, heaven is present within each person's heart, yet humans do not know this. Humans do not realize each self is divine in its all-embracing fullness. Though the natural tendency of humans (hsing) is to realize T'ien, ignorance causes perversity, misconduct, and serious disruptions in the balance of the universe. Though humans are fundamentally good by nature, their spiritual nourishment is often curtailed and hindered by selfish rulers, wrongful social relationships, and by other human atrocities against nature, humans, and the self.

The Confucian Strategy: Propriety

Still, Confucianism is optimistic: The human moral condition is not beyond redemption. Humans can achieve spiritual self-cultivation and exercise their Jen in human affairs through personal perseverance in study and through ritual.

Study. Though Confucius's advice on study is aimed particularly at rulers, it is applicable to all people. Human nature is ultimately malleable: Instruction can promote good and eradicate evil. Humans can become "superior persons" through long study and self-discipline. Inner knowledge of the will of heaven is awakened slowly. Study does not mean preoccupation with useless meditation or with learning trifles or particular skills. It is broad moral cultivation that engrains mystical sensitivity for fellow humans and an acute sensitivity to delicately balanced forces in the universe, not specialized competence. Only then can persons apply their knowledge, wisdom, and discipline to performing public duties, to improving the morals of others, and to restoring the balance of harmony to society.

Li ("Ritual" or "Propriety"). Performing the proper rituals and external ceremonies is the other discipline that helps persons transform themselves inwardly. Li ("Ritual") connotes all the formal and informal actions and duties by which people smooth social interactions with family, nature, and ancestors. Ritual alone is quite inappropriate, though. As Confucius said, "Ritual is more than jade or silk; music is more than bell and drum." When ritual generates the inner dynamics of human relationships, it is a powerful device for securing the harmonious human order. Ritual has to manifest reciprocity, a mutual exchange of gifts and favors between people where both parties gain from the transaction. It is a variation of the Golden Rule: "What you do not want done to yourself, do not do to others." One proper expression of reciprocity in ritual is the Rectification of Names, where persons are in reality what their title says. Just as a circle is a circle and a square a square, so fathers must properly father, mothers properly mother, and princes always carry out their duties and responsibilities in a princely fashion.

The Confucian Solution: The Chun-Tzu

The Confucian tradition does not put stock in a life after death, nor salvation through help from T'ien, nor does it strive for some distant future Utopia on earth. Someone who has mastered the self through study and ritual can obtain a good balanced life here and now. This is the Chun-tzu ("Superior Person"), who contributes to make society work fruitfully and harmoniously, thus enhancing the world which is already good and beautiful. The Chun-tzu fulfills the potential for peace, harmony, and happiness according to the design of heaven. Such self-fulfillment is the ultimate realization of human freedom and of the complete unity between humans and heaven. The Chun-tzu sets a standard of human refinement, consistently gracious and seldom giving offense. The Chun-tzu is the epitome of Jen and Chih ("Wisdom"). The superior person integrates loyalty and reciprocity, bringing serenity and refinement. The Chun-tzu desires benevolence, not profit, and seeks to draw out and perfect the good qualities of others.

The Taoist Problem: Going Against Nature

In the Taoist tradition, social institutions such as laws, education, ceremonies, rules of morality, and etiquette promote the tendency to force things in unnatural ways. The source of human unhappiness lies in the effort to control destiny, thereby impeding the natural flow of spontaneous events. In going against the givenness and spontaneous fitness of nature, humans experience suffering, frustration, and defeat. People have lost their sense of intimacy with nature's way, their most basic birthright. Living in a society with many laws distances them from the way that alone can make them prosper. Law-enforcers, teachers, and ritualists do the most to worsen human problems by imposing restraints on what should be natural or free. Forcing structure onto nature and themselves, humans are mired in an unnatural and disharmonious world and forget their potential for happiness.

The Taoist Strategy: Wu-Wei ("Active Passivity")

The way to overcome human disharmony is through wu-wei ("active passivity"), a combination of supreme activity and supreme relaxation. Humans who act with wu-wei have no wasted motion: Their behavior is spontaneous and natural. Wu-wei does not involve study or learning, for such activities only serve further to cloud over the mind and prevent it from being open to the flow of Tao. Humans who act with wu-wei go with the flow rather than try to swim against the current. In this way, in "letting it be," they take on Te, a new power that brings them in harmony with the mysterious energy of the Tao itself. With this energy, humans have no inner conflicts and no wasted movement. Their conduct is admirable in itself, apart from its consequences. Moving toward inward simplicity, their path avoids self-assertiveness and competition and is fully attuned to the rhythms of nature.

The Taoist Solution: Harmony With Nature

Lao Tzu's harmonious society is one based on the Tao, one that is least intrusive. Humans are at their best when social life is unadorned, when human rituals and conventions are few. The closer people can stay to nature and nature's way, the better off they will be. In a world lived according to Tao, there is a peaceful and well-ordered society, where people dedicate themselves to the aid and advancement of all people and, indeed, of all living things. In such a world, government is so natural and spontaneous that one hardly knows it is there. This can happen here and now.

Later Taoist religious tradition also advocates a place for the blessed after death, the so-called abode of the hsien-jen ("immortals"), located either on the Isles of the Blessed in the Eastern Sea or on the sacred mountain peaks on the western border. On the sacred Isles, the palaces and gates are made of silver and all animals and birds are pure white. If any mortal should attempt to approach, the islands suddenly collapse under water. The mythical mountain paradise is K'un-lun. Here the Queen Mother of the West frolics, riding geese and dragons, and the immortals abstain from eating cereals, feeding instead on the wind and dew. Here a peach tree confers longevity on anybody who has the good fortune to taste its fruit.

The Confucian Sacred Writings

Of the world religions in China, three have their own sacred writings. In this chapter, we will look at the sacred writings of Confucianism and Taoism, saving the Buddhist sacred writings for the next chapter.

Confucian Classics

The primary sacred writings in the Confucian tradition are the *Five Classics.* Four of these (Book of History, Book of Poetry, Book of Rites, Annals of Spring and Autumn) serve mainly for the moral training of the scholarly class. The fifth, *I Ching* (Book of Changes), is a book of divination with commentaries on a series of sixty-four diagrams formed by Yin and Yang lines that analyze and explain the patterns of change inherent in the universe. Other sacred writings include poems of romance and war, discourses on beauty and moral virtue, detailed accounts and philosophical meanings of the rituals of the ancient sage-kings. Still other texts include rites and ceremonies, chronicles of kings, and writings that describe a profoundly ethical view of life, with grave responsibilities for leaders in particular.

Analects. Recollections of the teaching of Confucius have been gathered by his disciples in *The Great Learning* (education for gentlemen) and *The Doctrine of the Mean* (the relation of human nature to underlying moral order of universe). The best known of the writings attributed to Confucius, though, are the *Analects,* a collection of sayings designed for training government officials, but applicable to all areas of social life. The Analects include no story of Confucius going off into the wilderness to fight against evil powers or to achieve some supreme destiny. Confucius worked as a minor government functionary to collect grain and livestock for taxes. For years he taught history, poetry, music, government, and moral conduct, and was a specialist in the I Ching. His ambition was to gain an important position with power where he could reform the government. He was no politician, however, and his candid criticism of superiors destroyed his chances.

Confucius describes himself as a person who forgets to eat when he is enthusiastic about something, disregards his worries in the enjoyment of pleasures, and dismisses old age in the delight of the present

Instructing young people in the classics of China's cultural heritage, Confucius trained them to be wise and generous public servants.

moment. According to one legend, he once asked his disciples, "If a ruler were to recognize your worth and give you whatever you wanted, what would you ask for?" One disciple answered that he would desire a kingdom, another a flourishing district, and a third would like to engage in ceremonies. The fourth student announced that he wanted nothing more than to take along half a dozen grownups and half a dozen youths to swim in the river in spring-time and, after bathing, to enjoy the breeze in the woods, and then return home loitering and singing on the way. Confucius heaved a deep sigh and exclaimed: "You are the person after my own heart."

Mencius. A short book attributed to Confucius's greatest disciple, Mencius, injects a profound note of compassion into Confucian humaneness. *The Book of Mencius* stresses the vitality of the sagely tradition, the necessity for well-established rituals, and the need for a stable political order. In his many stories and parables, Mencius stresses that the development and nurturing of the original and essential goodness of human nature is the key to the realization of social and political values.

The First Story: Bull Mountain and Humaneness

In his parable about Bull Mountain, Mencius argues that we are all born with innate feelings of righteousness and benevolence in our human relationships, although these are sometimes destroyed by outside forces. At one time Bull Mountain was beautifully wooded. Due to the nourishing influence of the rain and dew, the trees on its slopes grew buds and sprouts sprang forth. Because the mountain was close to a large city, though, its trees were chopped down for firewood or eaten by browsing cattle and sheep. That is why it now has a bare and stripped appearance. Looking at it now, people cannot imagine that anything ever grew there. But surely this is not the true nature of the mountain.

In the same way, Mencius asks, can it be that any person's mind naturally lacks humaneness and justice? If persons lose the sense of the good, then they lose it as the mountain lost the beauty of its trees, hacked away by axes, day after day. Yet, just as trees grow over the years, so humans grow, and in the still air of the early hours their sense of right and wrong is at work. If this sense is barely perceptible, is it because their actions during the day have destroyed it? Or is it because this sense of right and wrong has been disturbed and deprived by others? Like the trees, the true nature of human beings has to be allowed to grow: Given the right nourishment there is nothing that will not grow and, deprived of it, there is nothing that will not decay away.

The Story Magnified

Natural Goodness

With their innate humaneness and sense of right and wrong, humans instinctively feel compassion toward the sufferings of others and shame toward their own failings. Mencius clarifies this with another story. On seeing a child about to fall into a well, for example, everyone without exception experiences a feeling of alarm and stress. They will do all they can to save the child, not to gain the gratitude of the child's parents, nor to gain a reputation with neighbors and friends, but because they have within themselves the beginnings of the great virtues of humaneness and justice. Li ("Propriety") prompts them to act spontaneously without thought or calculation. Persons who perform this good action need no books to prod them: They are acting according to the true nature of their minds. And when their conduct is in conformity with their action, they are exercising their natural goodness and "delighting in the Way."

Nurture

In describing human nature as basically good, Mencius admits that humans still need education to restrain evil impulses. Though humans innately possess the beginnings of virtue, Mencius realizes that this virtue becomes clear and manifest when it is properly nourished through the transforming influence of education. For one who would teach humaneness, though, Mencius favors example and persuasion rather than meddling or compulsion. He tells the story of the farmer Sung, for example, who pulls up his corn because he is grieved that it is not growing long enough or fast enough. Having done this, he returns home, and announces proudly to his people: "I am tired today. I have been helping the corn to grow along." His son runs to look at the corn and finds it all withered. Some people, Mencius says, try to compel humaneness like the farmer Sung who interfered with the corn and forced it to grow. They have nothing to show for their efforts.

Nurturing humaneness, then, is an art. There are many ways to teach; in fact, teachers instruct by the very things they do not think worth teaching. Mencius, very conscious of his duties as a teacher, has his own method of teaching, which he elaborates in another story. He is leaning on a stool, he tells us, when a traveler, who wants to retain him to counsel the king, sits down nearby for a chat. Mencius says nothing. The guest says: "I passed the night here so I might talk with you. But you lie there without listening. I won't ever visit you again." Mencius replies: "If you will sit down I shall explain everything clearly." He proceeds to tell why he left the king's service: "When I was in your midst you did not appreciate me. Now I am leaving and you want to retain me. Go back to your king and tell him that I am still willing to assist him, but only if he gives me his confidence. As proof of this confidence I will only recognize a decisive change in his life. I have been insisting on this since my arrival in this country. If the king does not follow the principles I teach, how can I expect the people to listen to my words?" Mencius's method is successful because he goes beyond merely mouthing his teachings: Like any skilled teacher he is able to reach the best results because he finds ways to gain the attention of the students.

Attentiveness

With a reasonable amount of parental guidance and education in the classic Confucian virtues, then, humans will naturally develop the potential goodness with which they are born. Still, each person has to exert proper attentiveness to activate and develop this supreme virtue of humaneness. Though Jen is immediately at hand, Li must be learned. If education is going to nourish the growth of humaneness, it requires the concentration of the student's entire mind; merely going through the motions is not enough. Mencius explains this in his story about Chess Chiu.

Suppose that Chess Chiu, the best chess player in all the kingdom, is teaching two persons to play. One student gives his whole mind to the subject and bends all his will to it, concentrating intently on Chess Chiu. The other student, although he seems to be listening, has his whole mind focused on a swan that he sees approaching, and thinks only of shooting it with a bow and arrow. Although he is learning along with the first student, he does not measure up to him. Why not? Is it because his intelligence is not equal? Not so, says Mencius: Chess playing is but a small art, but unless one's whole mind is given to it, and the will bent to it, a person cannot succeed at it.

Humaneness

The soil out of which Jen grows is the elementary feeling common to all humans that they cannot bear to see others suffer. Mencius does not deny that many people are unruly and uncouth, but he places more weight on their innate possibility of experiencing the joys of the Way. Human nature essentially tends toward the good: "There is no person who does not tend to do good; there is no water that does not flow downward." We may strike water and make it splash over our foreheads, or we may even force it up the hillsides. This isn't due to the nature of water, though, but to the force of circumstances. Similarly, we may be brought to do evil, but it is because some force has been exerted on our nature.

Those who have been attentive and nurtured their own humaneness will exercise it in their reciprocal relationships and practice the Rectification of Names. Rulers will be benevolent, just as subjects will be loyal. Fathers will be kindly, just as sons will be filial. Husbands will be righteous, just as wives will be obedient. Elder brothers will be gracious, while younger brothers will be respectful. Elders will show humane consideration, just as juniors will be deferential.

There will be a proper sense of responsibility, reverence for the past, and no unfilial piety (e.g., not being lazy in supporting and caring for parents; not spending too much time in chess-playing; not showing too much fondness for wine, money, fighting, or reckless sports). Such a well-ordered family is a microcosm of the balance and harmony that is possible in the sociopolitical realm. No superhuman capacities are needed for acting humanely, only a compassionate heart. It is not something impossible, like lifting a mountain, but something possible, akin to massaging the knuckles of old folks.

The Taoist Sacred Writings

Taoist Classics

The fundamental text of the Taoist tradition is the *Tao Te Ching* (Book of the Way and Its Power). It is as necessary a complement to the Confucian classics as Yin to Yang. With sometimes deliberately esoteric language, the Tao Te Ching consists of eighty-one poems that are terse in style and paradoxical in thought. Traditionally attributed to Lao Tzu, the book is the result of many interpolations and repeated editing. The one who follows Tao is the "sage," that is, the truly natural person. With no ambitions, no desire for fame, the sage wants to be like an uncarved block. The sage knows that it is possible to achieve without doing: When things are allowed to take their natural course, they move with wonderful perfection and harmony.

The Tao Te Ching teaches non-intervention in dealing with others. Respect for the autonomy of all people and all things is the one way to peace and freedom. It is futile to push people around: The harder they are pushed, the harder they resist. So, stop pushing. True power is the power that comes from not contending with others. True wisdom is the wisdom that comes not from striving for personal ends. Lao Tzu teaches us indifference to power and rejection of public opinion. Wise persons never try to do good, because this requires having a concept of good, which leads to having a concept of evil, which leads to combating evil, which only makes evil stronger.

Lao Tzu. The Tao Te Ching does not tell us much about the legendary Lao Tzu (the "Old Master"). According to tradition, Lao Tzu disappears into the landscape, desiring to escape into the unknown.

This is thoroughly in keeping with the Taoist vision of how life should be lived. Lao Tzu, disillusioned with corrupt government, sets off for Tibet in his old age, but is recognized at the frontier by a guard who persuades him to write down some of his words of wisdom. As the story goes, Lao Tzu scribbles off the Tao Te Ching in a few days, then mounts his water buffalo, moves off to Tibet, and is never seen again.

Chuang Tzu. Whereas the Tao Te Ching is a collection of poems and aphorisms, the *Chuang Tzu* is replete with stories. Compiled by Chuang Tzu (369-286 B.C.E.) and his disciples, it is an anthology of whimsical humor, flights of fancy, and irony—a dazzling assault upon conventional systems of values and concepts. Exuberant and imaginative, Chuang Tzu tells us that he once dreamt he was a butterfly, content to hover from flower to flower. Suddenly he awakens and finds to his astonishment that he is Chuang Tzu. Or is he? Is he really Chuang Tzu who has only dreamt that he is a butterfly, or is he really a butterfly, dreaming that he is Chuang Tzu? He is a delightfully lighthearted non-conformist who laughs at pomp and circumstance and human foolishness. He gives our imagination the shock treatment, making us realize that up is down, asleep is awake, and that we are gross and dull compared with those who have lost themselves in Tao.

The Second Story: Cook Ting and Naturalness

Prince Wen Hui's cook Ting, Chuang Tzu tells us, is cutting up an ox. The ox falls apart with a whisper. The bright cleaver murmurs like a gentle wind. Every inclination of his shoulder, every step, is as carefully timed as the movements of a dancer. "Wonderful," exclaims the prince, "I could never have believed that the art of carving could reach such a point as this." The prince is enthralled and compliments Ting on his skill and method: "It is fantastic that your Chi ("craft") has reached such heights." Cook Ting lays down his knife and replies: "Method? What I follow is Tao, beyond all methods. I have left the Chi behind me." Putting away his knife, Ting continues: "I am a lover of Tao, and I have succeeded in applying it to the art of carving. When I first began to cut up oxen, I would see before me the whole ox all in a mass. After three years I no longer saw the mass, but I saw the distinctions. Now I see nothing with my eyes. My whole being apprehends. My senses are idle. The spirit follows its own instinct. My cleaver finds its own way. I cut through no joint, chop no bone."

He pauses for a moment and then cuts through the ox with a single deft stroke. "A good cook needs a new chopper once a year—he cuts—by then his blade is dented. A poor cook needs a new one every month—he hacks—by then his knife is broken. I have used this same cleaver nineteen years. It has cut up a thousand oxen, and its edge is as keen as if newly sharpened. When the blade finds the spaces in the joints, it goes like a breeze. True, there are sometimes tough joints. I feel them coming; I slow down, watch closely, hold back, and whump!, the part falls away. Then I withdraw the blade, I stand still and let the joy of the work sink in. I clean the blade and put it away." Prince Wen Hui is amazed: "This is it! My cook has shown me how I ought to live my own life!"

The Story Magnified

Spontaneity
Cook Ting's skill is a paradigm of the tranquility achieved by forgetting the self. By his carving he teaches that the Taoist art of living is a supremely spontaneous response that is undermined if it has to consider alternatives. This is a point easily appreciated in the case of physical skills: Grasping the Way is a matter of knowing how, not of knowing what. Ting responds to fine variations without analyzing or making considered choices: His work is effortless. Clearly he has a profound knowledge of his ox. His knowledge is much more profound than that of hackers, a knowledge so in harmony with the nature of the task that he does nothing at all. His self-awareness is a basic cosmic humility: He fully realizes his own nothingness and is totally forgetful of himself, like dead ashes or a dry tree stump. Yet he is not dull, but full of life, responding with boundless vitality and joy to all living things. He lives at peace with himself and with other creatures. He has not allowed society to complicate and confuse his existence, to cause him to become obsessed with what he is not. He is freed from judging everything in terms of his self. This is the Taoist ideal.

Chuang Tzu recognizes that persons cannot always control the conditions of life about them. In contrast to the Confucian plans of reform, he teaches that persons must live by freeing their selves from the world through discarding the empty baggage of traditional values. This is the classical Taoist course of action that is not founded upon any purposeful motives of gain or striving. It is really restraint from purposeful action in favor of action as spontaneous and mindless as nature itself. Humans become one with nature (or heaven, as Chuang Tzu calls it) and merge themselves with Tao or Way, the underlying unity that embraces humans, nature, and all that is in the universe.

Sacred Seriousness

Chuang Tzu desires to create a certain playful attitude toward life, looking on it as a game. He presents the cook's movements with a dance-like quality, with absence of strain. The easiest way to live is to go with what is natural: Naturalness, not willed striving, is primary. The cook's skill is to allow himself to be taken up by the Tao, to allow his work to become play. Totally absorbed in his work as play, he is totally at ease and relaxed. Losing himself in what he is doing, Cook Ting is the Taoist in action, his grace an outer expression of inner harmony. Finding the grain is much more than having sharp eyesight: It is a matter of spiritual perception, of sacred seriousness. Only seriousness in playing makes play wholly play.

Watching Cook Ting, the prince is compelled to exclaim: "This is how I ought to live my own life"—that is how he should rule his kingdom. The best thing a ruler can do for society is to drop almost all laws and regulations, rule by virtue, and leave the people alone as much as possible. The making of laws is a straight formula for making criminals. The best way for rulers to guide and to create a harmonious society is by wu-wei. Ruling a kingdom is like cooking a small fish: It requires a delicate touch. Above all, the fish must not be overcooked or stirred around too much. The best rulers are those who know not to meddle; they let others do what they are suited to do. They guide by their presence, and Te emanates from them.

Purposelessness

Chuang Tzu teaches a practical approach to life. Humans should embark on a totally free and purposeless journey, wandering through all of creation, enjoying its delights without ever becoming attached to any part of it. The sage, the natural person, avoids grief and pain and finds fulfillment by following the sort of simple and quiet life the world finds insignificant, just as the woodcutter and carpenter ignore a bumpy tree.

A certain Tzu Ch'i of Nan-poh, Chuang Tzu tells us, is traveling on Shang mountain when he sees a truly astonishing tree. It is so large that a thousand chariot teams could find shelter under its shade. "What tree is this?" cries Tzu Ch'i. "Surely it must have unusually fine timber." Looking at it more closely, though, he sees that its branches are too crooked for rafters and the trunk's irregular grain makes it valueless for coffins. He tastes a leaf, but it takes the skin off his lips, and its odor is so strong that it can make a person drunk for three days. "Aha, this tree is good for nothing, and that is how it attained this size. A wise person might well follow its example." Because the tree has gnarled roots, poisonous leaves, and wood unfit for building, it is "useless" and serves no purpose. But it is exactly this uselessness that allows the tree to grow so big and live so long, without being cut down at its maturity. It lives to ripe old age, while the straight, handsome trees go crashing to the ground, felled for builders or decorators.

Relativity

The Tao is the subtle, elusive, yet vital mystery underlying all existence that cannot be conveyed either by words or by silence. Still, only when one is in contact with this mysterious Tao can one really understand how to live. Both Cook Ting and the gnarled tree live the way of Tao, growing quietly in a simple, ordinary life. Cook Ting shows the prince how to live because he is not dependent on just one right way to do his work. The tree is not forced to grow in just one right way. Aloof from the "ten thousand things of the world," Chuang Tzu says that nothing is absolutely "right" or "good." Nothing should be clung to as an absolute: All things are equal in their right to be and to act.

When a limited view of "right" or "good" is erected to the level of an absolute, it immediately becomes an evil, because it excludes certain complementary elements that are required if it is to be fully right or good. No one is so wrong as one who knows all the answers. The greatest happiness consists precisely in doing nothing that is calculated to obtain happiness. Paradoxically, people never find happiness until they stop looking for it. Right and good are found everywhere, since Tao is, and until people can learn to act spontaneously and without calculation they cannot really be happy in anything. Human affairs are complex: Good to one person may be evil to another. The concepts of "right" and "good" and "happiness" are ambiguous from the start. From the moment they are treated as particular objects to be attained, they lead to delusion and alienation, just as beauty, when overdone, becomes ugliness.

Naturalness

Chuang Tzu does not teach that humans should avoid all action, but rather all hostile, aggressive action. Action should be undertaken without being intent upon results or being concerned with consciously laid plans and deliberately organized endeavors. The way to act is to be—then the powers of nature become one's own. The lightest touch at the proper time and place can do what heavy and forceful blows cannot. Action should be natural and spontaneous, like the activity of an athlete who runs or throws effortlessly and naturally. Using no force or violence, no straining or pulling, the action is completely free.

Taoism teaches that self-liberation from unnaturalness does not come through such Confucian values as humaneness or reciprocity. Indeed, these are harmful social and cultural constraints, and they are detrimental to the spontaneity of nature. Whereas the Confucian approach is concerned with particular details and has definite principles of right and wrong in human behavior, the Taoist view characteristically stresses the naturalness of all beings (e.g., to a duck, short legs are good, but to a crane, long legs are good). Taoists stress the identity of contraries: Yin and Yang are in tension but not opposition. Both are needed for the universe to keep functioning in a natural and harmonious fashion.

The Stories Exemplified

Other Stories

Many hagiographies have appeared in Chinese lore. These stories instruct Chinese on the paths by which they might realize their destiny and describe the rewards inherent in venerating those who gained entry into the celestial ranks. They also recount what happens to those who do not follow the path of the Tao. Tu Kuang-t'ing (850-933) tells one of these stories, for example, in his story of the magic bell in his *Records of Taoist Miracles*. When a military governor tries to remove the bell from the Taoist abbey where it has been used for years, the hero Hsu appears to the governor in a dream and tells him that his life is in danger. The governor returns the bell and goes to burn incense and confess his faults, but his sin in trying to steal the bell is too grave to be pardoned, and he dies in battle soon afterward. His theft has upset the way of nature and he is therefore punished.

Human Witnesses

Chu Hsi. Chu Hsi (1130-1200) is the major neo-Confucian thinker and synthesizer. His writings are based on a balance of religious reverence, ethical practice, scholarly investigation, and political participation. In *Reflections on Things at Hand* he teaches that humans must cultivate themselves to penetrate to the underlying principle of the whole universe, T'ai Chi, the Great Ultimate. The way to self-cultivation is through intellectual learning and through rectifying the mind: This requires a life of meditating, controlling desires, practicing humaneness, and exercising mutual respect in basic human relations. Chu Hsi was particularly critical of government abuses and accused rulers of failing in self-cultivation. Signs of this failure are plenty: shady dealings and vicious gossip in the palace, abuse of power by attendants, acquiescence of high officials, and greed of generals who fatten their pockets at the expense of their soldiers.

Chu Hsi himself sought to be above politics. Following Confucius and Mencius he coupled moral eminence with political failure. Indeed, he taught that a truly virtuous person should have little to do with unworthy government. He repeatedly refused to take public office, pleading illness, foot ailments, shortage of funds, and even his mother's old age. Chu Hsi affirmed the right of the Confucian scholar-official not only to criticize the government but to demand such high standards of political conduct that he could, in effect, always be justified in declining office. He preferred to guard his moral prestige by withholding support from the government rather than attempting to work for reform from within.

Chu Hsi wanted to be a person whose counsel would be universally respected and followed by those in power. When it became increasingly difficult for him to persist in refusing public office, he took a post as a minor official, bringing relief to starving people and trying to ease their tax burden. He showed himself deeply concerned with the economic and moral welfare of his people and incorporated a land-survey program to get rich and powerful families to pay their proper share of taxes. In the end his career offered an example of how one might serve both the Confucian way and the state without losing either one's self-respect or one's life.

Wang Che. Wang Che (1112-1170) was the founder of one of the major Taoist movements of the twelfth century, the Integral Perfection Order. He was adept at martial arts and an herbal medicine healer. Two mysterious encounters with Taoist immortals led him to dig a

hole six feet deep in which he lived for three years in deep meditation. After building a thatched hut where he slept on ice for another
four years, he suddenly burned down his hut and began to preach
his message. Wang's methods were apparently uncompromising
and even violent. He wished to shock people into enlightenment,
which necessarily entailed a complete break of the sort he had made
when he abandoned his wife, children, and career.

The seven disciples, the "Seven Real Persons," that Wang chose
for his small community were later portrayed as eccentrics. One
spent six years under a bridge neither moving nor speaking, eating
only when people offered him food. Another spent his nights in a
cave standing on one foot so as not to fall asleep. Wang's Integral
Perfection movement sought to synthesize the best of Confucianism
and Buddhism with Taoism. Wang preached Buddhist celibacy and
sitting-meditation in order to control the "apelike mind and horse-
like will." Like the neo-Confucians, he prized perfect authenticity as
the ultimate goal of self-cultivation. He was eminently Taoist,
though, in insisting that both one's hsing ("nature") and ming ("life
force") had to be nurtured, especially through physiological practices, the martial arts, and asceticism.

Communities

Popular Religion. Through the centuries Confucianism and Taoism
(and Buddhism) have remained the great religions of China in spite
of attempts at secularization, most recently under the Communist
regime. The Chinese people share and interact with many elements
of popular religion in their daily lives. They continue to perform sacred ceremonies which, according to their ancient beliefs, maintain
the harmony of heaven and earth and ensure the prosperity of the
four seasons. Very few belong to just one religious community.
They blend the religions together, tending to be Confucian in their
social life, Buddhist in self-cultivation, and Taoist in religious observances. Today popular religion is evident in Chinese attitudes of respect for family and elders, in loyalty to community and nation, and
in acceptance of reciprocity as the basis of human relations.

Religious Taoism. One community, Religious Taoism, has showed
complex development over the centuries, giving birth to numerous
currents in China, both scholarly and popular. It combined Taoist
rituals and theology with monastic organization and iconography
derived largely from Buddhism, absorbing superstition and magic

from a variety of native cults along the way. The Religious Taoists did not so much break with the fundamental conceptions of Lao Tzu and Chuang Tzu as transform them through a wide variety of medical, alchemical, and magical practices. Over the centuries they managed important cult centers on many of China's sacred mountains and were very popular among the pilgrims who came to visit them to take advantage of their divination practices and special techniques.

The Taoist Immortals used a wide variety of medical, alchemical, and magical practices in their attempt to attain physical immortality.

In an attempt to attain physical immortality, Religious Taoists developed hygienic techniques and drugs. A major text, *Pao-p'u-tzu* (The Master Who Preserves Simplicity) by Ko Hung (320 C.E.), describes how they availed themselves of magical formulas and charms to establish control over natural processes. They practiced alchemy, hoping to discover a liquid or edible gold which would circulate their ch'i ("vital forces") and confer immortality. Through breath control, gymnastics, and special diets and sexual techniques, they attempted to transform the body to its original state of purity and power, with its Yin and Yang forces in proper balance.

Twentieth Century

Modernization. The Chinese people have had a troubled search for national self-consciousness in the modern world. They have had to wrestle with the realization that they are no longer the center of all human culture. The forces of modern science and technology, the struggle between peasant nationalism and a more cosmopolitan vision of a democratic nation, and the problems associated with political and economic reform have all had their impact on the Chinese religions.

Several critical events early in the twentieth century hastened the political and cultural awakening of modern China, at least in the larger cities. The imperial government system was overthrown after 2000 years, and a student revolution in 1919 called for a new China, free of all traditional education and Confucian influence. Indeed, Confucianism came to stand for an anachronistic system of values, a millstone about the neck of progress. Confucian statesmen who had tried to save the Chinese spirit by limiting reliance on Western technology were perceived as disloyal and overthrown. When Chiang K'ai-shek (1887-1975) succeeded in establishing the Nationalist government in the late 1920s, he again reanimated Confucian flavoring and spirit as a matter of official policy. This revival, however, would not last long.

Religion Under Mao. Facing annihilation by the Nationalist forces of Chiang K'ai-shek, Mao Tse-Tung (1893-1976) led thousands of troops on a six-thousand-mile escape. About a quarter of his troops survived this epic Long March of 1934. Following the march Mao wrote most of the articles that comprise his *Selected Works* and rebuilt his troops for the revolution that would sweep through China after World War II. Driving Chiang Kai-Shek's Nationalist forces to Taiwan in 1949, Mao attempted to pulverize a great part of China's cultural heritage by imposing a communist regime. During Mao's tenure, the welfare of the people, rather than the benefits of the traditional family group, was stressed. The Marxist dialectic of history became a new version of the ultimate process of Yin and Yang. But, instead of bringing harmony, freedom, and prosperity, Mao's impassioned Red Guard brought a decade of senseless destruction and devastating damage—material, cultural, and psychological—in the 1960s and 1970s.

Though the Constitution of the People's Republic (1954) established the freedom both to support and to oppose religion, institutional religion was subject to intense persecution by the Maoists. With the Cultural Revolution of 1965, fanatical Red Guards stepped up their struggle to rid China of all old religious traditions. Religion was depicted along Marxist lines as "feudal superstition" that had to be rejected by those seeking to build a new China. The Confucian attributes of chung ("loyalty") and hsiao ("filial devotion") were reinterpreted as metaphors for submission to authority. Buddhism was deemed an instrument of exploitation of the masses, irrelevant to social and political movements. Religious Taoism was the object of government contempt, deemed superstitious and harmful to the new society. The efficacy of the gods of popular religion was called into question and temples throughout the country fell into disuse.

Mao Tse-Tung's government stressed the welfare of the Chinese people rather than the benefits of the traditional family group.

Beijing (Peking) Regime. The impetus of the Cultural Revolution came to an end with the death of Chairman Mao in 1976. China today is a nation racked by a crisis of values following the disillusionments of the Cultural Revolution, and the struggle continues to define modern Chinese identity. Since Deng Xiao-ping began his reforms in 1978, practical programs have been introduced to modernize China's schools and factories, its commerce, science, agriculture, and defense. Deng has shown great distaste for popular participation in politics and has not masked his deeply held conviction that dissent is synonymous with disloyalty. There has been a liberalization of policy regarding religion since he came to power. "In China religion is free," Deng tells his people, "I couldn't care less about people's belief as long as they observe the law and work hard." The state has paid for repairs to the temples and other houses of worship that were looted during the years of the Cultural Revolution. Salaries have been restored to some religious officials, and monks are no longer barred from living in temples. In recent years the moral validity of the Communist Party has evaporated because the ordinary people have become embittered by inflation, corruption, and injustices. There is remarkably little faith in communism in China today.

Human Rights. In the summer of 1989, Chinese students protested Communist Party rule. Gathering in Beijing in the square of its most

The gate at Tian An Men square in Beijing recalls the struggle (and subsequent suppression) of Chinese students in 1989 for a democratic form of government.

famous monument, Tian An Men ("The Gate of Heavenly Peace"), they struck an ancient chord from Chinese history. They became bearers of the tradition that scholars should censure the ruler for those evils in the kingdom that the ruler should put right. When the ruler would not listen, the scholars would take their own lives as a sacrificial witness to the higher good.

The students demanded that the government be more democratic and that economic benefits be spread more equitably. They rallied against rampant government corruption and abuse of power. Their biggest call for reform was with the education system in which they had no choice regarding academic major, no freedom to choose a place of employment after graduation, no possibility of marriage while they were still students. The students, now joined by workers from all ranks, received a jolt, and their enthusiasm, passion, and euphoria all came to a sudden end. In a bloody crackdown, Deng sent tanks of the People's Liberation Army rolling toward Tian An Men Square and troops fired on the crowds, killing hundreds and wounding thousands.

China's largely peasant population has had little exposure to the concept of democracy. The average Chinese tend to be more protective of their recently acquired right to grow cash crops than for the human rights for which the students were demonstrating. The Chinese have a saying: "The women hold up half the sky." Still, women in China do not share equal rights. For example, they are forced to retire five years earlier than men. The call for support of women's rights and equality has been raised, but it is largely unheard in a country that still has the adage, "Starving to death for a woman is a small matter, but losing one's chastity is a great calamity."

Ritual: The New Year's Festival

Chinese rituals are a part of the normal flow of family life. They participate in rituals to alleviate fear, strengthen hope, and reaffirm the total cohesion of the family. This is most obvious, perhaps, in the funeral rites, the binding force that holds the family together through generations. They perform rituals for their ancestors both to promote the prosperity of the family and to keep the memory of the ancestors alive. Sweeping their ancestors' graves is a family ritual that renews kinship with the past, assuring the comfort and well-being of the dead persons in their spiritual existence, and bringing new life and good fortune on their descendants. Death is a breach in nature, an element of disharmony, and the rituals function to fill that breach.

The most important and elaborate of all the annual universal festivals in China, though, is the New Year's festival. Celebrated for several weeks, it is a time of purification and new beginnings. During the festival the Chinese clean their houses to get rid of old dirt and bad influences. Debts are paid off and new clothes bought. People take vacations to return home to be with their families. In their homes a few days before New Year's day, the families burn a paper image of the God of the Kitchen Stove which is thus sent off to heaven to report to the Jade Emperor on the family's good and bad activities of the previous year. Its mouth is smeared with some sugary substance to insure only sweet words.

At midnight on New Year's Eve, families gather for a big feast, which is first offered to the spirits of the ancestors. Family members come forward in order of precedence to prostrate themselves to the family head and his wife. The family stays awake all night, talking and playing games. Everyone avoids words that sound even remotely like death or disease, for what they do and say that night influences good or bad fortune for the coming year. At dawn the fresh air of the New Year is let in, and the household gods are welcomed back with food and incense. For the next several days people pay courtesy calls and offer each other gifts, view ingeniously designed lanterns at local temples, and enjoy acrobatic troupes and parades of boisterous dragons. They set off firecrackers to scare away demons and offer prayers to the Jade Emperor for the welfare of the community.

The Stories Appropriated

The Confucian and Taoist stories are stories about harmony. They provide a context for meaning, not only for the lives of those within the Chinese tradition, but for those of us outside it. These stories present new ways for us to envision our own spiritual convictions. Reading the stories from Mencius and Chuang Tzu challenges us to respond in a personal way to our own religion on the basis of transformed decisions.

The stories of Mencius and Chuang Tzu spur us to recognize that the individual is a part of the whole: Gods, heavens, hells, society, nature, family—these are all parts of a single unity of which humans are the pivot. The stories hearten us to find a way of life that is as much natural and social as it is personal, a way of life that produces balance and harmony, serenity and proportion. They teach us that mastery of life is really the paradoxical union of detachment and constant attention. If our lives find the natural and spontaneous way of harmony, they are fulfilled, vibrant with meaning, too precious to end.

The Superior Person

Mencius's story of Bull Mountain teaches us that our human nature is basically good, but we still need education to restrain our evil impulses and to learn the guiding principles by which to regulate all human interaction. His story of the farmer Sung reminds us that the education we need in order to develop this human nature demands proper attentiveness. Our innate humaneness and potential goodness have to be nurtured properly, preferably through example and persuasion rather than through compulsion. Each person has the potential to become the superior person through rigorous learning and self-cultivation. The transformation into a superior person comes only through hard effort.

Becoming a superior person is the most genuine and authentic manifestation of humanity, and to ask the question of how to become a superior person is virtually identical with "How do I learn to be fully human?" or "How can I really know myself?" Because of the stress in our educational system on empirical problem-solving and on specialization for dealing with the issues of our complicated technological society, the efficacy of education for self-cultivation is often called into question. Still, the kinds of problems with which educated persons, and world leaders in particular, have to deal today require a basic understanding of our human nature and of the ethical relationships between human beings. Proper education in becoming a superior person requires that we recognize our innate humaneness and attempt to penetrate and thoroughly understand the ways of heaven and earth. In this way we can develop a sense of responsibility for nature and for others. We learn that a kind of doing, not merely a kind of being, makes for our fulfilled potential—we learn to use our knowledge to serve human society and the natural world.

Inner Teaching

Wisdom, the ideal of the superior person, is a goal that can be achieved by anyone, and is realizable within one's lifetime. This does not mean that anyone can become ruler; rather, it suggests simply the potential perfection of anyone's nature through education. Such perfection entails internalizing what we are taught and at the same time realizing our own internal moral and spiritual nature.

The vehicle for such education is in part the give and take of teacher and student, but the contact with an outer teacher serves only as a repeated, revitalizing spur to the inner teacher: If there is no inner master, the outer master has no power to transform.

Wisdom is a type of understanding in which human nature, the macrocosm, and human society are seen in unity, and a commitment is made to benefit them all. If we are wise, we can take on the trials and tribulations of other humans, work for the elimination of suffering, and speak out against corruption and the abuses of power. If we are wise, we recognize a larger order of things in which all humans are interrelated. We are also marked and charged by this larger order so that we can overcome many of the obstacles that prevent life from fully emerging. We embody Yin and Yang in never-ending alternation. At times, then, we can be a creative and a redeeming force in society and the world, bringing peace, security, and harmony. At other times, we will have to tear up the roots we have put down, knock over the things we thought secure, and sunder the bonds we have contracted in our sensitivity to the needs of others and our desire to give them a sense of worth and dignity.

Reverence and Reciprocity

Reverence and violence simply do not mix: Can we revere others and then torture them? There are reciprocal obligations in society. A reverential attitude toward human life has to be linked with forms of respect for others that are expressed in concrete relationships. The treatment to which we are entitled is defined in relation to a whole network of mutual responsibilities which the members of a family and a community owe to one another. In such a network, the emphasis is on loving, affective relations, not impersonal legalistic ones. Rights are based on equity in social relations, not equality: The relations between parent and child, for example, are equitable but not equal. These relationships, which are based on loving care rather than obedience or service, change in the course of time, and are sometimes returnable at a later stage of life.

The stories of Mencius strengthen our conception of human rights by tempering our priority of individual freedoms with communal and environmental duties. They teach us to recognize that individual autonomy does not necessarily enhance human dignity; in fact, the exaggeration of individuality may ultimately hurt the goal of human rights to protect and foster human dignity. The Chinese systems teach us to put ourselves in the other person's place, for there is no "me" in isolation. We are who we are only in relation to others: My life as a doctor can only be made significant by my patients, my life as a teacher only by my students, and so on.

We humans are molded by the ways in which we greet one another, work together, pay our respects, and venerate the powers sacred in our society. The stories of Mencius give us a profound appreciation of our ritual interactions and force us to take another look at the role law plays in society. In the Chinese model almost all human rights and duties are sustained by extralegal institutions and practices and are enforced by social pressures, such as courtesy and custom rather than punishments. The Confucian model does not express human "rights" in terms of "laws," but rather in terms of "rites" and reciprocal relations. Too much reliance upon application of law is fundamentally dehumanizing rather than a means of realizing human dignity, because it compromises our individual responsibility to define what conduct is appropriate and constricts the creative possibilities within our relationships.

Waiting

The secret of the complementary way proposed by Chuang Tzu—wu-wei—is non-action rather than the accumulation of virtue and merit. Cook Ting teaches us how we should live our own lives—his method is not to use a method. The easiest way to live is to go with what is natural, with absence of strain rather than willed striving. The cook's work is effortless: His skill is in responding to fine variations without analyzing or making considered choices. His spirit follows its own instinct just as his cleaver finds its own way.

This shows us the strength of waiting. Waiting makes for personal growth. The ideas and ideals to which we are committed (e.g., democracy, equality of women, peace among nations, nuclear disarmament, the end of hunger, etc.) may be the best in the world. Still, it is possible that we have something to learn about listening and human dignity and openness and patience before these objectives can possibly be real. While we wait, we can learn and grow like the gnarled tree, and become stronger than ever in our convictions.

Waiting is not about defeat or failure or frustration. It is about the virtue of hope. It leads us to compare what is probable with what is possible. Waiting is a call to conscience, to engage ourselves with an honest heart in our struggles, for or against, until there can be no disinterested bystanders, no free rides. Waiting proves the depth of ideas and does a great deal to cement convictions. Waiting time, in other words, is not passive time, but the time for developing real humility, which is simply the willingness to allow things to happen.

Meditation in Motion

If we learn to wait, we learn how to abandon and let go. This does not mean that we are all laid back or resigned to whatever happens to us. It means rather that we relinquish the conscious or willful controls that inhibit our subtler inner processes. Thinking is what makes us ruin one butcher knife after another, what makes us get caught up in our work so much that we are unable to act: a sort of paralysis by analysis. Learning to wait with a sense of relaxed attentiveness, we are completely at one with the self and the physical world with which we interact.

We can learn from the many Chinese people who bring this relaxed attentiveness into their lives through their practice of the graceful Taoist art of T'ai Chi Ch'uan, a type of "meditation in motion." Through a systematic succession of slow and smooth body movements, they express the quiet ease of the spirit of Taoism. Their esthetic movements improve their health by stimulating blood circulation, increasing pulse rate, and promoting mental relaxation. Although the movements are considered excellent for physical conditioning, they are not mere gymnastics. Instead, they are applying the body's internal energy not only to meditation, but also to general education, health, conflict-resolution, raising children, dealing with death, interaction with wildlife, and spiritual development. Life, they are telling us, is the harmonious interplay of opposites, and there is a little of each in the other.

Conclusion

The Chinese strive to achieve harmony with nature and with each other. Their ideal way of life produces balance and harmony, serenity and proportion. Their ideal life is as much natural and social as it is personal, preserving harmony in society through humaneness and harmony with nature through spontaneity.

Mencius, in the story of Bull Mountain, teaches that all are born with innate feelings of righteousness and benevolence in human relationships. The instinctive humaneness and compassion humans feel toward each other has to be nourished properly through the transforming influence of education by example and persuasion.

Chuang Tzu, in the story of Cook Ting, teaches that the truly sage person is one whose knowledge is in harmony with nature. The self-awareness of the sage is a basic cosmic humility, with full realization of personal nothingness and total forgetfulness of self. Yet the sage's life is not dull, but full of boundless vitality and joy. The sage acts spontaneously and without calculation, aware that happiness can be found everywhere, since Tao is.

Discussion Questions

1. Why do you think the author chooses the Great Wall as a symbol of Chinese religious unity and multiplicity?

2. What is the relationship between T'ai Chi, T'ien, and Yin and Yang?

3. Summarize the Confucian system of salvation in terms of ignorance, ritual, and the superior person, and the Taoist system of salvation in terms of going against nature, wu-wei, and harmony.

4. What essential aspects of the Confucian tradition does Mencius describe in his stories of Bull Mountain and Farmer Sung?

5. What essential aspects of the Taoist tradition does Chuang Tzu describe in his stories of Cook Ting and the Gnarled Tree?

6. Summarize the role of Confucianism, Taoism, and popular religion in China since the take-over of Mao Tse-Tung after World War II.

7. What can Christians appropriate today from the many stories of Mencius and Chuang Tzu?

8. Discussion Starter: What would Confucius say if he were to come into a modern university classroom after a lecture and see it scattered with cans and candy wrappings, student newspapers and professors' handouts, and chairs an erratic mess? What would he deduce about the quality of life in America?

9. Discussion Starter: While Chuang Tzu was fishing, the Duke of Chu sent two messengers to ask him to become his chief minister. Continuing to fish, Chuang Tzu replied: "I have heard that in Chu there is a sacred tortoise which has been dead for three thousand years and that the prince keeps this tortoise carefully enclosed in a chest on the altar of his ancestral temple. Now, I ask, would this tortoise rather be dead and have its remains venerated, or be alive and wagging its tail in the mud?" The two officials replied: "It would rather be alive!" "Go away, then," cried Chuang Tzu; "I too would rather wag my tail in the mud."

10. Discussion Starter: "More than a billion ants lived on a hill. One day when fire broke out, the only way to safety was to go down the hill. To save themselves from the fire, the ants clung to one another in a big ball and tumbled down the hill. The ants who were on the surface of the ball were killed by the fire, but most of the ants were saved." (Student leader at Tian An Men Square)

The Japanese perform elaborate rituals in the Todaiji temple in Nara, Japan, before the
Great Buddha of infinite space and infinite compassion.

Chapter Eight

BUDDHISM
Enlightenment and Compassion

Setting the Scene

Todaiji

Todaiji, the largest temple in Japan, dominates the city of Nara from the hillside out of which it is carved. The grand pageantry and annual festivals held at this revered Buddhist temple are a major attraction for swarms of Japanese. The temple's colorful, delicately-wrought statues are among the earliest examples of Japan's cultural heritage. Built by the emperor Shomu in the eighth century C.E. as the dominant temple for all of Japan, it became a force for national solidarity. The emperor laid the pagoda-like temple and his imperial palace in close proximity in the center of Nara (the capital city until Kyoto became the capital in 794). The rest of the universe revolved around this focal point.

The center and focus of the Todaiji temple is the Daibutsu ("Great Buddha"), the world's largest bronze statue. Staggering in size and physical opulence, this colossal forty-five-foot statue is not of the historical Buddha, but of Mahavairocana Buddha (known to the Japanese as Dainichi, the "Great Sun"). The source of light and life, Mahavairocana is the ultimate reality whose presence shines in all

things. This statue has special meaning for the Japanese, since Dainichi is Japan's name for itself and is part of its self-understanding.
The Mahavairocana Buddha is the universal monarch, the very
source of all Buddhahood. Arching over its deep still gaze is a gild-
ed wooden halo with representations of sixteen incarnations of the
Buddha, representing infinite space and infinite compassion. Here
the Japanese perform elaborate and aesthetically pleasing rituals, offering prayers and chanting year round. The Daibutsu at Todaiji
represents the culmination of the growth of Buddhism as it expanded eastward from India and symbolizes the significant contributions
that Buddhism has made to the cultural life of Japan.

Buddhist Roots in India

The focus of our study of Buddhism is Japan, which retains something of the common heritage of Buddhist doctrine, practice, and institutional life that began in India. More than 311 million Buddhists
in the world express their common roots in their prayer of the Three
Refuges: "I take Refuge in the Buddha, I take Refuge in the Dharma,
I take Refuge in the Sangha."

Buddha. The term "Buddha" refers to different realities: a human
being, an enlightened being, and true human nature. The "Buddha"
is first of all a human, Gautama (563-483 B.C.E.), called Sakyamuni,
who founded a community of wandering monks in the Ganges river valley that would eventually grow into the world religion we
now call Buddhism. He balanced the ideal of self-salvation with the
ideal of compassionate good will toward all living beings and practiced that compassion himself. Heir to the spirituality of India, he
experienced release from the snares of desire and karma through a
meditative insight that he expressed in terms of the Dharma. With
his enlightenment, Gautama became a wandering teacher and guide
who oversaw the founding of the sangha, the Buddhist community.
Later, "Buddha" refers to anyone who has attained release from this
world of recurring rebirths, that is, to anyone who has achieved liberation from this world of suffering. Finally, the "Buddha" refers to
the recognition that true human nature and, indeed, all of life is
identical with Absolute Reality itself.

Dharma. Dharma ("Truth") is also a term that refers to many different realities in the Buddhist tradition. Dharma is the collection of canonical texts of the different Buddhist communities. It is also the
collection of teachings, described as enlightenment, formulated by

the Buddha and based on an intuitive vision achieved through meditation. These teachings contain the Four Noble Truths, the Eightfold Path, and the Middle Way. Dharma teaches the nonexistence of any kind of independent self, the impermanence of all things, and the universality of suffering. Dharma also encompasses the Buddha's teaching on the "conditioned co-production" or "dependent co-origination" of all existence, that is, the truth that every event is caused by something prior in an interrelated process. Finally, Dharma is the law of the universe encompassing all that nature and humans do.

Sangha. Early Buddhism in India rejected the caste system and accepted people of all classes and both sexes into the community (sangha) of those who were willing to dedicate themselves totally to seeking enlightenment. Through history, the sangha has been the monastic organization providing a social basis for the persistence of Buddhist thought and values. It is the vital community of fellow Buddhists who encourage and critique each other, thus supporting and contributing to each other's development. Buddhism expects the lay people to feed and assist the monks in the sangha. In return the sangha perform rituals for them, including ceremonies for birth and death and ceremonies for all the promising or threatening events that favor or deeply disturb villages, homes, and individuals.

Buddhist Traditions
Buddhism has largely disappeared in India since the twelfth century C.E., surviving mainly in its architectural ruins. Its demise has several possible causes: isolated monasteries, revival of Hindu devotional movements and Tantric practices, Muslim invasions, and change of language from Pali to Sanskrit. Buddhism developed in different cultural areas outside India. While transforming these cultures it was itself intensely changed, taking on a distinctive flavor in each region. In the course of its journeyings the original teachings of the Buddha were reinterpreted, adapted to changing times and cultures, and even completely transcended.

Over the centuries two dominant strains have developed in Buddhism, each internally highly pluralistic. These are the Theravada and Mahayana traditions.

In Theravada and Mahayana, the poles of Buddhist spirituality—disengagement in wisdom and involvement in compassion—together constitute a basic belief that has run down the centuries like a continuous thread, binding the schools of Buddhism together. In passing, we might note a third type of Buddhism, Vajrayana ("Vehicle of the Thunderbolt"), active today mainly in Tibet. In Vajrayana Buddhism, awakening comes like a lightning flash through direct experiences guided by a guru. The guru involves the adherents in various rituals that utilize mandalas (sacred circles), mantras (sacred chants), hypnotic spells, magic gestures, and sexual union.

Theravada. Theravada Buddhism ("Way of the Elders") is found mainly today in Sri Lanka and Southeast Asia (e.g., Burma, Cambodia, Thailand, and Laos). Theravada claims that its doctrines derive

Monks teach, chant sacred songs, and bring spiritual power to the Theravada community at The Temple of Dawn in Bangkok, Thailand.

from the teachings of the historical Buddha himself and thus constitute the only true path. Important in Theravada is the interrelationship between the monastic community and the lay people, with each group living in a certain dependence on the other. The monks need the support of lay people in terms of food and security, while the lay people need the services of monks who teach, chant sacred songs, and provide spiritual power to the community. In supporting, maintaining, and cheering on the small percentage who belong to the sangha, lay people reap the benefits of the monks' meditation struggles for wisdom and earn a good deal of spiritual merit. In Theravada, liberation through meditation is a matter of self-reliance and individual striving.

Mahayana. As Buddhism gradually moved out of India, Mahayana ("The Great Raft") became the dominant branch of Buddhism in China, Korea, Vietnam, and Japan. The various branches of Mahayana hold that the rigid teachings believed essential for enlightenment of Theravada Buddhism are much too traditional and defensive. Mahayana has more colorful rituals and less austere practices. It includes a much greater number of sacred texts, a greater number of Buddhas, and expresses its goal in a variety of ways: Nirvana, rebirth in Pure Land, becoming a Buddha, or achieving the "Great Emptiness." In Mahayana, where the fate of one is linked to the fate of all, compassion for others is the key virtue. In providing greater lay effort and a more realistic, existential response to the quest for enlightenment, they pursue not a Nirvana secluded in the cells of monasteries, but a Nirvana attained here and now by a life of self-forgetful activity.

Buddhism in Japan

When Japan gained access to the advanced civilization of China, the Japanese people took over the Mahayana Buddhist texts and images, already present for several centuries in China, as part and parcel of the Chinese culture. The Japanese were irresistibly attracted by the exciting literature, rich art, emotionally satisfying rituals, and fresh insights in every field of human thought and action—including logic, medicine, and social service. In the sixth century C.E., Buddhist schools began to flourish, a thousand years after Buddhism's birth in India. It took firm root and has had an important impact on Japanese social, cultural, and religious life.

In Japan Buddhism has always participated in the experience of religious diversity, coexisting with the successive waves of other religious traditions that have swept into the islands of Japan from overseas. Buddhism was significantly modified and took on particular Japanese traits as it was assimilated into the Japanese culture, especially in its interaction with Shinto, the Japanese popular religion. While most of the 125 million Japanese claim that they belong to no religion whatsoever, more than three-fourths also maintain that they are affiliated with Buddhism (and fifty percent also affirm allegiance to one of the Japanese "New Religions").

To most Japanese, different religions meet different needs and operate in different areas of life. Allegiance to two religions, sometimes three, is the common course. Families will often celebrate a child's coming-of-age or marriage in accordance with the rites of Shinto. They look to Confucianism to implement moral and political tendencies in affirming authority, filial piety, and duty. They still consult the Taoist calendar for magical techniques and divination practices. They make their way to centers of new, energetic religious movements for a sense of prosperity and well-being. They look to the Buddhist vision of life, with its final goal of liberation and the peace of Nirvana, as the focus of their intellectual commitment.

Faith and the Gods

Absolute Reality

The Absolute Reality in Buddhism is one's Buddha-nature or Dharma. As the Buddha nature, it is not a potentiality that all beings have, but the reality that all beings essentially are. In the Buddha's words, the highest reality is not a doctrine, but a truth to be known and lived by. As the Dharma, it is the true essence of everything that inevitably leads to salvation when it is realized. Still, it is not correct to say that Buddhists "have faith" in Buddha-nature or Dharma. Nor do they have gods, for Buddhism is very self-consciously non-theistic. If Buddhists have faith, it is faith in the Three Refuges: They will find liberation and salvation by committing themselves totally to this threefold treasure by a life of meditation and compassion.

For Gautama, attempting to answer the question of whether there are gods is inappropriate to the human situation. In his *Parable of the Arrow*, he teaches that approaching this question is fruitless. It is like coming across a person who has been shot with an arrow and is dying from loss of blood and asking questions like "Who shot the arrow?" or "From what direction did it come?" or "What are the materials that comprise the arrow, the shaft, the head?" All these questions are irrelevant to the pressing need of the person who has been shot. What is needed is for someone to remove the arrow as quickly as possible and stem the flow of blood. It is a matter of life and death calling for appropriate action, rather than questioning or belief.

The Japanese do revere the bodhisattvas and petition them for favors. The female bodhisattva Kannon (in China: Kuan-Yin), the "Perceiver, or Hearer, of the Cries of the World," in particular, is the object of intense devotion. Often shown standing on a lotus, riding on a cloud or gliding on a wave of the sea, Kannon hears the cries of distress of all suffering beings. She is often depicted with ten heads and a thousand arms with an eye in the palm of each hand, symbolizing her readiness to extend a hand of assistance in the direction of those who cry out in their suffering. She promises to save humans from all forms of calamity and to grant them health, fertility, wealth and security in life.

Shinto Kami

The Japanese people look instead to their native religion, Shinto, to interact with their gods. Shinto is the local religion that meets the daily and immediate needs of the people. In Shinto, the people do not have faith in a system of dogmatic beliefs nor do they follow a

The torii is a gigantic curved arch that serves as the gateway into the sacred Shinto shrine of the kami, the Japanese protective spirits.

definite code of ethics. Shinto is rather a set of traditional rituals and local ceremonies. Shinto means the "way of the kami." The kami are deified forces of nature and humanity, who bestow life and promote all growth and creativity. Not considered as universal gods or supreme creators, the kami are the many awe-inspiring supernatural beings who have animated the world from the beginning. Some kami bring misfortune, but most are protective spirits, usually well-disposed toward humanity.

The eighth-century C.E. Shinto sacred writings, the *Kojiki* ("Record of Ancient Events") and the *Nihongi* ("Chronicles of Japan"), describe the role of the kami in the ethos and meaning-structure of Japanese religion. The Japanese believe that their islands, people, and emperor have all descended from the kami, and are thus all bound together in the sacredness of Japan. Amaterasu ("the heavenly shining one"), the sun goddess and ancestress of the imperial family, enjoys the central position in the pantheon of Shinto kami, though not even she is absolute in power and authority. Amaterasu brings peace and order to the world of nature and humans. The masses of pilgrims to her main cult center at Ise revere her three precious symbols: a sword, a string of ancient pearls, and especially the mirror she gave her grandson when he descended from heaven to earth to found the imperial dynasty.

Human Salvation

The Problem: Suffering and Clinging

The Buddha's first and second Noble Truths declare that all life is dukkha ("suffering"), and that this suffering is due to tanha ("clinging") to the belief that humans are independent selves. That is, unhappiness comes from saying "I" or "mine." The "I" is a mere figment of the imagination, as is the idea of "belonging." Humans are constantly afraid that they will lose what is important to them. The Buddha compared human craving and attachment to the monkey who hops restlessly from tree to tree in order to satisfy its craving for fruit. The monkey can never get enough. Humans too try to hold on desperately to fleeting pleasures, even to life itself. Since everything is passing, however, there is nothing to cling to. Humans therefore lose what they try to hold on to, experiencing suffering, frustration of desire, and emotional pain in the process.

Grief and loss, pain and misery accumulate like possessions. Sorrows cannot all be explained away. The suffering in existence is characterized by change and instability. All life is anicca ("impermanent"): Moments of happiness and joy are real, friendships and family joys are genuine, but they all pass away. Human lives are suffering—violated relations, fractured intimacies, failure. There is the suffering the mind creates in its anxiety of possible future suffering and regret of past suffering. There is public pain too, although it is not so apt to be easily identified: violence, the death sentence, indigent mothers.

The Strategy: The Eightfold Path

How can persons be released from the burning, the strangling, the poisoning, the persistent restlessness of their craving and desires? While the Buddha's Third Noble Truth describes the Solution, it is the Fourth Noble Truth that proclaims how desire can be extinguished.

This Truth teaches that it is possible to arrive at wisdom and complete liberation by following the Middle Way between excessive sensuousness and excessive asceticism, that is, by following the Eightfold Path. In its shortest representation, the Eightfold Path consists of right understanding, right attitude, right speech, right action, right livelihood, right effort, right mindfulness, and right meditation. The Eightfold Path of wisdom and compassion thus regulates proper views and intentions, directs moral behavior and conduct, and concentrates awareness on the still point at the center of the turning world.

In addition to the Eightfold Path, the Mahayana tradition in Japan has developed a sophisticated range of techniques and elaborate teachings to help people rise above ignorance and face reality as it is. Mahayana teaches that methods are highly relative, and to seize upon only one method is also a form of attachment. In some forms of the Mahayana vision all beings are one in the ocean of life, and merit achieved by one can be shared with others. Each individual must tap into the communal resource of saving power that helps on the path of final release. This power is made available through the use of mandalas and recitation of mantras, or through faith and chanting. In other forms of Mahayana, each individual must rely on one's own powers and the abilities to see the Buddha-nature within. That is, there is no outside goal to be attained, no purpose for which to strive. Each individual has to come to awareness within the pure mind of Buddhahood and to experience satori ("awakening") through zazen ("sitting meditation") or the use of a koan ("paradoxical question") or mondo ("riddle-like story").

The Solution: Nirvana

The Third Noble Truth concerns Nirvana, the goal of Buddhism. Expressed negatively, Nirvana ("annihilation" or "cooling") does not come about by overcoming or mastering the self but by "annihilating" the idea of an independent self. Expressed positively, Nirvana is the realization that there is no independent self. It is "cooling" refreshment to a person who is hot with desire, whose passions are on fire. It is the transformation of life that results from seeing the "suchness" of reality, the Buddha quality that is inherent in every moment of existence. Later Buddhist thought describes this experience of the nonexistence of the self in the doctrine of Sunyata ("emptiness"): All reality is empty or lacking in self-nature.

Nirvana is enjoyment of the freedom from concern that comes to persons who are simply what they are and who accept things simply as they are. Nirvana can be found in the midst of the world. It is neither the extinction of existence nor a state to be experienced only after death. Beyond pleasure and pain, beyond happiness and sorrow, Nirvana can be attained in normal daily living. It is the experience of full life and meaning that comes through eliminating all forms of grasping, desire, and attachment. Nirvana is complete freedom from conditions and limitations, permitting life to be lived in the full richness of the present moment without fear or anxiety.

As the Buddha expresses it: "Having achieved Nirvana is like a deer living in a forest who might lie down on a heap of snares but is not caught in it....It is like a deer roaming the forest slopes who walks confidently, stands confidently, sits down confidently, goes to sleep confidently."

Buddhism does teach about life in the heavenly realms but it too is conditioned, for the ultimate goal of enlightenment and fulfillment transcends even the highest of the heavens. The Buddhist heaven is part of the transitory world, an intermediate and temporary state between one earthly existence and another. There are many realms of heaven, varying with modes of meditative attainment, graphically described as a bountiful land with lotus-filled lakes, permeated by pleasant music, and adorned with exquisite gems.

The Sacred Writings

Theravada Texts
The normative writings in the Theravada tradition are the *Tripitaka* ("Three Baskets"). These include the Discipline Basket, which articulates an effective rule for monastic discipline, and Higher Dharma Basket, a collection of philosophical texts. The most important Basket is the Discourse Basket, which contains middle-length and long

discourses by the Buddha, plus aphorisms in the *Dhammapada* ("Path of Virtue") and the *Jataka Tales*. The Jatakas recount incidents in th234e Buddha's previous lives and are an important part of Theravada preaching and artistic expression. They are a compilation of 547 stories told as fables in which the central character (whether human, animal, or semi-divine) practices one of the ten virtues that must be perfected on the way to Buddhahood.

The Historical Buddha. In the composite portrait that emerges from these texts, Buddha is a sensitive and compassionate individual, a human teacher to be followed, and a saint to be imitated. Gautama lives a sheltered life as a young prince, and his father surrounds him with the pleasures, comforts, and luxuries of life. He marries at a young age and fathers a son. Out riding in his chariot on different occasions, he sees an old man, a sick man, and then a corpse (these will become the three signs of the classic Buddhist description of the human condition). Later he sees a yellow-robed ascetic, a wandering beggar dedicated to a life of poverty and meditation. Gautama, understanding him as the sign of the way beyond life and death, is inspired to do the same.

The Great Renunciation. Gautama's series of shattering encounters leads him in his early adulthood to forsake the path of earthly enjoyment and power in exchange for the life of a hermit. With his growing awareness of misery in the world, he renounces his life of luxury to search for enlightenment. At the age of twenty-nine, silently bidding farewell to his wife and son, Gautama dons the yellow robe of a mendicant monk. He resolves to seek enlightenment because he is deeply convinced that human life, in spite of its joys, brings in its wake the untold sufferings of old age, sickness, and death. He spends his time begging, practicing self-mortification, and consulting with teachers. After six years, near starvation and dissatisfied with ascetic teaching and techniques as ways to truth, he begins to eat again and sits down beneath a tree at Bodh Gaya to seek enlightenment.

The Enlightenment. The Buddha's quest for enlightenment beneath the tree is the master story of Buddhism. It is related in the *Buddha-carita*, a transitional work containing both Theravada and Mahayana ideas. Gautama takes his beggar's bowl, dons the ascetic's garb, and sits beneath the tree to await illumination. He makes a resolution:

The dome-shaped stupa (architectural monument) where Gautama delivered his first sermon at the Deer Park near Banaras recalls the roots of Buddhism in India.

"Though my skin, my nerves, and my bones should waste away and my life-blood dry, I will not leave this seat until I have attained Supreme Enlightenment." Mara, the devil-god of Death and Desire, summons all the powers at his disposal to detain Gautama from achieving enlightenment. He takes the form of a messenger to tell Gautama to return home to restore order in his father's kingdom. Next Mara unleashes a flood, casts down burning ashes and coals, and causes a thick darkness over the earth. Still unable to dissuade Gautama, Mara offers him lordship of the earth and summons his daughters (Desire, Delight, and Pining) to dance seductively before him.

Through all these temptations Gautama's heart is not moved from his quest. During the watches of the night, he reaches knowledge of his former states of being, obtains the eye of omniscient vision of all levels of cosmic and material existence, and grasps understanding of the chain of causation of all rebirth and suffering. Finally, at daybreak, he attains perfect enlightenment, the insight of the Middle Way between indulgence and asceticism.

Having solved his life's problem of how to conquer death, disease, and old age, he is tempted once again by Mara who encourages him to enjoy his own Nirvana without bringing his message to others. The Buddha dispels him, however, and resolves to teach all who would listen. He expounds the Four Noble Truths and the Middle Way in his first sermon to his small band of followers at the Deer Park in Banaras. He spends the next forty-five years organizing his sangha and effectively teaching the Dharma, usually in dialogue or story form.

Mahayana Texts

The Mahayana tradition includes more than 2000 other mostly philosophical sacred texts in addition to the Theravada canon. Although these texts are purportedly the Buddha's own teaching given to his most advanced disciples, they date from a much later period. They present the richness and complexity of the new Mahayana perspective and refine their understanding of Dharma as both truth and path. Mahayana sutras ("short, clipped sentences") include *Perfection of Wisdom*, *Pure Land*, and *Vimalakirti*. Two parables from the *Lotus Sutra of the Wonderful Law*, a very popular sutra in Japan, exemplify how the Buddha used stories to get his followers to grasp his message.

The Burning House. A father returns home, the Buddha tells us, to discover that his house has caught fire and will be engulfed any moment in flames. His children are playing happily inside the house, totally unaware of their imminent disaster. His warning shouts elicit no response and he has no time to search for them all. Panic sets in. What can he do? Suddenly he has an idea: He shouts to his children that he has bought all of them gifts. This draws their immediate attention and they rush out to get their fabulous toys. The children are disappointed when they see nothing. Nevertheless, the father is overjoyed and goes into town and buys each of them a chariot, far more splendid than the carts he originally promised.

By tricking his children, the father is able to rescue them from the flames. Even if he does not give them carts or chariots, he is justified in his action, for it brings rescue to his children. As the father says to himself, "I will get my children to escape by a skillful means." That they are not only rescued but given even more glorious gifts only adds more emphasis to the superabundance of the salvation offered by the Buddha.

The Prodigal Son. A prodigal son has left home, the Buddha tells us, and wanders aimlessly for many a year. In the meantime his father has become a wealthy merchant. Eventually the son happens by the town where his father now lives in wealth. Despite his rags and care-worn features, the son is recognized by his father. When the father tries to approach him in the desire to accept him as his true heir, the son is struck with terror at the unexplained attention he receives. Realizing the psychological state of his son, the father has to adapt skillful means. He orders his servants to offer the boy some menial task so that he can earn some money. Meanwhile, the father takes off his noble garb and puts on a worker's garments so that he can be near his son incognito. Gradually the son is given increased responsibilities until he is eventually made the chief steward of his father's estate. Finally, when the time of the father's death draws near, he summons witnesses and divulges the true family relationship to his son, who now enters into his inheritance.

In this allegory, the compassionate rich man is the Buddha and the son represents his disciples. Just as the son is not prepared emotionally or mentally to receive the full truth until there has been a period of preparation, so the Buddha has to mold disciples little by little. There is no falsehood or deceit in his contrivance, for the lasting truth proves to be richer and fuller than any of the forms in which it is partially conveyed. The consequence is not anger, but joy, surprise, and gratitude.

The First Story: Hui-Neng and Enlightenment

Though these two parables show the essence of Buddhism, I want to indicate the abundance of riches in the Buddhist sacred writings by studying two other stories. The first story, from the Chinese *Platform Sutra,* is a well-known classic in Japan. It is attributed to Hui-Neng (638–713), an authoritative transmitter of the Zen Buddhist spirit. The narrative section of the Platform Sutra, describing the events leading to Hui-Neng's selection as the sixth patriarch, precedes his lengthy sermon which forms the builk of the text.

Having gone on pilgrimage to the flourishing school of enlightenment on East Mountain to learn the Way, Hui-Neng, a young man of little or no education, is harshly received by the monks and is assigned to grind rice. After about eight months, the fifth patriarch, Hung-jen, comes to the monastery to transmit his role and dignity to a successor. He asks each of his monks to compose a verse that will show insight into Zen. Presumably the one whose verse shows the most authentic enlightenment will be worthy to succeed him as patriarch.

During the night the master of the monastery, Shen-hsiu, who is the popular favorite to succeed as patriarch, secretly writes a verse that he posts on the monastery wall: "Our body is the tree of perfect wisdom, and our mind is a bright mirror; at all times diligently wipe them, so that they will be free of dust." The next morning Hui-Neng hears the uproar of the monks shouting approval of their master's poem. He himself reacts strongly against the inadequacy of the verses, however, and that night composes his own verse: "The tree of Perfect Wisdom is originally no tree; nor has the bright mirror any frame; Buddha-nature is forever clear and pure; where is there any dust?"

The patriarch Hung-jen recognizes Hui-Neng's insight and secretly calls him to his room the next day. Transmitting the patriarchal robe and insignia to him, he tells Hui-Neng to leave the monastery immediately to avoid physical danger at the hands of the other monks who feel their master should be the next patriarch. He instructs Hui-Neng that attainment of the highest wisdom comes from freeing the mind of all attachments, but counsels Hui-Neng not to spread this teaching for three years. Thus does Hui-Neng become the founder of the Southern School of Sudden Enlightenment while Shen-hsiu's Northern School of Gradual Enlightenment will decline and gradually disappear. Hui-Neng propagates the Dharma of the Buddha in the temple and surrounding areas for thirty-seven years, attracting thousands of followers, among them the most famous Zen masters in Chinese history. The title "Zen Master of the Great Mirror" is bestowed on him after his death.

The Story Magnified

The Two Verses

Though the story depicts Hui-Neng as winner and Shen-hsiu as loser, we should note that the two verses are really complementary, giving us a fuller picture of the two major types of Zen that will later develop in Japan. Shen-hsiu's stanza emphasizes the process of emptying as a continuing, active vigilance in polishing the mirror of enlightenment. Hui-Neng's verse, on the other hand, emphasizes the state of being empty from the very start and looks at everything from the standpoint of perfect tranquility.

Where Shen-hsiu advises the cleansing of the mirror, the paradoxical verse of Hui-Neng points to the nothingness of all things, including the exercise itself. Shen-hsiu remains attached to the learned study of the sutras, always acknowledged as a valid way to full enlightenment. Yet Hui-Neng criticizes Shen-hsiu's dust-wiping operation—where dust represents passions, thoughts, and images— as likely to reduce meditation to mere temporary suspension of consciousness or perhaps a self-absorbed ecstatic state.

The Mirror

Hui-Neng minimizes building temples, giving alms, studying sutras, and making sacrifices, and reduces Buddhism to a pure concern with the mind alone. No, not the mind either, for purifying the mind is irrelevant, since the true mind is no-mind. A pure and polished mirror is completely transparent, receiving everything into itself without distortion and reflecting all objects as they appear in it. In the same way, the enlightened mind is completely receptive and filled with wonder, seeing everything as if for the first time. The mirror-mind is like the mind of a child, totally open and never fixed on one thing. Who, then, can wipe the mirror clean?

When Hui-Neng rejects the "mirror-wiping" concept of meditation, he is not rejecting all meditation. Rather, he is rejecting what he believes to be a totally wrong attitude to meditation, one that gives primacy to ego-consciousness or an empirical self that views its thoughts as a kind of object or possession. The mind, then, is regarded not as something I am, but as something I own, and then the self resolves to purify the mirror of the mind by removing thoughts from it.

There is no mirror as such, only what it reflects. The perfect clarity of the mirror, its total "emptiness," is precisely what gives it the capacity to contain the whole universe within it. While reflecting all things equally and equitably, without prejudicial stance, the mirror nevertheless reflects each thing and each person in its uniqueness. Precisely because the mirror, the mind, is totally empty, it is totally full! The fully enlightened mind—the fully emptied person—thus perfectly contains the universe in its fullness and totality.

Enlightenment

Hui-Neng revolutionizes Buddhist spirituality by discounting the practice of formal and prolonged meditation. His Buddhism is not a mysticism of introversion and withdrawal, by which persons seek to exclude the external world and to eliminate distracting thoughts. Nor is it sitting in silence, emptying the mind of images, and concentrating on the purity of one's own spiritual essence, whether or not this essence is regarded as the mirror of divinity. Instead, Hui-Neng considers all of life as prajna ("awareness"), and the goal is to be the one life that lives in all.

For Hui-Neng, the awakening that occurs in a single second through naturalness and through letting go makes all effort superfluous. He eliminates all stages and exercises along the way to enlightenment and discards the idea of an endless journey of sentient beings in gradual ascent toward enlightenment. No practices are necessary to attain enlightenment, since the mind already possesses enlightenment within itself. Enlightenment is "attained" by total self-forgetfulness and total self-emptying in the existential present of life here and now.

The Second Story: Vessantara and Compassion

Our second story comes from the *Vessantara Jataka*. This particular story is retold in every Buddhist language, both in elegant literature and in popular poetry.

Vessantara, one of the Buddha's previous incarnations, already speaks at his birth, causing the gods in the heavens to take notice. "Mother," he asks as he leaves her womb, "what gift can I make to the world?" Indeed, from very early in his life he desires to be generous. He wants to give away something of his own, something not given to him by another—perhaps his eye or his flesh. Later, happily married to Princess Maddi, with a son and daughter, he gives away the national treasure—a magic, white, rain-bringing elephant—to a nearby kingdom. The elephant can ensure adequate rainfall for those people who are suffering from a prolonged drought. When the gods see his noble act, they shake the earth and fill the skies approvingly with thunder and lightning, but his fellow citizens are so distressed by the loss of their animal that they rebel and have him banished. Giving away all his possessions—his 700 elephants, 700 horses, 700 chariots, 700 slaves, and everything else—he takes his family to live as an ascetic in the foothills of the Himalayas.

There too, while his wife Maddi is away gathering food, Vessantara makes a gift of his two beloved children to a hideous and despicable old Brahmin, Jujaka, who is harried at home by a young wife who demands her own servants. His children lament as they are led away. Maddi, when she hears what Vessantara has given away this time, also weeps and frantically searches for the children the whole night long. Sakka, the king of the gods, fearing that Vessantara may yet give away his wife too, disguises himself as a brahmin and asks Vessantara to give her to him. This is Vessantara's final act of renunciation, and Maddi submits since she knows that this will fulfill his greatest wish for non-attachment. On receiving Maddi, Sakka immediately gives her back to Vessantara.

As Vessantara now has his wife as a gift, he is no longer forced to give her away in his pursuit of total generosity. When his exploits become known, he is asked to return to resume his kingly role. The city and palace are decked out for him, and amnesty is proclaimed for prisoners. Every creature is set free; a shower of jewels fills the ground up to waist height so that he can give them away to his subjects when they ask him for supplications. In the end, his children are returned to him, and the gods restore all his gifts a hundredfold. He puts away his hermit's robes and reigns gloriously for many years before he dies, remaining a symbol of generosity for all time.

The Story Magnified

The Bodhisattvas

Vessantara is a bodhisattva who embodies the virtue of generosity. Intense practice of generosity is the first of the ten stages or perfections that the bodhisattva has to traverse before final liberation. In the prevalent popular view in Japan, bodhisattvas are heavenly beings far advanced in the path of enlightenment who accompany, protect, and assist countless persons on their way to the liberating state of peace where they are no longer attached to the turmoil of the cycle of rebirth. The bodhisattvas are beings who vowed many existences ago to become buddhas. Each time they die, they delay final liberation and choose freely when and where to return in another incarnation, for the sake of others, until all are saved. Out of love and pity for suffering humanity, they strive to awaken the Buddha-reality in others and to help them along the road to final enlightenment.

In their rebirths ever since, the bodhisattvas live in such a way as to acquire stores of merit. They work ceaselessly for the welfare and salvation of all living things by transferring their inexhaustible merits to them, as the need arises. They grant their merits especially to those who express devotion to them or call upon them in prayer. Among the bodhisattva's ten perfections are wisdom, skill in means, and compassion. Through their wisdom they skillfully use

At Kyoto, more than a thousand images of Kannon, the bodhisattva of mercy, line the longest wooden building in the world.

all kinds of marvelous upaya ("means") to show their love for the world and to benefit the world by conveying the truth to others. By helping others become enlightened, they attain their true enlightenment. In the story of Vessantara's use of generosity as his skillful means, all Buddhists have a model to follow in renouncing and giving away everything that is "his" or "hers" and thus to achieve non-attachment.

Compassion

Vessantara's generosity is a manifestation of compassion, the most important of the bodhisattva's virtues. Vessantara turns his entire attention toward the world, moved by an all-embracing karuna ("compassion"). He has compassion for all beings that suffer because of attachment, and he desires to be united with all living beings in their joys and sufferings, struggles and hopes. Through his generosity, Vessantara characterizes the reality of interdependence in placing the needs of others before his own. Vessantara says that it does no good to give something away if you regret it. The point of his generosity as a bodhisattva does not lie in the nature of his gifts—certainly he does not want to be rid of his children and wife—but in becoming so free from attachment that he does not mind parting with anything. Though he gives material gifts to others, his compassion dispels spiritual, rather than material, impoverishment. His real gift is the message that those who are on the way to enlightenment can attain it only by freedom from any and all desire.

The Stories Exemplified

Other Stories in Japan

The artistic Japanese Noh dramas develop many of the Buddhist stories in a sophisticated way. Noh is the theater of contemplation, withdrawing the spectators from their busy, crowded lives into ceremonial quietness to look, calmly and with dignity, upon a few beautiful objects and actions. All is flux, the dramas say, all is change. The *Tale of Genji*, by Lady Murasaki Shikibu (c. 1000, C.E.), develops the fundamental tension between the inner life, where feeling and taste are supremely important, and the outer life of society, where all must conform to obligations built into the social structure. Genji is a generous and amorous prince of supreme sensitivity who has adventures with many ladies, especially one vivacious young maiden to whom he sends love poems in a mood of wistful love. Attachment to life, even to the memory of passion, the tale tells us, is pain. Another Buddhist narrative popular in Japan is *Monkey*. This humorous novel of Chinese origin extols the compassion, wisdom, and power of the bodhisattva in recounting the adventures of the restless and roguish genius Monkey and the exploits of Tripitaka ("Three Baskets").

Communities

Of the dozens of different Buddhist schools and traditions in Japan, Pure Land and Zen are perhaps the best known today. These religious communities both came to Japan from China and developed during the Kamakura period (1185-1333), at a time when the warlords of the samurai class gained political power. Today Pure Land and Zen are clear expressions of Buddhism with a distinctively Japanese cast, one emphasizing the way of salvation through simple faith in the compassionate bodhisattva Amida, the other through the way of meditation.

Sand gardens are spontaneous and natural, allowing the Japanese to rise above the limits of relativity and have a glimpse of eternity.

Pure Land Buddhism. A way of salvation for the common people, Pure Land is the most widespread and numerous of the Japanese Buddhist communities. Popularized in Japan by Honen (1133-1212), Pure Land arose at a time of widespread belief in mappo (an era of irreversible decline and frequent natural calamities). Pure Land taught that it was not possible for humans to achieve enlightenment by self-power (jiriki); instead they had to rely on the power of another (tariki). It replaced lofty speculation, elaborate rituals, and meritorious deeds with a simple act of faith in the saving action of the bodhisattva Amida. Once a person has abandoned reliance on the powers and accomplishments of the self, then faith alone is sufficient for salvation. This faith springs up spontaneously from Amida's spiritual presence in the hearts of the Pure Land believers, and they express their wholehearted reliance on the mercy of Amida through reciting the Nembutsu ("Praise to Amida").

Rebirth in a heavenly paradise, where all beings will be reborn and achieve enlightenment without fail, replaces the traditional Buddhist goal of attaining Nirvana. Amida presides over this paradise, the Pure Land, and freely admits to it those who beseech him in faith and recite the Nembutsu. Rebirth in the Pure Land is not yet Buddhahood, but those reborn there will never again be born to lower states of suffering, and they will achieve Buddhahood in just a few more lifetimes.

Zen Buddhism. Though Zen is not as popular in Japan today as Pure Land, it is the Buddhist tradition that is the best known in America. Zen firmly retains the Buddha's more traditional notion that enlightenment is gained through one's own endeavors. As in Pure Land, scholarly research, good works, and performance of rituals are of little merit. In fact, they are often a hindrance to true insight into the Buddha-reality. In Zen, salvation comes through meditation into one's own nature. Every technique is merely a finger pointing to the moon, a device to induce satori ("surprised awakening"), when the mind breaks through to a wondrous new awareness. Satori comes by a flash of insight through contemplation.

Satori involves a total change in one's view of reality, a turning point in life. Satori is self-realization, that is, seeing into one's own being and true nature. The satori in Zen is the sudden experience or actualization of the oneness of all reality. When persons see into their own nature in a moment of awakening, there is a blinding realization, like a flash of lightning, an insight transcending all rational limits, that "I" and "not I" are one: Both are aspects of Buddha-reality. In satori persons realize the universal Buddhist essence: The Buddha is not other than I am, here and now. Satori is a spontaneous and natural experience; it is grasping life with bare hands. It is the affirmation of everyday life in everyday words: "When hungry, I eat; when thirsty, I drink." The satori experience of self-realization is not communicable to others. All a teacher can do is show the way.

Rinzai Zen. Two major types of Zen are Rinzai and Soto. Though Soto is numerically the larger, the distinctive features of the Zen outlook are most dramatically represented in Rinzai Zen. Eisai (1141-1215), who was the first to bring tea to Japan from China, also stimulated Rinzai among the Japanese.

Rinzai uses the techniques of the koan ("paradoxical question") and the mondo ("riddle-like story") for meditation. The value of koans and mondos is that by means of a cryptic assertion, paradoxical statement, meaningless remark, or baffling action, a seemingly irreconcilable conflict situation is set at wit's end. These verbal puzzles are intended to challenge ordinary thinking and frustrate rational thought. They are techniques that help persons see directly into their true nature. Everyday reasoning has to be transcended for persons to stop clinging to objects (the self included) and realize their Buddha-nature.

Ming tombs portray venturesome Japanese warriors who were attracted to Zen for its virtues of self-sacrifice and single-minded devotion.

"What is the sound of one hand clapping?" "What was your face before you were born?" These and several hundred similar koans are the principal weapon used in the battlefield of the spirit. The koans and mondos agitate and stir the mind to impatience, counting on a flash of sudden insight to bring the person to no-mind. In the words of Hakuin, the classical master of the koan, one experiences "the great root of faith, the great ball of doubt, and the great strength of tenacity." A person who lacks one of these is like a three-legged pot with one leg broken.

Eisai's form of Zen was popular among the adventurous samurai (warrior class) who found Zen particularly congenial to their way of life. The attraction for Japanese warriors revolved around self-sacrificial and single-minded devotion to emperor and country. The spiritual attitude in both Zen and swordsmanship is the same: In doing dramatic battle with ego, desire, and illusion, no mental image should cloud the spirit of the swordsman, who must immediately respond to or anticipate every movement of his opponent. Rinzai Zen provided a foundation for the Bushido Code ("way of the warrior") in which the true warrior spirit forgoes the option of attack in favor of taking a defensive initiative. This Japanese code of behavior utilized the method of private self-discipline, inspiring the warriors to act bravely and fearlessly in battle, with a spirit of loyalty and sense of honor that was never to be compromised.

Soto Zen. Dogen (1200-1253) provided the intellectual foundation for Soto Zen in Japan. In marked contrast to Eisai's use of the koan, Dogen taught that Zazen ("just sitting") was the means to attain sudden enlightenment. Enlightenment can be attained even in secular life: Since persons already possess the Buddha-nature or are the Buddha, all they have to do is to awaken to that nature. This silent illumination comes through the practice of sitting meditation. The person meditates with legs crossed in the traditional Buddha posture, with the hands held in one of several ways, in the fashion of a strong, sturdy tree well-rooted in the earth. This practice—sitting straight without entertaining vain thoughts—is the enlightenment.

Going directly to springtime images of seed, growth, and coming to flower, Soto emphasizes patience and nurturing. Soto is like a farmer patiently taking care of a rice field, one stalk after another. Perhaps this is why Soto has been a more powerful political and social movement in later Japanese history and more influential than Rinzai among common people. Many lay people are drawn to spend a period of time in temples and monasteries with the monks. A further aid is used to deepen Zazen in the temples: Monitors strike the shoulders of those in meditation with a specially designed paddle. For those deep in Zazen the paddle can be a source of great stimulation. There are also regular group sessions with the master, during which they devote time to chanting, exercising and attending to the teacher's instructions.

Human Witnesses

Shinran. Shinran (1173-1262) is the most famous proponent of the Pure Land form of Buddhism. As Shinran grew aware of Amida's compassion surrounding him, he became identified with this power of compassion. Indeed, for Shinran, the experience of compassion was itself rebirth in the Pure Land. Filled with compassion, he no longer sought peace and happiness for himself nor waited for rebirth;

rather, he was compelled to lead others to Buddhahood. Shinran emphasized the all-encompassing and absolute mercy, the saving power of the bodhisattva Amida. He was convinced that the compassionate Amida had already completed salvation: All persons are already saved, although they don't realize it.

Shinran went so far as to say that wicked persons might be more acceptable to Amida than good ones, since the former threw themselves entirely on the mercy of the bodhisattva, while the latter might be tempted to think that their chances of salvation were improved by their own meritorious conduct. Unquestioning faith alone in Amida brought salvation. Accordingly, chanting the Nembutsu was regarded as an expression of gratitude rather than a practice that might lead to the Pure Land. Building a society on this basic principle, he deliberately ignored the rules of monastic life by marrying and raising children. The new school he established for the integration of secular life and the religious quest remains one of the most powerful Buddhist institutions in Japan today.

Hakuin. Though highly esteemed for his paintings and works of calligraphy, Hakuin (1686-1769) is most famous for his creative use of koans. For him, koans were indispensable for those aggressively seeking enlightenment. In contrast to sitting in quiet meditation, Hakuin emphasized meditation in the midst of activity at all times and places. He accentuated disciplined meditation on koans under a teacher's guidance for those who wished to see into their true nature. He claimed those who just sat would meditate one minute and then fall asleep for a hundred, and during the little bit of meditation that they managed to accomplish, their minds were beset by countless delusions. Without a koan to focus upon, persons accomplished very little just sitting because they tended either to go to sleep or to let the mind wander.

Hakuin is also the main character in several koans. Hakuin is approached one day by Nobushige, a soldier, who asks him: "Is there really a paradise and a hell?" Hakuin replies: "Who are you?" Nobushige answers: "I am a samurai." "You, a samurai!" exclaims Hakuin. "What kind of a lord would have you as his guard? You look like a beggar!" Nobushige becomes so enraged that he draws his sword. Hakuin continues, "So, you have a sword. It is probably too dull even to cut off my head." When Nobushige brandishes his weapon, Hakuin then remarks, "Here, open the gates of hell." At these words the perceptive samurai sheathes his sword and bows.

"Here, open the gates of paradise," says Hakuin.

Though koans are not meant to be explained, it is easy to see that heaven and hell are the contents of everyday life. Unless persons are aware, Hakuin is saying, they do not fully live. They have ears, but do not hear; they have eyes, but do not see. Oftentimes they are merely existing. Awareness means awareness of life. Because of this and similar koans, all Rinzai Zen masters today trace their lineage to Hakuin.

Twentieth Century

Modernization. Until a little over a hundred years ago, Japan was a tightly ordered society sealed off from the rest of the world. After the American, Commodore Perry, sailed his ships into Tokyo Bay in 1853, treaties opening Japanese ports to Western trade were quickly negotiated. This marked the beginning of the irreversible process of modernization that has made Japan one of the world's economic leaders today. The Meiji government (1868-1912) attempted to develop a national consciousness and cohesion in face of the transitions needed to industrialize and modernize the state. With a series of radical changes in the political, economic, and religious spheres, the Meiji rulers aspired to restore the actual rule of the emperor in a modern context.

The Meiji government established Shinto as the state religion, a sort of non-religious national cult. The government claimed that the loyalty and obligation to the emperor and the state took priority over individual goals and should be expressed through Shinto myths and rituals. Various other means, especially military training and public education, were utilized to promote the sacred "legacy of the kami way."

Legally, Buddhism no longer possessed the privileged status that it formerly enjoyed. It became one tradition among others in a religiously pluralistic society. Thus Buddhism was deeply affected both negatively and positively by the rapid process of modernization, for at the same time it was being rejected as a state religion, its organizations became actively engaged in educational and social work projects.

New Religions. Along with political, social, and cultural changes at the end of World War II, full-scale religious freedom was introduced into the Japanese nation. The post-war period in Japan was a time of uncertainty, poverty, and loss of confidence. The time was ripe for the so-called "new religions." Literally thousands of new religions have since sprouted up, each claiming to offer mundane happiness, tightly knit organization, healing, and readily accessible divine agents. The new religions have been very successful in concentrating attention on the concrete needs of mass society during Japan's heavy trend toward urbanization and modern industrialization. Promising benefits through magical practices and faith, they support popular aspirations for democracy and peace. They attempt to win the minds of people through indoctrination and extensive publishing efforts.

One new religion, Soka Gakkai ("Value Creation Society"), now claims a third of the nation's households, and is unquestionably the liveliest religious movement in the country. Its large number of middle-class followers are active in political affairs. Soka Gakkai has medieval roots in the Buddhist tradition founded by Nichiren (1222-1282), which taught that merely reciting the title of the Lotus Sutra enabled persons to receive the power and blessings of Buddhahood. Today it is embraced by the merchant class and those with a strong propensity toward active political and social involvement. Soka Gakkai stresses immediate attainment of all worldly goals and interprets the ancient Buddhist goal of enlightenment as something akin to "happiness." Its intense small groups have sessions and rituals that emphasize group solidarity. They are convinced that their religion meets their mundane needs in the modern industrial world, offering salvation here and now. They operate the largest temple in the world at the foot of Mt. Fuji. Thousands of pilgrims each day come there to chant the traditional invocation to the Lotus Sutra and to gaze at the magically powerful mandala designed by Nichiren.

Human Rights. In the half century of Meiji government, the Japanese sought and achieved a constitution, modern law courts, and religious freedom, all modified by Shinto traditions and values. Setting up Shinto as the state religion was a ploy to allow the government to claim its place as a modern nation that guaranteed human rights, including religious freedom. Japan's new constitution was created in 1947 in an attempt to make Japan a bastion of democracy and individual freedom in the Western pattern. The feudal aristocracy was abolished, and women were given economic and political rights (e.g., suffrage). Many of these changes were the direct result of Western legal influences.

Just as visible today, though not so much in the legal system, is the enormous influence of the Buddhist vision of self-realization through individual self-emptying. The social dimension of the Mahayana traditions stresses a lack of possessiveness, rather than personal and individual rights. Today in Japanese society individuals do not exist outside the tissue of social structure unless they pay the price of severe alienation. Japan is an excellent example of how a modern industrial nation can build social relationships on the model of the family. The ritual announcement that summarizes Buddhism—"This is not mine, I am not this, this is not myself"—is quite prominent in Japan today and is at the core of modern Japanese management techniques.

The Japanese have developed a successful management style because they recognize basic human needs. Their Buddhist backgrounds give them an awareness of human relationships and an openness to its subtleties. Managers recognize that humans want to feel useful and important at the workplace, to satisfy their basic aspiration to belong and experience a sense of fulfillment. Managers help workers develop self-reliance and respect and give them the chance to develop their well-being and sense of wholeness. They provide a creative environment where all may contribute according to their abilities and personalities. Encouraging initiative from the bottom up, they make use of untapped human resources and involve workers in the tedious process of maximum consultation and collective decision making. They give incentives to meet the goals that the employees themselves help establish. They treat ordinary business problems patiently and unobtrusively: The notion of achieving change gradually runs deep in Japanese culture.

Ritual: Tea Ceremony

The Japanese people feel close to nature, love poetry and the arts, and observe numerous traditional rituals. Their religious life continues to focus on family values and on observances performed in the home. Still, the Buddhist tradition, with its individual meditative exercises and discipline of self-knowledge, has had a profound transforming effect on Japanese culture and rituals. Their rock gardens and landscapes are spontaneous and natural. Their flower arrangements are expressed in a simple and subtle manner, with a deep contemplative effect. Their elaborate mandalas and chromed images of the bodhisattvas are works of lasting refined beauty. Their haiku poetry, in its bare seventeen syllables, is crisp, direct,

Capturing the spirit of Buddhism, the Zen tea ceremony is a stimulant to meditation, encouraging a relaxed atmosphere and natural awareness.

and enigmatic, usually about nature or daily beauties and sorrows. Everyday commonness is veiled exquisitely with the mist of transcendental inwardness, and the mind is lifted wonderfully above the perplexities of life. In their culture and rituals, the Japanese find a corner, however humble, in this world of struggles and vanities where they can rise above the limits of relativity and even have a glimpse of eternity.

One Japanese ritual that captures the spirit of Buddhism is the tea ceremony. The setting, the preparations, and the ceremony all incorporate the prime characteristics of Buddhist teaching. In the garden leading to the tea hut the visitors are aware of stepping stones, a stone water-basin, and a stone lantern. Each of these silently teaches the lesson of selflessness—the stone lantern's wick, for example, being consumed in flame in order to illumine, however faintly, a dark corner of the garden. Before entering the tea hut, the visitors pass by a small outdoor toilet and under a small jutting roof that protects them from the shifting weather, both graphic reminders that life is everlasting variation and constant change. Once inside, the visitors are greeted by a festival of the senses. Incense and scroll paintings catch the imagination and magically transform the atmosphere. Fragrances, faint wisps of ever-rising smoke, and flower arrangements all point to the infinite, to the bliss of Nirvana.

In the actual preparation of the tea, the host pays special attention to the fire and the water, but especially to the spoon and the bamboo whisk. The spoon for measuring the powdered tea and the whisk for stirring it both require care and delicacy in order to ensure a perfect balance. When the proper measures of tea and boiled water are poured into the clay cups and stirred with the whisk until exactly right, the visitors lift the cups in both hands, feeling the texture and warmth. They drink the tea, not in one gulp but in small sips, savoring the refreshing liquid. The tea ceremony is a stimulant to meditation: The atmosphere is relaxed, awareness is unhurried, and the conversation is non-argumentative. The purpose of the ritual is to be all there, to be one with the tea, developing attitudes toward existence and nature that ought to permeate one's entire life. As the Zen masters were accustomed to say, "Religion is a most ordinary thing."

The Stories Appropriated

When Gautama Buddha concluded his teachings at the Mount of the Holy Vulture, he raised a lotus blossom as a way of summarizing all that he had been teaching. None of his disciples understood his meaning, except one, Mahakasyapa. This first of the patriarchs said nothing and did nothing. He only smiled. But in so doing, he indicated in the most appropriate manner possible that the transmission of truth had occurred. The Buddhist stories of Gautama, Vessantara, and Hui-Neng continue to transmit truths, not only for those within the Buddhist tradition, but for us outside it. These stories present new ways for us to envision our own spiritual convictions. Reading about compassion and meditation can help us to respond in a personal way to our own religion on the basis of transformed decisions.

The Religious Quest

In the master story of the Buddha, Gautama had to face temptations and dangers from the demon Mara when he withdrew in meditation to seek enlightenment. Only after he had successfully undergone several trials did he experience a spiritual rebirth and acquire a new power and a new vision that he could then share with others. Our own quest for religious wholeness always involves a struggle.

We all seek the way to happiness, the secret of good living, the transformation of consciousness. We all seek liberation from suffering and from the arbitrary intangibles in life. Winning through to enlightenment involves a long quest and many battles against adverse forces, forces that will tempt us to be satisfied with superficial answers.

We have to reach down to our spiritual depths to achieve insight in spite of temptations that beset us during the very times we retreat from everyday activities in order to meditate on our spiritual lives. Just as Gautama took refuge in his own immanent Buddha-nature, so can we intuitively realize our own divine nature. Like Gautama we can take on a new power to use as a healing gift in community. We can make the meaning of our sacred vision a part of other people's lives by bringing them into contact with our insight.

Solitude

The religious wholeness we seek does not involve accumulating more information, but an education centered on self-understanding, through which we experience the oneness of our knowledge and our being. For this we have to meditate—something that most of us find very difficult to do. We are transfixed by all the diversions of the media and of technology. The information explosion swamps us with too many new facts to absorb. Technology increases our heartbeat. Our lives are filled with so much to do that we lose sleep, and with too little sleep there are too few dreams. Meditation can calm us down and enable us to accept things as they are without injecting our ego-centered desires.

Meditation demands solitude, yet many people fear solitude, thinking it is the same as loneliness. Whether we experience our time of being alone as loneliness or as solitude depends on whether we view it as the product of our free choice. Loneliness results not only from a lack of choice but also from not knowing how to occupy time alone. Time can seem to stretch out endlessly like the monotonous tick-tocking of a clock, without meaning or purpose. In their loneliness many people become prey to feelings of inadequacy in their lives. Solitude, though, is good for us at times. Only in solitude can we achieve an unobstructed, undiluted awareness of our true selves. Solitude offers us the opportunity to gain a stronger sense of who we are and what we are capable of becoming. Private moments allow us to function in the social world without losing ourselves in the process.

Liberating Wisdom

When Hui-Neng dismisses the "mirror-wiping" concept of meditation, he is not rejecting all meditation. His opponent emphasizes the process of emptying as a continuing, ongoing event, as active vigilance in polishing the mirror of enlightenment. This is what Hui-Neng criticizes, for it gives primacy to ego-consciousness, to an awareness of an individual self. This self views its thoughts as a kind of object or possession: The mind is something I own that I must purify by removing thoughts from it.

Hui-Neng proposes a liberating style of meditation for us in which all polarities (suffering versus comfort, conflict versus harmony, good versus evil, life versus death) are overcome. With liberating wisdom we fully accept each situation in its eternal fullness, and we are at peace with ourselves and with the whole universe. This wisdom is the fount of genuine compassion, latent in all of us, and its awakening enables us to realize our lives fully.

Interdependence

Vessantara's generosity is so great that he tries to give away his wife as a final act of renunciation, as the fulfillment of his wish for non-attachment. The point of his story does not lie in the nature of his gifts but in his becoming so free from attachment that he does not mind parting with anything. Vessantara says that it is no good for us to give something away if we regret it. For our generosity to be worthwhile, we have to place the needs of others before our own, and thus practice the virtue of interdependence.

Crucial to interdependence is an egoless self (the not-self) that is released from any kind of self-centeredness. Nothing—the giver, the gift, the receiver—exists in isolation; there is an interconnectedness with all existence. With interdependence we experience an intense feeling for all living beings who suffer pain, anxiety, ignorance, or illusion. The self-fulfilled individual (i.e., one enlightened as to selflessness) automatically wills to share that happiness of release with others by aiding them in their own quest for enlightenment. This lesson of the bodhisattva on universal compassion flies in the face of our tradition with its stress on individual rights—personal, human, and civil. The interdependence that comes with compassion means we mustn't be numb to the real suffering of others: the poor, the hungry, the exploited, the victims of structural and actual violence. Compassion is the obsession for justice, the rightful indignation at the suffering of fellow living beings.

The bodhisattva's generosity and sense of interdependence extends beyond humans: It provides the necessary foundation and demonstrates respect for all of nature. Selfishness abounds, arrogance becomes rampant, and violence to nature ensues if there is no basis of emptiness. A sense of interdependence, though, radically changes our relationship with nature and reverses the acceleration toward ecological self-destruction. A single blade of grass, a single tree, a single dust particle—each contains Buddha-nature. Even in drops of water we see reflections, smaller ones and bigger ones, like in a house of mirrors: We see the same thing, the same nature, reflected in different ways.

Recognition of interdependence of all life leads to an expression of gratitude. The Japanese express gratitude and a profound appreciation for all of life and nature in various acts of compassion and thanksgiving. Whether in good times or bad, the Japanese preface their greetings, opening remarks, and responses with "How grateful I am." Gratitude, we learn, is essential for a truly human life. It is the recognition that whatever our present circumstances, fortunate or unfortunate, we live by virtue of the working and sacrifices of countless others, including the blessings of nature. Just to be here, to be alive, is a blessing and a gift.

Conclusion

The Buddhist story of disengagement in wisdom and involvement in compassion has come down the centuries, binding the schools of Buddhism together, from its beginnings in India to its modern forms in Japan. Buddhism balances the ideal of self-salvation with the ideal of compassionate good will toward all living beings. Pure Land and Zen are clear expressions of Buddhism with a distinctively Japanese cast, the former emphasizing the way of salvation through the way of meditation and the latter through simple faith in the compassionate bodhisattva Amida.

The story of Hui-Neng and the mirror teaches that the enlightened mind is completely receptive and filled with wonder, seeing everything as if for the first time. His style of meditation brings a liberating wisdom in which all polarities are overcome.

The story of Vessantara's generosity is the story of compassion. His generosity as a bodhisattva teaches that persons have to become so free from attachment that they do not mind parting with anything. Those who are on the way to Enlightenment can attain liberation only by detaching themselves from any and all desire.

Discussion Questions

1. Why do you think the author chooses the statue of Mahavairo-cana at Todaiji as the symbol of Buddhism?

2. Explain the prayer of the Three Refuges: "I take refuge in the Buddha; I take refuge in the Dharma; I take refuge in the Sangha."

3. Summarize the Buddhist system of salvation in terms of suffering, the Eightfold Path, and Nirvana.

4. What essential aspects of the Buddhist tradition are treated in the story of Hui-Neng in the Platform Sutra?

5. What essential aspects of the Buddhist tradition and the bodhi-sattva are described in the Jataka tale of Vessantara?

6. Summarize the role of Buddhism and Shinto in Japan since the Meiji restoration.

7. What can Christians appropriate today from the stories of Gautama, Hui-Neng, and Vessantara?

8. Discussion starter: "The Bodhisattva holds a spade in his hands and yet the tilling of the ground is done by him empty-handed. He is riding on the back of a horse and yet there is no rider in the saddle and no horse under it. He passes over the bridge, and it is not the water that flows, but the bridge." (D.T. Suzuki).

9. Discussion Starter: "One day Banzan was walking through a market. He overheard a customer say to the butcher, 'Give me the best piece of meat you have.' 'Everything in my shop is the best,' replied the butcher. 'You cannot find any piece of meat that is not the best.' At these words, Banzan was enlightened." (Hakuin)

10. Discussion Starter: When the poet Basho was questioned by his master about the ultimate truth of things, he saw a frog leaping into an old pond, its sound breaking into the serenity of the whole situation. Basho's reply in a seventeen-syllable haiku captures the essence of Buddhism: "A frog jumps into the water. Plop!"

The pyramid of Kukulcan, the plumed serpent, in the central courtyard at Chichen Itza, expresses the richness of the Maya civilization.

Chapter Nine

MAYA AND UGANDA
Sacrifice and Death

Setting the Scene: Maya

Chichen Itza

A marvelous pyramid of Kukulcan, the plumed serpent, towers in the center of the broad open plaza at Chichen Itza in the Yucatan peninsula of Mexico. Four steep staircases ascend the pyramid, each beginning on the ground with two colossal serpents' heads, ten feet in length, with tongues protruding from wide open mouths. At certain times of year, when the sun hits the seven flights of steps going up the pyramid at just the right angle, the stairs resemble a serpent's tail wriggling down from the heavens. Atop the narrow steps is a small level space for a temple supported by serpent columns. On the stone jaguar throne inside the temple the Maya made contact with the gods.

A paved roadway leads from the pyramid to the cenote ("sacred well"). Chichen Itza ("mouth of the well of the Itza") is the cenote of sacrifice to the gods. Surrounded by vertical cliffs sixty-five feet high, the cenote is a limestone cavern 200 feet in diameter where the surface of the earth has collapsed, exposing an extensive underground water hole. It is the only steady source of water in the region. Revered by the Maya who were always anxious about rainfall, the cenote was a door to the watery underworld inhabited by Chacs ("rain gods") and Balams ("jaguar spirits"). The dark depths of this murky, green pit hide countless prized possessions the Maya sacrificed to their gods, including gold pieces, jade ornaments, and belts encrusted with gems.

Off to the side of the pyramid is another part of the ceremonial precinct, the great ball court, a long field where athletes played a soccer-like game using a small, hard rubber ball. The ball court was the fusion of the religious, aesthetic, political, and athletic aspects of the Maya culture. Target rings were mounted high up on the side walls of the ball court, and the players had to pass the rubber ball through the hole in the ring. The sloping walls flanking the court are decorated with stone carvings. The carvings show two teams of warrior-players, or shaman-priests, performing human sacrifices along with their supernatural overlords, all with flamboyant head-dresses and accoutrements. Riotous movements of hooked-nosed war chiefs and plumed serpents bring out the excitement of Maya warfare. In one carving, a man, presumably the winning captain, holds a knife in one hand and the head of his victim, the leader of the opposing team, in the other. From the victim's head sprout six serpents and a plant, symbolizing fertility and renewal—the religious purposes of the ritual.

The Maya Civilization

The Maya today still observe many of the customs of their ancestors, following the ancient calendar, and living in the slow, soothing rhythm of their distant forebears. The Maya culture flourished for around a thousand years, until its sudden and still unexplained demise around the time of the Spanish conquest in the sixteenth century. The conquistadors wiped out the majority of the Maya Indians and brutally forced the conversion of the rest to Christianity.

Calendar. Maya advances in astronomy, art, and architecture, and their early use of the zero in mathematical calculations still stand as lasting cultural achievements. The Maya devised an accurate 365-day cyclical calendar a thousand years ahead of other cultures in the New World. They counted not only in days, months, and years, but also in much larger periods of 20 years, 400 years, 8000 years, and more. They had two main cycles, one of 260 days, the other of 365 days, whose sequences meshed like gear wheels, repeating approximately every 52 years.

Since their culture was tied to the needs of corn cultivation, the Maya used their calendar to predict the seasons for farmers and astronomical events for religious rites. The learned shaman-priests provided weather forecasts and calculated the duration of the harvest year, telling the people when to burn and plant their fields. They also intensively studied and charted the annual motion and phases of the sun, moon, Venus, and various constellations, and accurately computed the dates for eclipses. Keeping track of the calendar, they accommodated the gods and knew when to celebrate religious festivals, hunt, and go to war. The Maya believed that events were repeated in successive cycles. Because they used their calendar to predict the structure of events in the future, people had no control over their fate. They even intervened in history to make events conform to the cycles. Time had a special and miraculous significance.

Faith and the Gods of the Maya

The Maya gods did not grant favors, but traded them for sacrificial offerings of incense, food, and blood. The devout people had the duty to provide human blood to give the gods strength to perform their tasks. Their dominating sky god, the creator and framer of the universe, was Itzamna ("Iguana House"). Lord of day and night, Itzamna's serpent-like body encircled the plane of the earth's surface and passed through the underworld each night in the guise of a jaguar. There were actually four Itzamnas, each assigned to a world direction and color. The Maya prayed to Itzamna at times of drought and famine.

The Maya also prayed to the rain gods (Chacs). The four chief Chacs rose to preeminence each springtime by sending life-giving rains, thus maintaining life. With faces of stylized serpents, long pendulous noses, and projecting tusks, the Chacs were frequently depicted on monuments and pottery. The Chacs were both beneficent and death-dealing, with the power to bring gentle rain and abundant harvests or devastating cloudbursts, floods, and rotting harvests. Associated with them were the chacmools—lifelike stone figures sculpted in a reclining posture, with knees up and hands holding a receptacle in which human hearts may have been placed during sacrificial ceremonies.

Kukulcan (in Yucatan) or Gucumatz (in Guatemala) was the Maya manifestation of the central Mexican deity, Quetzalcoatl, the feathered serpent. Discoverer of maize and inventor of writing, he

Stylized serpents and iguanas represent the Maya gods who sent life-giving rains in the springtime.

was the wind god and the messenger of the gods. His heart was consumed by a bonfire that he built himself. It rose skyward to become the planet Venus. Of the few goddesses among the Maya, by far the most important was the moon goddess Ixchel. The goddess of medicine, she ministered to women in pregnancy and childbirth. The goddess of weaving, she invented the loom.

Human Salvation: Maya

The Problem: Evil Spirits
Humans are prevented from living in harmony with animals, plants, and sacred forces because evil and failure are built into the world. Such evils as illness, disease, death, crop failure, and misfortune are caused by the magic and sorcery of evil spirits. Human evils, such as crimes, are due to thoughtless negligence toward the divine order. The earth is supported by four gods who can cause the earth to tremble as a punishment to the people for such forbidden transgressions. These gods might shift their burden when tired, causing earthquakes that bring malnutrition, related childhood diseases, and death.

The Strategy: Sacrifice
Every feature of Maya life had its religious aspect, designed to rees-

tablish contact continually with the sacred sources of power. The Maya had to perform a perpetual round of sacrifices of food, drink, animals, and incense to keep the gods nourished and satisfied. Ritualistic drinking of fermented honey, for example, was more than a release from tension: By this holy act they drove evil from their bodies, and the resulting physical and spiritual exaltation brought them in closer touch with the gods.

The Maya also regularly sacrificed human blood to give the gods strength to function benevolently, particularly the sun god who needed to be clothed with flesh when he emerged each dawn. Human sacrifices—prisoners of war, slaves, criminals, or even devout volunteers—sated the divine appetites. Such human sacrifices, carried out for the glory and benefit of the community, were expedited under conditions of maximum spectator participation, pomp, and ceremony. Human sacrifices were necessary in times of public calamity (e.g., to avert drought and famine, to prevent the recurrence of a hurricane, or to prolong the life of a sick ruler). The human sacrifices in the cenotes and on ball courts, such as at Chichen Itza, assured abundant rainfall and sufficient crop growth. The sacrifices satisfied the gods responsible for wind, rain, sunshine, and fertility. Victims generally cooperated with the sacrificers, for they were guaranteed a happy place in the afterlife.

In addition to sacrifices, the Maya also depended on the chilams (shaman-priests) to play an important role in combating evil. Through an elaborate initiation and training period the chilams acquired visionary powers and the ability to fall into trances spontaneously or through the use of narcotics. In their state of ecstasy they received divine inspiration from sacred powers. With this power they consulted the Maya calendar to predict future events, establish auspicious times for the holy rites and days favorable for such matters as celebrating puberty or marriage ceremonies, and for burning and planting their fields. Most of all though, they used this sacred power and knowledge to perform communal sacrifices, heal sicknesses, and combat witchcraft and sorcery.

The Solution: Harmony with Life Forces
The primary concern for the Maya was with fullness and wholeness in human existence as it was given from their ancestors and from sacred powers. The goal they sought was a life in harmony with these forces rather than a different state of life after death. When the Maya talked of the afterlife, they described it as a delightful place

where good people would go and where nothing would give them pain. There were seven layers of heavens above the earth, ruled by the Lords of the Heavens. There they would have an abundance of foods and drinks of great sweetness. They would rest under a sacred tree that gave cool shade, and cease forever from labor and worries in life. A special place of honor was reserved for warriors who fell in battle, for victims of ritual sacrifices, and for women who died in childbirth.

Maya Sacred Writings

Most of the ancient books (codices) of the Maya were destroyed at the time of the Spanish conquest in the sixteenth century by Christians in a pious rage to wipe out all traces of the "heathen" culture. Of the few works of Maya lore that have been preserved, the most notable are the *Chilam Balam* ("Jaguar Priest") books of Yucatan and the *Popol Vuh* ("Council Book") of Guatemala. The Chilam Balam books, written down after the Spanish conquest, contain material on the Maya shamans as well as some prophecies and historical material.

Popol Vuh
The Popol Vuh abounds in mythical creatures of unsurpassed imagination and creativity. It narrates how the gods created the world and, after three unsuccessful attempts, how they finally created humans in order to have someone visit their shrines, give them offerings, and call them by name. In addition to recounting the origin of rituals for the veneration of ripened corn and deceased relatives, the Popol Vuh contains stories of tribal wars and records of historical rulers. It depicts the duel of an elder pair of hero brothers who are defeated by netherworld demonic powers, yet later avenged by a younger pair of hero brothers. These younger hero twins undergo boyhood trials, discover their true calling, descend into the underworld, and gain ultimate victory over the Lords of Death.

The Maya Story: The Hero Twins and Sacrifice

The story of these younger hero twins, Hunahpu and Xbalanque, begins when their father and uncle, themselves twins, offend the lords of Xibalba (the Underworld) with the noise they make while playing ball. The father and uncle, One Hunahpu and Seven Hunahpu, are lured by the lords of the Underworld, Death and Seven

Death, with the challenge of a ball game. With the home court advantage, the lords plan to defeat them, injure them, and steal their ball equipment. Since the lords riddle the path to the underworld with traps, the elder twins fail to maneuver past all the obstacles and do not arrive in time for the game. The demons of the underworld therefore call off the ball game and instead sacrifice the twins the next day. They bury the twins at the Place of Ball Game Sacrifice, except for the severed head of One Hunahpu, which is placed in the fork of a tree that stands by the road. Immediately transformed, the head is indistinguishable from the calabash gourd-like fruits of the tree.

A maiden, Princess Blood, happens by and admires the tree, desiring to pluck one of the gourds. The head in the midst of the tree questions her if she indeed wishes the gourd. When she replies affirmatively, the head spits in her hand, making her pregnant in this fashion with the younger pair of twins. While the fragrance of the burning blood-red sap of a rubber tree stupefies the lords of Xibalba, she is able to escape from the underworld to earth.

Her twin sons, Hunahpu ("Hunter with Blowgun") and Xbalanque ("Jaguar Sun"), quickly get involved in an amazing series of adventures. They kill Seven Macaw with a blowgun, and then pull out his teeth and remove metal disks from around his eyes. They make a mountain fall on the chest of one of Seven Macaw's sons, and lure his youngest son ("Earthquake") to his death by having him follow the delicious aroma given off by roasted birds. The twins even get revenge on their half-brothers who had pulled some pranks on them. After they kill some birds with blowguns, they persuade their half-brothers to climb up into a tree where the birds have been snared. As they climb, the tree grows taller and bigger. The half-brothers call out in fright because they can't climb back down. Hunahpu and Xbalanque tell them to loosen their loincloths, tie them below their stomachs, and pull the long ends from behind. They do so, but the loincloth ends become tails, and the half-brothers are turned into monkeys.

These escapades are merely training exercises for their real heroic adventure, the vindication of the deaths of their father and uncle. They capture a rat, who in exchange for a share of stored crops, reveals to them that their father and uncle have left a set of ball game equipment (rings, gloves, and rubber balls) tied up under the rafters of the house. When they begin playing ball with this equipment at the Great Abyss, they disturb the lords of Xibalba, just like their father and uncle before them. Summoned to the underworld, they leave behind some ears of corn for their grandmother. These are to be kept as a sign that corn remains alive throughout the year, even between the drying out of the plants at harvest time and the sprouting of new ones after planting. They teach their grandmother how to ensure the fertility of the corn by burning incense before the consecrated ears of seed corn.

When the twins come to a crossroads on the descent to Xibalba, they do not fall for the tricks that had killed their father and uncle. In the ball game the next day, the Xibalbans insist on putting their own ball into play first. The ball is covered with crushed bone and has a weapon hidden inside: This is the White Dagger, the instrument of sacrifice. After playing well for a while, the twins allow themselves to lose. Their penalty is to spend the night in Razor House, which is full of blades looking for something to cut. They then have to survive stays in Cold House, Gloom House, Fire House, and other houses of ordeal. At Bat House, Hunahpu's head is taken off by a bat. After Xbalanque replaces the head with a carved squash, the twins are ready to play ball again. The Xibalbans put the original head into play as the ball. Xbalanque is able to retrieve it secretly when it is hit into the woods and put it back atop Hunahpu's shoulders. The squash he substitutes for the ball eventually wears out and splatters seeds on the court, revealing to the lords of Xibalba that they have been played for fools.

Knowing that the lords of Xibalba are devising a plan to burn them for their trick, the twins instruct two seers on what to say when the Lords seek advice on how to dispose of their remains. The twins accept an invitation to see a great stone pit where the Xibalbans are cooking the ingredients for an alcoholic beverage. Skipping a challenge to leap clear across the pit, the boys jump right in, cutting the deadly game short. Thinking they have triumphed, the Xibalbans follow the advice of the seers and grind the bones of the boys and spill the powder into a river. After some days the twins reappear, though, disguised as vagabond actors. They gain fame as illusionists, setting fire to a house without burning it and performing a sacrifice without killing the victim. Unaware of their true identity, the underworld lords invite the two actors to show their skills at court. The twins accept with pretended reluctance. The climax of their performance comes when Xbalanque sacrifices Hunahpu, rolling his head out the door, removing his heart, and then bringing him back to life.

Thrilled by the experience, the lords go wild with delight and demand that they themselves be sacrificed: "Do the same with us—immolate us also." They too want to experience the thrill of rebirth. The twins oblige—but this time their sacrifices are real and they do not restore the demons to life. The twins reveal their true identities and declare that from now on the offerings received by any Xibalbans will be limited to animals or to incense made of sap. From now on, Xibalbans will have to limit their attacks on human beings to those who have weaknesses or guilt.

After their speech to the defeated Xibalbans, the twins go to the Place of the Ball Game Sacrifice to revive Seven Hunahpu, their elder, whose head and body still lie buried there. The full restoration of his face depends on his ability to pronounce the names of all the facial parts. He can get no further than the mouth, nose, and eyes, though, so the twins have to leave him in the land of the dead. They do promise that humans will remember his day. Hunahpu and Xbalanque are then glorified by becoming the moon and sun.

The Story Magnified

Center of the World

Archaeological remains testify to the ceremonial character of the Maya ball game. Ball courts were included within ritual centers and associated with special temples. Figures and reliefs represented the ball players adorned with elaborate ritual decorations and headdresses. Through their history, Hunahpu days were set aside for the veneration of the dead, as promised by the twins, and graveyards were called by the same word as the ball courts of the Popol Vuh. The ball game was a ritual, then, that took place at the mythological center of their world. It was performed at their axis mundi, the place around which the whole world turns, in order to command greater immediacy and attention of the gods.

Played at the heart of the universe, the Maya ball game had astronomical significance. The ball court represented the center of the universe where the divine beings played with the stars as their ball. While the hero twins symbolized the sun and the moon, the flying ball represented the motion of the stars and planets. These celestial movements signaled seasonal changes as well as the daily cyclical interchange of the sun and moon. The Maya tradition holds that civilization, like the cosmos itself, is enmeshed in an ongoing cycle of creation, destruction, and recreation.

A disc of a ballplayer from an altar in Chiapas shows the Maya enthusiasm for sport contests of skill, strength, and perseverance.

Recreation

The Maya considered recreation an essential part of their civic life. The ball court presented a circumscribed area of controlled striving and, in a limited sense, was a model of the good society where rules were respected and excellence was rewarded. As a small universe of rule-regulated behavior, the ball court always maintained a conspicuous and important place in their city plans. The enclosed place was a vestigial memory of paradise, a place of freedom and play.

Purifying themselves before the game in a ritual sweathouse and uttering incantations over their equipment, the Maya were deadly serious in their ritual ball game. The sport contests of skill, strength, or perseverance were a ritual that incorporated discipline, dedication, and enthusiasm, good for both body and spirit. Their skilled exertion, movement, and bodily grace stretched their human boundaries and provided an intense drama for human excellence. The game piqued their awareness of the pains and joys of life and death. Death was not disguised or evaded; instead, it was recognized as simply the end of the game. Their play transcended time, evoking that fragile moment in which they experienced a oneness between themselves, their community, and the universe.

Sacrifice

Sacrifices were crucial to the twins' ball game. The lords' ball was a skull with the instrument of sacrifice hidden inside. When the twins lost a game they had to survive a sojourn in the sacrificial Houses. There were sacrifices when they jumped into the stone pit and when Hunahpu's head was taken off by a bat.

The murals on the ball court at Chichen Itza also contain several hints of the importance of sacrificial death, and a gold disk dredged from the sacred cenote depicts the ceremony of removing the heart. On one frieze, the blood of one who lost, represented by snakes and quetzal (bird) feathers, fans out from a decapitated body. Many victims were sacrificed on the playing field itself, with the decapitation performed either by the shaman-priests or ballplayers dressed in jaguar attire. The skull of the victim was placed on a pole at the ball court in a ritual reenactment of the execution of One Hunahpu, whose head was placed in a calabash tree. The victim's sacrifice to the gods ensured the fertility of the land and the people.

For centuries, scholars believed that sacrificial victims, most frequently children or virgins, were thrown into the sacred cenote at Chichen Itza while still living or with their hearts already torn out. The understanding was that it was customary to smear the hearts and blood of the victims on the face of the idol that received the sacrifice, with the idea that the gods fed on the offering. Today, however, most scholars believe that this is romantic fiction. People did die there, but not necessarily as offerings. Recent exploration of the well has revealed hundreds of tiny rubber dolls that were probably propitiating images thrown down during certain ceremonies. The famous sacrificial cenote was probably not a place of human slaughter, but of symbolic sacrifice to the gods.

The Maya Story Exemplified

Twentieth Century

Survival. The crumbling pyramids, vine-shrouded walls, and fallen monuments of the Maya are scattered over Latin America. Not much has been done to improve the lot of the surviving Maya since the Spanish conquerors imposed a colonial economic, political, and cultural system in the sixteenth century. Their blood diluted and their past forgotten, the Maya manage to survive in scattered villages, having lost much of their highly developed cultures and brilliant civilizations. Guatemala remains the heartland of Maya civilization with three million Maya, more than the other countries with Maya heritage (Mexico, Belize, Honduras, and El Salvador).

The Maya have suffered massacres over the centuries, especially as the result of various peasant uprisings that attempted to set up communal local governments. Especially burdensome was the War of the Castes, in which they struck back at hacienda owners in a prolonged revolt that officially ended with an uneasy peace in 1901. With the Mexican Revolution of 1910, the Maya regained most of their ancestral property, which had gradually passed into the hands of the Ladinos (Mexicans of Spanish descent).

Suffering from hunger, unemployment, and economic injustices, the Maya manage to survive today in scattered villages.

Human Rights. The Maya today are mainly campesinos (poor farmers) who still practice slash and burn cultivation, dependent on the sometimes benevolent, sometimes cruel and capricious behavior of nature. Similar to the majority of people in other Latin American countries, they suffer from hunger, unemployment, inhuman living conditions, infant mortality, and diseases. Hunger and economic injustices are rampant and keenly felt. Wealth is concentrated in the hands of a few, and multinational corporations, who want cheap natural resources and cheap labor, make the network of oppression still larger. Overt racism and appalling poverty make the structures even more oppressive.

Widespread devotion to the Blessed Virgin of Guadalupe testifies how the Maya combine their ancient beliefs with Christianity.

The religion of Latin America today is primarily Christian. Fundamentalist missionaries have recently been successful in converting some to their form of Protestantism. By and large, however, the most visible Christian movement in Latin America is liberation theology. To correct a situation where humans are thoroughly exploited, systematically and legally despoiled of their humanity, the people have turned to this grassroots approach, and small charismatic communities committed to social action—base communities—have sprung up all over Latin America. These small groups study the Christian Scriptures to apply them to their experiences. The groups attempt to confront injustices through collective action wherever possible. They strive to create a society where justice, peace, and love are not just preached but also practiced. They stress the social, political, and even revolutionary dimension of Jesus' teachings and deeds. They believe in God neither as all-powerful nor as a powerless sufferer, but a God who has shown a "preferential option for the poor."

Ritual: Carnival

The descendants of the Maya still practice the sacred rituals of their ancestors. They offer corn tortillas to their ancestral gods who live inside the mountains. They ceremoniously mix ground corn with water, pour it into gourds and pass it around as a holy drink for the Chacs. Corn is not only a staple of food and drink: It is a miracle gift, the sunbeam of the gods, and its kernels a means of divination.

Once the Maya had been coerced into Catholicism by Spanish threats of violence, they found the new religion remarkably compatible with their own. Catholic ritual seemed quite familiar, though more abstract than the blood sacrifice practiced by Maya priests. They associate the sun with Christ and the moon with the Virgin Mary. Catholic saints have become the supernatural guardians of Maya fields, homes, and health, and shamans fuse them together with the mountain gods in their prayers. Mounds of shelled corn in the fields bear small wooden crosses at harvest time, and storage bins of corn are topped with crosses in the family compound.

Carnival, a major religious festival among the surviving Maya in Chiapas, shows how a combination of ancient beliefs and Spanish Catholicism still permeates their lives. At this springtime festival, groups of men parade around dressed in bright red costumes that mimic the vestments of bishops. While some people wear images of Christ, the Blessed Virgin, and the saints, others wear carnival masks rigid with expressions of Maya valor and Spanish greed. Carnival gives the people a strong sense of community that imparts meaning and constancy to their lives. Their revelry fills them with religious passion and prepares them for Lent and Holy Week, building in intensity toward Good Friday, when they ritually share in the sufferings of Jesus.

Like their ancestors before them, the Maya continue to measure the count of time, discerning a meaning for the present out of the patterns of the past. Though their religion has been altered through interaction with Christianity, they still retain their rituals and their master stories. Many religious cultures throughout the world have intermingled with Christianity over the centuries. Some have lost their traditions altogether, some have retained them, and some have combined them with Christianity in fascinating and exciting ways. In studying the Baganda people of Uganda we find an interesting example of blending that has been at times a difficult struggle and at times a splendid affair.

Setting the Scene: Uganda

The Kabaka's Tomb

On the outskirts of Kampala, the capital city of Uganda, near vast papyrus swamps and plains of elephant grass, the rutted road runs by banana groves and densely packed cardboard and tin shacks up to the sacred burial ground of Kabaka (King) Mutesa I. The tomb is built in the style of a vast hut in the center of a courtyard. Inside, on festive occasions, a leopard's skin is spread in front of the kabaka's spears. These spears point upward to the apex of the thatched roof, which mounts in an irregular curve more than fifty feet above the ground. Baganda women brighten the scene with their boldly colored, winged-shouldered, one-piece outfits gracefully swathed around their bodies.

The tombs of the kabakas (kings) of the people of Buganda are generally considered sacred shrines, the palaces of spiritual beings.

Founded in the fifteenth century, the Kabakaship was the central institution and dominant part of the religious system in the kingdom of Buganda (the source of the name "Uganda"). The people believed that the kabakas—thirty-five in a 500-year period—were somehow responsible for the fertility of the land and the welfare of the people. The kings were symbolically identified with the country as a whole, hence their well-being was essential to the well-being of the kingdom. The kabakas were surrounded by ritual prohibitions that were intended to keep them in a state of health and ritual purity. Their tombs are generally considered shrines, the palaces of spiritual beings.

Christian Missionaries

The source of the Nile was discovered in the 1870s, during the reign of Kabaka Mutesa I. The first Christian (and Muslim) missionaries came to Uganda soon after, at the king's request. The pioneer Anglican (British) and Catholic (French) missionaries were opposed to each other on religious and political grounds, but both groups thought that everything African—religious practices, morals, dress, music, dance—was uncivilized. In spite of these deterrents, the missionaries converted the majority of the Baganda to Christianity over the next century, bringing them better knowledge of health care and medical care. The missionaries also aided development in many other areas: education, the economy, clothing, houses, and food. Though the traditional local religious systems still remain the basis of social and cultural life, there are virtually no people in the region who are unaffected by Christianity (or Islam).

Uganda

Like many African nations, Uganda is the product of imaginative lines arbitrarily drawn on maps by European colonial officials. Rich in minerals, climate, and fertile soil, with dense jungles, dusty plains, and snowcapped mountains, Uganda is home to more than a dozen tribes, mainly agrarian but also pastoral. Uganda was formed at the end of the nineteenth century when four kingdoms of diverse peoples—long divided against each other and each having its own history, language, and traditions—were grouped together under British protection. The most prominent and politically centralized of these Bantu kingdoms of Uganda was Buganda. The Baganda tribe, which formed the kingdom of Buganda, is still the largest tribe in Uganda today, comprising more than a quarter of the sixteen million people there. The Kabakaship of the Baganda was outlawed when Uganda was declared a republic in 1967.

Faith and African Gods

African Traditional Religion

There are about 1000 tribes in Africa, each with its own religious system and cultural practices. Because the traditional societies are sometimes pastoral, sometimes agricultural, and sometimes hunting cultures, and because their religions are self-contained and apparently unrelated, it is impossible to describe them as one "African religion." The African religions have no sacred writings, no definitive creeds or dogmas concerning beliefs and practices, and no individual founders or reformers (with the exception of individual cults). Consequently, there is great flexibility and tolerance for pluralism.

The religious dimension pervades all aspects of life in African societies: To be human is to be religious. African systems of meaning and values—including their tools and utensils, architecture, work activities, clothing, hair styles, kinship structures, and language— are centered more in humans than in gods or in nature. Ideally, humans have within their power the means for a happy and significant life. They find fulfillment as participants in family and community relationships, in their stories, rituals, festivals, dances, artistic expression, and deep respect and veneration for ancestors.

In African traditional religions the gods are both close and remote. The gods have created everything and are present everywhere in creation directly or indirectly, through nature and human ancestral spirits. Each tribe has its god who is close and continues "to blow life into human beings all the time" or "snaps off their pumpkin" and "stops them from snoring any more" when they die. By and large, though, the Absolute Reality is remote. After creating the world, the high god retires from the detailed affairs of daily human existence. This ultimate principle behind all things usually has no cult, images, temples, or priesthood. In matters concerning everyday affairs, the lesser gods and ancestors are more immediately involved.

The Baganda Gods

Prior to the coming of Christianity, the Baganda saw their gods in the same way they saw their kabaka, who traditionally ruled the people through ministers to whom he delegated certain powers. The common people had little contact with the gods. Their creator god was the Master and Giver of life, the Supernatural Shepherd, the Great Eye that sees all things, and the Omniscient Owner of the sky. When the rain was heavy and lightning severe, the Baganda made smoky fires to keep the clouds from falling, and they beat drums to let Gulu, the god of heaven, know where they were, so that he would not hurt them with lightning. Only the kabaka could make offerings to Walumbe, the god of death, in order to prevent him from killing people wholesale. In principle, over seventy tribal gods were available to the Baganda people.

Among the goddesses, Nalwayga's chief function was to assist childless women to become mothers. The Baganda took samples of their withered fruits to the temple of Nagawonyi, the goddess of hunger, to show her how needy they were. She was able to end drought or famine because of her influence with Gulu. The Baganda people hold the "lubaale" in high esteem. These were the hero gods who were once historical figures noted for their skill and bravery and afterwards deified and invested with supernatural powers by the people. The Baganda gods are still consulted today about a variety of personal troubles, such as illness, crop failure, loss of money, and loss of employment.

Human Salvation: The Baganda

The Problem: Witchcraft

The Baganda believe that humans are largely responsible for their own misfortunes whenever they create tension, disharmony, or disruption within the community, especially the family. Many sufferings in life, including demonic possession, sickness (e.g., smallpox), and death are due in part to evil human intentions. When anyone breaches the community's customs, laws, or regulations, or breaks the taboos that govern conduct in society, they are committing evil, for they are injuring and destroying the accepted social order and peace. Where the sense of corporate life is so deep, the solidarity of community relations must be maintained. Otherwise, there is disintegration and destruction because the powers that originated everything eventually get used up.

Evil also arises when humans offend their dead ancestors. The ghosts of the dead are more concerned to punish than reward and they are responsible for witchcraft and sorcery. When the ghosts of the dead lose their links with humans, or are not properly buried, or have a grudge, or are neglected and not obeyed, they take revenge and punish the offenders by bringing evil into the world. The Baganda people fear the ghosts who are active in the world, diffused like the wind, bringing calamity to those who injured or offended them while they were alive. They will not approach the heights of the Mountains of the Moon because ghosts dwell there. They try to prevent road-builders from felling certain holy trees inhabited by ghosts, for fear that the life of the whole village will be endangered.

The Strategy: Divination

The Baganda, even those who are Christian, often still visit the Bafumu (medicine men or witch doctors) for diagnosis and protective medicine against witchcraft and misfortune. They pay a fee to the Bafumu, who practice divination through oracles, trances, and consultation of omens. The Bafumu tell what remedies are needed and what additional costs are involved to make the remedy effective. The remedies are usually certain medicines or the performance of a ritual action or sacrifice. Customarily, sacrifices are the offerings of an animal (cow, goat, or chicken) and banana beer that is sprayed over the participants as a blessing.

The Solution: Obuntu ("Humanization")

Rather than speak of overcoming evil and suffering through salvation in an afterlife, the Baganda speak of the acquisition of Obuntu ("humanization"). Obuntu is really the process of human self-transcendence. Whatever else salvation might be, it is first and foremost a process by which the high god turns humans into beings possessing essential humanity, capable of morally responsible choices, kindness, tolerance, patience, generosity, and forgiveness. The god, propitiated by sacrifices, brings renewal to human affairs here and now and makes the people capable of respect, freedom, responsibility, wonder, and worship. This in turn helps the people reestablish contact and communion with their sacred beings, ancestors, and other sources of power.

The Baganda do not expect the future to usher in a golden age or a radically different state of affairs. Indeed, the future has no existence, since it has not yet acquired any concrete reality. The Baganda do not long for spiritual redemption or for closer contact with God in the next world. The best and most fulfilling life for human beings is to be found here on earth, nowhere else. Life after death is not a time of extinction, but a period full of activities and happenings going off into the distant past. The afterlife is the inevitable continuation of life, generally no better or worse than life in the present world.

African Sacred Stories

In traditional African religions, beliefs and traditions exist in people's hearts and minds, in their stories and their rituals, rather than in sacred texts. The most extensive accounts of African myths are found scattered in monographs written in the early decades of the twentieth century. These monographs contain the data gathered by anthropologists and ethnologists who lived among the people to learn their languages and ways of life. Revealing religious traditions that are both rich and compelling, these reports are superior to earlier ones by explorers, tradesmen, and naturalists who had only a marginal interest in religious matters, and those of missionaries who, though better qualified to investigate religious beliefs, were too often prejudiced by contempt or pity for the "heathen."

African stories evoke a religious experience without which life itself is diminished in spirit and purpose. The stories have a sense of immediacy, for the features of their ways of life and accumulated wisdom are held in the minds and memories of the living members. Their main focus is to teach proper values and maintain the proper patterns of group life. The stories explain and give the weight of supernatural origin and authority to tribal customs, ceremonies, and beliefs.

In the stories of the Baganda people, the cultural hero and first ancestor is Kintu. Exciting stories about Kintu describe the many trials he has to undergo before he can marry the daughter of the sky god Gulu and the many struggles he endures in his unsuccessful attempt to keep death from coming into the world.

The Baganda Story: Kintu and Death

When Kintu first comes to Uganda, the only food he can find is the little that his one cow supplies him. He builds a small hut and lives for some time on the products of his cow, till one day he sees the sons of Gulu and their sister, Nambi, coming down from the sky. When Nambi notices Kintu, she quickly falls in love with him. "Kintu is good," she tells her brothers, "I like him—let me marry him." They demur, asking whether she is sure that he is really a human being. Nambi replies that she knows he is a man because animals don't build huts. She tells Kintu: "I love you, Kintu; let me go home and tell my father that I have seen a man in the jungle that I would like to marry." Still objecting to the marriage, her brothers tell their father that Kintu does not eat ordinary food and is certainly a suspicious character.

Gulu decides to test Kintu before he will consent to the marriage. He steals Kintu's cow, and Kintu is forced to eat different kinds of herbs. Nambi finds the cow, though, and goes back to earth to invite Kintu to return and take it back. When Kintu reaches heaven,

Nambi's brothers persuade their father to test him further to see if he really is worthy of her. They cook up an enormous meal of mashed plantain and a thousand bulls, along with a thousand gourds of banana beer to drink. Kintu is locked in a house where he has to eat everything or be killed as an imposter. What can he do with the leftovers? Suddenly the earth in the middle of the house magically opens up, Kintu throws the superfluous food into the pit, and the earth closes back over it. He then calls the people to take away the empty baskets.

Other trials quickly follow. Gulu makes Kintu cut firewood from a rock and fetch water that comes from dew. Next Kintu has to pick out his cow from the herd. How can he do this from a herd of twenty thousand? His helper this time is a large bee that buzzes in his ear: "The one whose horns I alight on is yours." Kintu watches the bee go through different herds till it finally settles on his cow. Then he claims the cow. The bee next perches on some calves (which his cow has produced). Kintu claims them too. Gulu is amazed and finally laughs: "Kintu, you are a wonder; take your cows; no one can deceive or rob you, you are too clever for that. Take my daughter who loves you, marry her, and go back to your home on earth."

Gulu strongly warns Nambi not to turn back once they leave heaven for their home on earth if she wants to live in eternal peace and happiness with Kintu and the children that will be born to them. They must not return, even if they have forgotten something. "Hurry back to earth before Walumbe (Death, one of Gulu's sons) comes; he will want to go with you, and will only cause you trouble and unhappiness." On their way to earth, Nambi tearfully tells Kintu that she has forgotten the grain for the chickens: "I must go back for the grain for the fowl, or they will die." Kintu tries in vain to dissuade her: "Your brother Death will be on the watch and see you." Refusing to listen to her husband, she returns to heaven to get the chicken feed, thus disobeying Gulu's command. Though she tries to steal away to earth unnoticed, her brother Death trails her down from heaven.

Nambi and Kintu have several children. One day Death demands that Kintu send one of his daughters to be his cook. Kintu refuses. Death is silent and goes away, but again repeats his demand, and again Kintu refuses. Death seeks vengeance: "I will kill the children." Kintu hears this, but doesn't know what it means. Shortly after, one of the children falls ill and dies, and from then on the children begin to die at intervals. Kintu returns to Gulu and accuses

Walumbe of being the cause of the deaths of the children. Gulu replies: "I told you so. If only you had obeyed me, you would not have lost any of your children." After Kintu's further entreaties, Gulu sends Death's brother Kaikuzi ("Digger") to prevent him from killing any more children. Gulu commands Death to return to heaven, but he refuses to go without his sister Nambi. Kaikuzi tries to take Death away by force, but Death slips from his hands and takes refuge underground.

Kaikuzi and Death struggle for some time. At last Kaikuzi feels he can capture Death, so he tells the people to remain in their houses and not to let the animals out while he goes on a final hunt. He further tells them that if they see Death they must not call out nor raise any cry of fear. Just as Kaikuzi is about to capture his brother, some boys see Death in the goat pasture and call out in fright. Thus warned, Death escapes underground. Kaikuzi complains to Kintu that he is tired of hunting Death and wants to return home. Realizing that nothing more can be done, Kintu thanks Kaikuzi for his help and hopes that at least Death will not kill all the people: "If he wants to kill humans, let him—I, Kintu, will not cease begetting children, so that Death will never be able to make an end of my people." From that time Death has been allowed to remain on earth and kills people whenever he can.

The Story Magnified

Family and Kinship

Nambi's brothers investigate Kintu and handle the arrangements for her engagement. Her father Gulu tests Kintu before giving his consent. Her brother Walumbe wants to accompany her to earth after the marriage. This family or clan involvement is still current in Uganda: The two families of the couple still come together to make arrangements and exchange gifts prior to the marriage. Kinship creates a sense of sacred obligation to the clan and determines the behavior of individuals to each other. The kinship system cushions the people against calamity and develops a feeling of deep rootedness. They extend their sense of solidarity even to plants, animals, and non-living objects, and each clan has its own "life-carrier" or "totem"—a frog, grasshopper, or monkey, for example. Kinship, reckoned through blood and marriage, is still a strong force in the family groups, though the sense of belonging to a specific clan is gradually disappearing.

The Present

Gulu strongly warns the couple not to turn back once they leave heaven for their home on earth if they want to live in eternal peace and happiness. They must not return, even if they have forgotten something. When Nambi discovers that she has forgotten the grain for the chickens, however, she is compelled to return to heaven for the grain. This is characteristic of Ugandan life, which is an existence-in-relation here and now. Individuals consciously bind themselves, their family, their clan, and their environment together day in and day out. They maintain vital relationships with nature, the gods, ancestors, and their extended clan. The present moment is the arena of life in its fullness. They express their generous living and loving here and now in the course of day-to-day living. They do not defer anything to the unknown and unforeseeable future: Anything too far in the past or in the future has no appeal.

Rejoicing in simple human presence, the Baganda people receive visitors warmly into their mud-caked homes with straw-thatched roofs.

The concept of time in Uganda is event-centered and human-centered rather than linear. Moments are charismatic, not chronological. Because the present moment is central, the people fill their encounters with each other with significance. They enjoy each other's presence without fuss or pressure, whether in conversation or in silence. Visitors are never an interruption. They just enjoy every moment they can. I have seen children chase each other aimlessly through the elephant grass on an endless summer day, as though they had all the time in the world. The people in Uganda understand human presence as a debt they owe each other. In the afternoons, after teaching religion to high school boys or collecting statistics at the local hospital, I would relax on the veranda overlooking Lake Victoria. A dozen or so young children came by each day on their way home from school. They would come onto the porch and just kneel down beside my chair, up to half an hour, without saying a word. There was an extraordinary stillness and reverence in their presence, and they exuded a joy just to be seen with and recognized by another human being.

Death

Nambi and Kintu break Gulu's taboo for chicken feed. By returning to heaven they bring death into the world. Since then, death has remained upon the earth and kills people whenever possible. Not even married love, indeed, not even the god Gulu can take away death or save humans from dying. For the Baganda, dying is like packing up their bags and moving on to a different residence. This does not mean that they are not afraid of death. In fact, their fear of death is almost reverential. Rather than bury a dog killed by a car on the road, for example, they are careful to throw grass and sticks on it, thinking that they can prevent the evil spirits of the dead from escaping. In the days before independence, Ugandans buried parts of the body of a deceased kabaka (his saliva, nails, and hair) lest they be used in malicious ways, and preserved other parts of the king's dead body (his jaw, skull, and genitals) for use in ritual ceremonies or consultations with the reigning ruler. They also sacrificed people, usually prisoners. They gave their victims a special kind of drugged beer to dull their senses, then led them to the place of sacrifice and speared or clubbed them to death, leaving their bodies for the wild beasts and birds.

The Baganda believe that humans continue to exist after death and to influence the affairs of those who survive. Living persons are happier than the departed because they are alive, but the departed are more powerful. Because of their sensitivity to the spirit world, the people in Uganda bury the dead as soon as possible so that the corpse can make contact with all significant relatives. They often wrap a dead body in banana leaves, with the outer layers of plaintain stems joined together, end overlapping end, and fix it to the back of a bicycle. They then transport the corpse to a burial site, usually in the immediate vicinity of an anthill or a stream, both of which are understood as symbols of renewal and continuity of life. Though Walumbe remains on earth and kills humans whenever he can, Kintu continues to beget children and life goes on: Death will never be able to make an end of his people.

The Baganda Story Exemplified

Human Witnesses

In 1885-86, within ten years of the coming of the first missionaries, thirty-two African Protestants and thirteen Roman Catholics were burned to death by order of Kabaka Mwanga II. They are commemorated as the first Christian martyrs of Uganda. There may have been another hundred whose names are not known, who were willing to suffer brutal martyrdom rather than betray their new-found Christian faith. They went to their deaths with the praises of the Christian God on their lips. Earlier, Mwanga's father Mutesa I had martyred several dozen Muslim converts because of the zealousness of their faith and the threat it posed to his exercise of authority. With this precedent, Mwanga II did not hesitate to kill Christians when they ventured to rebuke him for his vices. Suspicious of their independent behavior and absolute faith, and furious that they placed their Christian faith above their allegiance to the throne, Mwanga used the excuse that they gave him an "improper greeting" when he returned from a trip. Each one was executed individually: The wood was piled higher and higher on their pyres, and they were burned slowly so the flames would cause great pain.

Twentieth Century

Modernization. The people in Uganda, like most African peoples, are scrounging for scraps of modern life. Their patterns of family and social life, their system of education and upbringing, their modes of production and daily life, have all undergone erosion. The drums of modern communications and mass media are beating a new and rapid rhythm, and nothing can slow down its tempo. They find themselves dancing between two positions: the traditional solidarity that has supplied their land, customs, ethics, rites of passage, customary laws, religious participation, and historical depth, and a modern way of life that has not yet acquired any solidarity. The role of traditional religious values and insights has in many cases been undermined by political conflict and divisions among various groups and newly established nations.

Human Rights. Uganda gained independence in 1962 and a new constitution in 1967. After Idi Amin's ascendance to power in a coup d'état in 1971, Uganda went through a period of misrule, economic decline, social disintegration, massive violations of human rights, and the murder of 300,000 tribal rivals. Idi Amin was overthrown eight years later by the Uganda National Liberation Army and succeeded by Milton Obote. In the four-year reign of terror that followed, Uganda became a mass killing field as Obote slaughtered more than 500,000 tribal foes. The majority of his victims were Baganda people whose skulls and bones Obote placed on display for years along rural highways. Yoweri Museveni became president in 1986, vowing to end the rancorous tribalism that for two decades had stained Uganda with blood.

The roads in Uganda are filled mainly with bicycles, usually draped with bananas, but occasionally laden with corpses being transported for burial.

Ravaged by war, hatred, and repression, Uganda today continues to be unstable, still suffering the effects of an impoverished economy and from divisions within the government itself. The traditional subsistence agriculture has been gravely damaged by lack of attention, drought, and locusts. Like more than half the African nations, Uganda is poorer now than before independence. Agricultural stagnation, racial wars, and land mismanagement have brought a downward spiral of poverty and poor economic performance. There is no incentive to work because wages are so low and inflation so high. Though roads are slowly being repaired, hotels renovated, and industry restarted, most young people literally have nothing to do.

Christian missionary clinics are trying to eliminate malnutrition by showing the Ugandans how to prepare balanced meals and find sources of protein in peanuts, beans, and fried termites. The mission groups help the Ugandans dig wells and give them advice about seeds, fertilizer, and insecticides. They train the people in candle and soap making and provide treatment for widespread tropical diseases. They encourage those with any skill in reading, writing, cooking, or hygiene to teach others. These projects in development are commitments to social justice, geared to give the people a sense of their human rights.

AIDS. Wars and famines and other human rights problems have solutions, however elusive. Sadly, the same thing cannot be said about the "slim" disease, AIDS. The AIDS epidemic in Uganda is pernicious, cutting down young adults just as they are emerging from their long, dark passage of economic and social breakdown. Uganda has the highest number of identified cases of AIDS in Africa, and the number of victims is growing exponentially.

AIDS in Uganda is spread through heterosexual intercourse and affects men and women equally. The virus is often transmitted from mother to infant. The number of parentless children has escalated to the point where boarding schools and orphanages have been set up to provide for them. Suicide (often by drinking poisonous pesticides) among identified AIDS patients is growing at an alarming pace. Uganda's few hospitals cannot cope with the numbers of patients, and the traditional medicine men and witch doctors are useless. Most AIDS victims are cared for by their families, who keep vigil over them as they slowly waste away. Though public meetings are held to discuss AIDS, warning leaflets printed ("Love carefully" and "Zero grazing" are popular slogans), and an AIDS curriculum incorporated into school education, the epidemic threatens to unravel the social fabric of the nation. Whole villages are being decimated, and the nation faces genocide in the next decade.

New Christian Movements. Though about half the people in Uganda today are Roman Catholic and another third Protestant, they go back and forth to their traditional religions with a certain ease or nonchalance, especially for divination and healing practices. While missionary hospital clinics are still filled to capacity, the Christian churches have been effectively reduced to a marginal role in African politics. The mainline Christian churches are concentrating their efforts on Africanizing Christianity rather than Christianizing Africa. At the same time, several new religious movements have recently appeared and successfully organized themselves.

In this century several prophets in Uganda, possessed by local spirits, have formed independent religions or church groups as protest movements against either British colonial rule or the national government. These groups seem to get closer than missionary Christianity to traditional African aspirations and religiosity. Possessing a messianic and charismatic authority, the leaders preach a message of hope and healing and promise a new society free of sickness and poverty. The Balokole ("the Saved Ones") are a prominent revivalist and fundamentalist movement within the Protestant churches of Uganda. Their evangelism is uncompromising and their proselytizing aggressive. The Seventh Day Adventists also crisscross Uganda, spreading the vision of a fiery apocalypse. For people who have lived through Uganda's bloodthirsty dictatorships, it is not hard to accept the notion that the end of the world is at hand.

One popular prophet in Uganda in the late 1980s has been Mama Alice Lakwena. With a strange mixture of Christian theology and African witchcraft, she has attracted a band of followers who refer to her as "her Holiness." Lakwena (the name means "messiah"), they believe, was sent by God to preach the gospel of the Holy Spirit, to heal people, and to topple the Ugandan government. Her Holy Spirit movement is filled with puritanical rigor: The members are forbidden to smoke, drink, have sexual relations, or take medicine. Her troops, which number in the thousands, are armed only with sticks and stones: They do not fire bullets in battle but only sing hymns, relying on the Holy Spirit to protect them. They believe that their wads of mud and bean paste will turn into grenades and that they can ward off the bullets fired by government soldiers by coating themselves with oil. Their weapons and defenses have been useless, though, and Mama Alice's religious group has been reduced drastically by death and desertion.

Ritual: Marriage

Rites of passage are the very foundation of African religions. They accompany changes in social position and in the individual life cycle. Through these rites the African tribes have moved their people into new social roles and maintained significant patterns in their enduring social institutions. The tribes publicly mark life's critical moments—birth, puberty, marriage, old age, death, and ancestor-hood—with suitable observances to impress the significance of the transitions on the individual and the community. Many of these rites have lost much of their former importance and are performed somewhat perfunctorily today. Still, they contain valuable lessons, as we can see by examining the Baganda marriage ritual as it exist-ed prior to Christianity.

The marriage ritual began when the suitor approached a girl, usually in her teens, with a present of meat or salt. If she accepted the offering, he would address himself to her brother who then con-sulted with a paternal uncle regarding possible marriage. If ap-proved, the suitor took an oath to treat her well, not desert her, and not to wander from one chief to another.

The girl then performed the legally binding action of the mar-riage: She poured out beer for her brother and uncle to drink. She then promised to be faithful to her husband and to cultivate a gar-den and cook for him. The uncle and the brother then told the girl's parents that their daughter was engaged to be married and told them about the suitor and his circumstances. The clan was called to-gether to settle the dowry amount—usually goats, pots of beer, and blankets, but especially the hundreds of brightly colored cowrie shells (a type of currency), which were precious and hard to get.

The bride began the day she was to be taken to her new home by going to the well, drawing a pot of water for her mother, gathering a bundle of firewood, and bringing sweet-smelling grass to carpet her parents' floor. After being arrayed with ornaments, she was car-ried to the bridegroom's house. That first night, as a sign of mutual affection, she had to demand cowrie shells several times and he then had to provide them. This occurred upon entering, sitting down, eating the evening meal, and again before retiring to bed. After the marriage was consummated on the third night, the husband sent the marriage blanket to his in-laws along with a present of goat meat.

The young bride stayed in seclusion for some weeks after the marriage. Afterward she would sit near the door for several days so that her husband's male friends could call and offer congratula-tions. Finally the bride was allowed to visit her own family. On this visit her parents gave her a chicken—an indispensable act that re-minds us of Nambi and Kintu but, more important, served as the fi-nal ratification of the marriage. On her return to her husband, she presented him with the fowl and cooked him a feast, a token that she accepted him as her lord. The last ritual act of the marriage was the young wife's visit to the bridegroom's mother. Going at dawn, she was given a hoe and told to dig in the garden. She had to continue until the mother-in-law sent for her to come and eat. Given a present, she then returned home.

The Stories Appropriated

The Maya and Baganda stories of the twins' ball game and Kintu's marriage and struggle against death provide a context for meaning for us who are outside those traditions. The stories present new ways for us to envision our own spiritual convictions. Reading about sacrifice and dying challenges us to respond in a personal way to our own religion on the basis of transformed decisions.

Conquering Time

Time had special significance both for the Maya and the Baganda. The Maya calendar helped them celebrate religious festivals and told them when to perform social activities. The Baganda consider the present moment charismatic and they enjoy each moment as they can. In our modern society of staggered work schedules and VCRs, seasons and individual moments no longer seem to matter. Chronological time itself is something of an anachronism. Schedules are less rigid now than in the past, and there is a real possibility of a dateless, hourless, calendarless future.

The Maya and Baganda stories remind us that moments of time are fragile in their sweetness and piercing in their pain. Some moments are jagged and some are gentle, and some point toward those rare and haunting times that transcend the limitations of our own experience. Some moments emerge alone, resisting interpretation or definition. When we squeeze individual moments and hours out of our lives, the loss is a cause for regret.

Sacrifice

The sacrifices in the Maya ball game make us reflect on the need for sacrifice in our own lives. While we do not perform ritual sacrifices to appease the gods, we do have to pass through ordeals that demand sacrifice. Transitions from old to new—graduating from high school, changing jobs, marrying, moving to a new city—usually involve a period of testing and hardship. In these situations we struggle with demons to see the possibilities before us. Many times we do not know where we are headed, nor are we aware of the special tasks that our friends or our community may ask of us. If we are able to absorb and integrate the new forces we encounter through our sacrifices, we experience an almost superhuman degree of masterful control over our selves. There is a dying and a rising, a putting aside of previous goals in exchange for the challenge and stimulation of a new and higher life.

Both the story of Kintu's courtship and the Baganda marriage ritual show how humans have to endure trials in the service of love. Kintu's tasks—eating an enormous meal, cutting firewood, recovering water, picking out his cow—are a necessary part of an initiatory process of formation and struggle before he is allowed to share intimacy with Nambi. Kintu's tale is the story of the human joy born of victorious effort. Kintu says "yes" to the unknown powers that help him in his tasks—the earth that magically opens to hide his unconsumed food and the large bee that alights on the horns of his cow and its calves. Kintu's opening up to unseen powers teaches us the secret of every successful marriage. In the transition from concern for the self to love for another person, we cannot refuse to enter into a relationship that is, at its base, a mystery. In the inner world of relationships, we have to commit our selves to the unknown if we are to be successful and generate new life. The sufferings of love are a privileged mode of understanding and being.

Every married couple knows that it takes years for the initial commitment to penetrate the very distinct levels of personality: The purifying fires of love slowly sink onto deeper and deeper levels. Somehow in deep marriages wounds and sufferings undergo a kind of healing transformation. Love seems to heal, yet without violating our human integrity and independence. Married love develops a kind of mutual harmony where each intuits the other's deepest needs and aspirations.

Rites of Passage

The period of time before Kintu can marry Nambi is a time of great opportunity and great danger, with possibilities for better or for worse. The time between the Baganda girl's acceptance of the marriage proposal and her visit to her mother-in-law is also a time of decisive change. Each period is a time of engagement, a time to learn self-commitment to a loving and caring relationship with another person. All religious societies ritualize such dangerous transitional experiences of life.

The rites of transformation that accompany changes of place, state, social position, and age follow a threefold pattern. First, those undergoing the change are secluded from the others in the society where they experience a sense of loss and disorientation. The second stage is a liminal period, a time of ambiguity, in which the initiants endure some kind of suffering. In many African cultures, for example, before entering adulthood, the initiants have lines cut across their forehead that scar them forever. The painful marks indicate that the transition to adulthood is permanent, and that the society has successfully imprinted itself upon the individual. In the third stage of the ritual, the initiants are reincorporated into the society as new persons. Now they have clearly defined rights and obligations, and they are expected to behave in accordance with certain customary norms and community standards.

The Baganda marriage myth and ritual taught the people the responsibilities of their new phase of life and got them in touch with the deeper values of their own life and community. Formal rites of passage into adulthood have largely disappeared from our modern society. There are scant reminders in our marriage ceremonies, for example, of undergoing "mortal" wounds that signify the "death" of individual self-importance for the sake of the new life of the couple. Aside from a minister's occasional remarks, marriage ceremonies hardly ever recognize the ordeals involved in the transition from single life to married life. Too often engaged people today spend their time poring over the invitation list, hiring the reception hall, the musical group, the photographer, and planning the honeymoon. We have much to learn from these "primitive" people about a new life of purpose and joy that somehow inevitably, yet appropriately, encompasses all the cosmos.

Acceptance of Death

Kintu's story describes the inevitability of death in the world. Not even the high god Gulu can take away death or save humans from their fate. The story helps us realize that death is one of the necessary alternating rhythms of life, one of the many changes we go through in the process of living. Life and death are phases of the grand process of nature in which death can no more be avoided than life. Death is a turning point, a rite of passage, similar to marriage. Both accepting death as part of life and giving the self in marriage teach us to take joy in the existence of beautiful and desirable things without wanting to possess them. Though we cannot prevent death, we can still make it a part of life. It is natural that life comes to an end.

When we live with the realization that we grow older each day and that death comes as an expected guest, not as a dreaded stranger, there is a peaceful and serene submission to what cannot be changed. We are spiritually enriched if we reach this awareness before we die. We can love life before death, have passion for life in all its fullness, and take up its cause wherever it is injured, desecrated, and destroyed. We can live our lives neither as a preparation for tomorrow nor a remembrance of yesterday, where today somehow gets lost in the shuffle. We can enjoy the present with its varied tasks and distractions. Even in old age, we can enjoy adventures of the heart, mind, and spirit.

Conclusion

Both the Maya and Baganda stories teach that the inclusion of a divine dimension in human stories is not an imperfection but a necessity: It is part of their responsibility of finding the traces of divine movements in their own deeds. The Maya story of the ball game is a story of sacrifice. By placing their story and rituals at the mythological center of their world, the Maya do not disguise or evade death; instead, they recognize it simply as the end of the game. In their awareness of the sacrifices and joys of life and death, they evoke that fragile moment when they experienced a oneness between themselves, their community, and the universe.

The story of Kintu's marriage and his attempt to conquer death is the story of life as existence-in-relation. Consciously binding themselves and their environment together, the Baganda celebrate the present moment as the arena of life in its fullness and, as such, to be celebrated now. Life and death are phases of the grand process of nature in which death can no more be avoided than life.

Discussion Questions

1. Why do you think the author chooses the pyramid at Chichen Itza and the Kabaka's tomb as symbols of the Maya and Baganda religions?

2. In what ways are the Maya gods Itzamna and Chac as well as the Baganda Gulu manifestations of the Absolute Reality?

3. Summarize the Maya salvation system in terms of evil spirits, sacrifices, and harmony with life forces, and the Baganda system in terms of witchcraft, divination, and Obuntu.

4. What do the Maya stories of Hunahpu and Xbalanque teach about the religious dimensions of sacrifices and recreation?

5. Show how Kintu's sacrifices in the myths of marriage and death point to important themes in rites of passage.

6. How have the struggles for liberation theology in Latin America and against the AIDS epidemic in Uganda affected concerns for human rights in those countries?

7. What can Christians appropriate today from the Maya and Baganda stories for their own understanding of time and presence?

8. Discussion starter: "If we who presently claim to be human were to forget our efforts to find the traces of divine movements in our own actions, our fate should be something like that of the wooden people (one of the first three attempts to create humans) in the Popol Vuh. For them, the forgotten force of divinity reasserted itself by rising up against them and driving them from their homes. Today they are swinging through the trees." (Dennis Tedlock)

9. Discussion starter: "Old age is teaching me to take joy in the existence of beautiful and desirable things without wanting to possess or even savor them. I have not enjoyed the sight of beautiful women in the past as I do now. The same is true of the new magnificent buildings, paved plazas, fountains and flower beds. Life seems richer now." (Eric Hoffer, at age 73)

10. Discussion starter: "What, then, is the right way of living? Life must be lived as play, playing certain games, making sacrifices, singing and dancing, and then humans will be able to propitiate the gods, and defend themselves against their enemies, and win in the contest." (Plato)

CONCLUSION

We have studied the world's major religions through selected stories from their sacred writings, stories that radiate a deeper symbolic meaning beyond their literal wording. In their complexity they both assimilate the core experiences of their particular religious traditions and provide relevant insights for those within other religious traditions who are attempting to live spiritually.

Information

The study of these stories is informational: It increases our global awareness and helps us gain a basic knowledge of the world's major religions. The stories give vigor and intensity to each tradition's beliefs regarding Absolute Reality and to their systems of salvation and rituals. They help us understand the teachings, ethical systems, experiences, and other practices of various religious traditions. The stories show us how people express and respond to the recurrent problems and permanent mysteries of human existence, and thus find spiritual meaning, value, and self-esteem in their lives.

Though the core stories of the world's religions deal with similar themes, we cannot reduce all the religions to one voice. The more we know about the religions, the less we can maintain that they are all the same. The world's religions are complex, multidimensional phenomena, and their fundamental differences cannot be glossed over in the name of unity. Hindu interest in Dharma and Karma meet head on with Pauline freedom from the Law, for example. In contrast with the Confucian ideal of the polished sage, the details of the Muslim ideal of submission to Allah seem almost fanatical. The Buddhist quest to escape from the ceaseless cycle of birth and death confronts Jewish involvement with God in the work of a new creation and Christian concern to realize eternal life. Attempts to transform the self by letting go of the world in some religious traditions clash with attempts to transform the material world in others. Different religions place contrasting emphases on stability and freedom, punishment and reward, love and justice, rights and responsibilities. Their various expressions of faith in Absolute Reality and models of salvation are complementary.

Transformation

The study of these religious stories is also transformational: It enriches our spirituality. The stories sensitize us to themes hidden, perhaps, in our own religious traditions or in our own lives. The tap root from which religion springs is the basic human motivation to derive meaning from chaos. The stories aid that quest for meaning. In them we find intense images around which to organize and control our lives and profound symbols to broaden and heighten our struggle in the face of mystery. Stories enhance our self-esteem by showing us how mysterious and absorbing human existence can be. The truths in the religious stories are not truths for each particular tradition only: They are universal truths to which one religious tradition or another happens to call our attention in a particularly poignant way. The stories become a source of new life, creating a world unlike our own to a greater or lesser extent, and inviting us to allow the horizons of our own world to merge with those of that other world.

Each of us gives different weight to certain aspects of religion rather than others in our gradual spiritual development. At different times we may perhaps be attracted to the institutional, the intellectual, or to the experiential side of religion. At different times we place more weight on sacred writings than rituals, on ethical guidelines than doctrinal teachings, or on the origins, rather than the goals, of religion. As we grow into a mature spiritual life these dimensions all continue to flourish maximally: We become ever more fully conscious of the dimensions and closely integrate them so that they mutually enrich each other. The stories further this growth in spiritual transformation by reaching into our physical, psychological, and religious depths, and touching our deepest feelings and convictions. They affect the whole of our spiritual and religious experience, our beliefs, patterns of thought, emotions, and behavior in respect to what is ultimate.

The Religious Kaleidoscope

The stories provide a kaleidoscope through which we can perceive all our human relationships in a mature spiritual way: our relationships to God, to our selves, to others, and to the world itself.

Relationship to God. Those who strive to be spiritual recognize that the Absolute Reality pervades their very being. They realize that their experience of this Absolute Reality is fundamentally a mystery at the foundation, the center, and the end of their human existence. They actively attempt to harmonize their entire lives with this Absolute Reality that remains always surprising and never fully known. They integrate their experience of God into their motivation to carry on a full and satisfying human life. Described in an abundance of different images and ideas—as "being itself" or as "no-thing," as transcendent or immanent, as personal or impersonal—this Absolute Reality is what Christians call God. Familiar and comforting, bringing joy and deepening the passion for freedom, it is always available in communion and presence.

God widens the horizons of spiritual persons with a call that often breaks into the ordinary day-to-day activity of human existence, interrupting what has up till now seemed normal and important. Just like Moses on his wilderness journey, they are sent off by God in a completely new and perhaps disturbing direction. Their spiritual growth involves overcoming sluggishness and indifference to this call.

Though they may not, like Paul, be knocked off a horse and blinded, they suffer absolute darkness and emptiness in the call. Then comes the light, a new conviction about the way they should live. The initiative comes from God, whose action liberates and creates a new relationship that empowers them to reconcile their individual consciousness with the universal. From this new and larger perspective they find a new freedom to live, seeking only God's glory and a way of living with compassion for others. Through a conversion that brings disruption into the lives they had planned, they develop a personality focusing on the transcendent, rather than human, dimension.

This conversion requires a struggle, what Muhammad calls the "greater jihad." This is the continual holy war to conquer all that opposes God's will and to establish God's design in the world. Religious persons are the caliphs or representatives of God in this trial that will culminate in that all-embracing peace that belongs to those who are inwardly at peace with the will of heaven and outwardly at war with the forces of sin and selfishness.

Relationship to the Self. Those who strive to be spiritual struggle to transcend all self-centered needs. They set aside any selfish claim to their own lives and commit both their achievements and the many things they have left undone to the Absolute Reality, becoming enriched through personal transformation. Paradoxically, by sacrificing a part of their selves, they become completely receptive to the wonders of the universe. Their experiential horizons are broadened and their minds enlightened. Working for something with no direct reward, they possess a wider vision of human mutuality, reciprocity, and interdependence. Religion increases their self-realization, helping them to attain the highest potential of love, freedom, and other experiences of which humans are capable.

By self-forgetfulness in daily life, they attain what Hui-Neng calls liberating wisdom. This wisdom fully embraces each situation in its eternal fullness, overcoming opposition between sickness and health, riches and poverty, success and failure, life and death.

Valuing anything in the visible world primarily, if not solely, for its capability to move one forward on one's journey to the Absolute Reality parallels the martyrdom of Husain. Such martyrdom manifests the power of innocent suffering without worldly expectations, the highest degree of self-sacrifice for the sake of religious principles.

Conscious of sacrificing themselves at every moment in time, spiritual persons are what they are and they accept the consequences of being themselves. Their selflessness leads to that calmness in the midst of strife that Krishna proclaims as the beginning of restoration to divine intimacy. Through their dutiful detachment and sacrificial death, nothing—no activity, no human psychological event—can separate them from the vast texture of which they are a part.

Saying "yes" to the unknown power that helps them in their tasks, they experience a human joy born of victorious effort. Like Kintu, their passage to new life is a continual series of dyings and risings: This helps them respect the immediacy of religious experience. The present moment becomes central, and their encounters with other persons are filled with the significance of the present moment.

Relationship to Others. Those who strive to be spiritual surrender their sense of self-importance out of regard and respect for the needs of others. For them, religion promotes a form of self-transforming, other-embracing behavior. It challenges them to search for their welfare and happiness through their concern and care for others and to anchor their lives in the history of others within a community in virtue of a shared vision. This vision shapes their moral sensitivities, attitudes, and imagination. They seek to discover experiences that are ethically, politically, and religiously acts of resistance to social injustice, indeed, to all instances of social inequality between men and women and between people of one culture and another. Their engagement in promoting human welfare (for peace and human rights, against hunger and discrimination, for example) grounds their resolve and inspires their hope. This commitment extends to their care for persons and communities whose future they will not share.

They embody the compassion toward others' sufferings that Mencius believes is part and parcel of the great virtues of humaneness and justice. Their priority for reciprocal obligations and correlative responsibilities and their full commitment to wanting what is best for all gives them serenity and poise. They express respect and benevolence for others through loving, affective relations, not through impersonal and legalistic ones.

Restless until all creatures have found peace, they give generously of themselves, as Vessantara does. They live in a world of interdependence that is only realized on the basis of emptiness, where self-centeredness cannot exist. Their sense of interdependence encompasses an intense feeling for all living beings who suffer pain, anxiety, ignorance, and illusion. It places the needs of others before their own, leading them to the spiritual depths of universal compassion.

Like David, they endure a total transformation in the crucible of life. They are the constantly changing product of what they were, of what happens, what they do, and what they are called to do or undo. Undergoing reversals in life brings them a maturity manifested in their feelings of empathy with others.

Their transformation in human maturity and wisdom moves

them beyond estrangement, from revenge to forgiveness. They recognize the message of Jesus that forgiveness, not revenge, is the triumph of wisdom. Though forgiveness is a difficult social gift, they recognize that harboring resentment makes for a stunted spirituality. Forgiveness may not necessarily be an act of forgetting, but it is certainly an act of remission that allows life to go on.

Relationship to the World. Those who strive to be spiritual become attuned to the whole of creation. They participate and believe in a meaningful cosmic order and purposeful world. They regard the world with fascination and marvel, finding a spiritual presence and power in the most ordinary things and places. They regard the environment of the planet as a complex web of relationships between earth and sea and sky; between plant and animal life; between past, present, and future. By saying "yes" to the world as a whole they receive sustenance from the whole. With this power they struggle against crises that threaten the welfare—even the existence—of the world as we know it, especially the nuclear crisis that could destroy all life and future life and the ecological crisis that could destroy the life-sustaining capabilities of mother earth herself.

Having lost their self-important seriousness, they live in awareness of the cosmic dance and move in time with the cosmic dancer. Like Ganesha, they find joy and spontaneity through living in union with the cosmic player, whose play is manifested in the inexhaustible richness of the world. Their ability to perceive humor, no matter how brief the glimmer, releases them from the prison house of the self. They are free to laugh, and in that freedom their lives open up to a different light and larger perspective on the cosmos.

Their action is really non-action: They are neither intent upon results nor concerned with consciously laid plans and deliberately organized endeavors. Like Chuang-Tzu, they have an empathy with nature: They use no force or violence, no straining or pulling. Their way of life produces balance and harmony, serenity and proportion, coming spontaneously from letting things alone and not intruding their personal desires to bend events to their wishes. Their way to do is to be, effortlessly and naturally.

They are cognizant that the cosmos is enmeshed in an ongoing cycle of creation, destruction, and re-creation. Just as Xbalanque and Hunahpuh of the Maya tradition have to descend to the underworld before they can be re-created as the planets in the celestial sphere, they realize that life and death are phases of the grand process of nature in which death can no more be avoided than life. They accept death as part of life, dying to self-destroying pride, vanity, and unmerciful power and finding new and joyful life in the existence of the world around them.

Christian Appropriation

Those who are striving to develop a mature Christian spirituality attempt to embody the story of Jesus. Following Jesus and his way faithfully today, they live the same way he lived—making God present in the world with their compassionate love and message of social justice.

After studying the stories in other world religions, they remain bound by the same basic Christian story: They are still challenged to deepen their participation in the cross and resurrection and to sustain their responsibility as signs and servants of the kingdom of God. Still, the way they appropriate that story in their personal lives varies constantly with the times. In our generation their personal Christian story can find its fulfillment only through a real encounter with the riches and insights of the stories of other world religions.

The stories from the world's religions challenge Christians to reflect critically upon their own religious tradition and the contemporary world. Creative awareness of and appropriation of basic insights from other religions nourishes their spiritual growth. Their spirituality continues to grow from that foundation as it moves back and forth between prayer and social action, the two irreducibly distinct experiences of the spiritual life. Each of these is incapable, unless aided and complemented by the other, of being an adequate script for our own personal religious and spiritual stories.

READING LIST

In addition to the books on particular religions that I list below for each chapter, I want to make special mention of several overviews of the world's major religious traditions. These are not the only overviews, but they are the ones that I used extensively in writing this book. Each of them provides an abundance of detail that I can only hint at in this short book. Also, I want to mention that my source for the estimates of members for each religion is the *Encyclopaedia Britannica*, Book of the Year 1990.

Tosh Arai and Wesley Ariarajah (eds.), *Spirituality in Interfaith Dialogue* (Maryknoll, NY: Orbis Books, 1989).
   A collection of testimonies of believing Christians who have integrated spiritual disciplines from other religions into their own religious odysseys. The challenge and enrichment they received through awareness and appropriation of discoveries and insights from the other religions leads them to explore issues of social justice.

Denise Lardner Carmody and John Carmody, *The Story of World Religions* (Mountain View, CA: Mayfield Publ. Co., 1988).
   Introduces the religions through the narratives, tales, and myths, great and small, that have offered meaning and guidance to the peoples of the world. Great narratives are the sacred writings or central myths; the small narratives are scenarios from individual lives, famous or obscure. Chapters on religious traditions of prehistorical peoples, recent nonliterate peoples, early Europeans, and Marxists.

Mary Pat Fisher and Robert Luyster, *Living Religions* (Englewood Cliffs, NJ: Prentice-Hall, 1991).
   This survey of the modern religious world includes personal interviews

with followers of each tradition and incorporates extensive quotations from primary sources. Provides discussions of the feminine in religions, a chapter on surviving indigenous religions, and an original framework for understanding new religious movements.

Theodore M. Ludwig, *The Sacred Paths: Understanding the Religions of the World* (New York: Macmillan, 1989).
Thematic questions about identity, ultimate reality, human nature, and the right way to live provide background for the master stories of the religion, its historical development, its ideas and teachings, and its ritual and ethical practices.

Niels C. Nielsen, Jr. et al, *Religions of the World* (New York: St. Martin's Press, 1983).
Each religion treated by a specialist. Comprehensive treatments of the history, philosophy, social, and political aspects of religion. Theological issues are balanced with discussions of myth, ritual, and folk traditions. They pay great attention to the contributions and roles of women in the world's religions.

Leroy S. Rouner (ed.), *Human Rights and the World's Religions* (Notre Dame, IN: University of Notre Dame Press, 1988).
Reveals the critical differences in the world religions in the dynamics of human rights. A particular culture's notion of rights is not understandable without recognizing what a society believes about the individual's place in it. The contributors represent many of the major world religions.

Robert F. Weir (general editor), *The Religious World: Communities of Faith* (New York: Macmillan, 1982).
Written by a group of specialists in the major religious traditions. Concentrates on the world's living traditions. Includes separate chapters on Native American religions, African religions, and new religions in America.

I also want to cite three recent series of textbooks on world religions that provide in-depth treatment of the major world's religions.

The Prentice-Hall Series in World Religions.
Edited by Robert S. Ellwood, Jr. Specialists examine each religious tradition as a cultural system that includes historical, intellectual, ritual, and social forms. They provide insights into particular personalities, movements, and historical moments. They foster an understanding of the worldview, lifestyle, and deep dynamics of practicing religious cultures.

The Religious Life of Man Series (Wadsworth).
Edited by Frederick J. Streng. Experts present the depth and richness of religious concepts, forms of worship, spiritual practices, and social institutions in the religions. The variety of religious expressions and the similarities in

the structures of religious life are interpreted in terms of their cultural context and historical continuity.

The Religious Traditions of the World Series (Harper & Row).
Edited by Byron Earhart. They introduce an overall interpretation of the religious traditions without presupposing prior knowledge. They consider the distinctiveness of each tradition within a comparative context, discussing the history of the traditions, interpreting them as unified sets of religious beliefs and practices, and giving examples of religious careers and typical practices.

Chapter One
APPROACHES TO RELIGION

John B. Cobb, Jr., *Beyond Dialogue: Toward a Mutual Transformation of Christianity and Buddhism* (Philadelphia: Fortress Press, 1982).
An intriguing discussion of how Buddhist thought might help to reshape Christian understanding in creative ways.

Harvey Cox, *Many Mansions: A Christian Encounter with Other Faiths* (Boston: Beacon Press, 1988).
His experiences and dialogue with Hindus, Buddhists, Muslims, Jews, and Marxists broaden and deepen his conception of the divine, especially an appreciation for the feminine aspects of God. In dialogue, Christians must not downplay the particularity and centrality of Jesus.

John Hick, *An Interpretation of Religion: Human Responses to the Transcendent* (New Haven: Yale University Press, 1989).
Incorporates and integrates most of his earlier efforts on the topic of religious pluralism. Analyzes the function of religion in individual human life: the transformation of individuals from ego-centeredness to reality-centeredness.

Paul F. Knitter, *No Other Name? A Critical Survey of Christian Attitudes toward the World Religions* (Maryknoll, NY: Orbis Books, 1985).
A sincere exploration of numerous Christian responses to new awareness of the world's richly varied religious traditions.

Alan Race, *Christians and Religious Pluralism: Patterns in the Christian Theology of Religions* (Maryknoll, NY: Orbis Books, 1982).
A survey of the main explanations of the relationship between Christianity and other religions: those who think allegiance to Christ excludes other religions; those who hold that Christ is in some measure already present in other religions; and those who count the different religions as independently valid communities of faith.

Wilfred Cantwell Smith, *Toward a World Theology* (Philadelphia: Westminster, 1981).

There is an emerging religious consciousness, where persons recognize that all of us in the various discrete religions are companion participants in one human religious process. Still, participation in one particular religious community will not be superseded and the particular faiths must not be diluted.

Leonard Swidler (ed.), *Toward a Universal Theology of Religion* (Maryknoll, NY: Orbis, 1987).
A state-of-the-art account of Christian approaches to interreligious dialogue: "Though it seems that a universal theology of religions cannot be done, the work of dialogue must continue, with a playful sense of joy and discovery."

Chapter Two
STORIES IN SACRED WRITINGS

Joseph Campbell, with Bill Moyers, *The Power of Myth* (New York: Doubleday, 1988).
A combination of wisdom and wit in conversations that range from the hero's journey to modern marriage, from savior figures to virgin births. It deals with the first storytellers, the gifts of goddesses, the masks of eternity, and with the suffering that alone can open the mind to all that is hidden to others.

Robert Coles, *The Call of Stories: Teaching and the Moral Imagination* (New York: Houghton Mifflin, 1989).
The benefits of linking stories and values. Enduring stories touch universal chords of human experience and exercise the moral imagination.

Wendy Doniger, *Other Peoples' Myths* (New York: Macmillan, 1988).
Draws on biblical parables, Greek myths, Hindu epics, and modern mythologies to celebrate the universal art of storytelling and the rich diversity of stories by which people live. Myths are true stories that represent the deepest values of a culture.

Mircea Eliade, *The Sacred and the Profane* (New York: Harcourt, Brace and World, 1959).
Combines philosophical, anthropological, phenomenological, and psychological approaches to the nature and history of religion, to the significance of religious myth, symbolism, and ritual within life and culture. He traces manifestations of the sacred from primitive to modern times, in terms of space, time, nature and the cosmos, and life itself.

C.G. Jung (ed.), *Man and His Symbols* (New York: Doubleday, 1964).
Approaches to archeytpal patterns in ancient myths, legends, and primitive rituals. Jung's theory of the importance of symbolism, and his insistence that humans can achieve wholeness and be happy only when their conscious and unconscious sides have learned to live at peace and to complement one another.

Amos N. Wilder, *Theopoetic: Theology and the Religious Imagination* (Philadelphia: Fortress Press, 1976).
Theology has to relate itself not only to philosophical ideas but to symbolic life and creative impulses. For powerful new forms of spirituality, we have to get at the imagination and the deeper dynamics of the religious situation (myths and symbols) rather than doctrines and social forms.

Clemens Thoma and Michael Wyschogrod (eds.), *Parable and Story in Judaism and Christianity* (Mahwah, NJ: Paulist Press, 1989).
Experts on parables and narratives show how the ability to interpret narratives becomes a key to unlocking the deeper meaning of texts which can then be shared between different religious traditions and enrich their mutual understanding.

Chapter Three
JUDAISM: PRESENCE AND HOPE

Walter Brueggemann, *David's Truth in Israel's Imagination and Memory* (Philadelphia: Fortress Press, 1985).
Offers distinctively different modes of truth about David: the trustful truth of the tribe, the painful truth of the man, the sure truth of the state, and the hopeful truth of the assembly.

Marc H. Ellis, *Toward a Jewish Theology of Liberation* (Maryknoll, NY: Orbis Books, 1987).
Claims that normative Jewish theology community today is no longer centered on rabbinic theology, but on the issue of empowerment within the context of the Holocaust and the state of Israel.

David Hartman, *Conflicting Visions: Spiritual Possibilities of Modern Israel* (New York: Schocken Books, 1990).
Essays reflecting enthusiasm for exciting ways to expand the spirit of covenantal Judaism in the State of Israel. New opportunities for the Jews to live the Torah commandment in full visibility before the nations of the world.

Paul Johnson, *A History of the Jews* (New York: Harper & Row, 1987).
An insightful and impassioned blend of history and myth, story and interpretation, covering the impact of Jewish genius, imagination, and achievement through the ages.

Conrad L'Heureux, *Life Journey and the Old Testament: An Experiential Approach to the Bible and Personal Transformation* (Mahwah, NJ: Paulist Press, 1986).
Establishes fresh connections with the Bible's power to transform human lives. Cites both the positive contributions and limitations of the historico-critical method. Has chapters on David's story, and on the response to God's call.

Jacob Neusner, *Between Time and Eternity: The Essentials of Judaism* (Belmont, CA: Dickenson Publ. Co., 1975).
Calls for a return to rabbinic Judaism which maintains that the Torah endures amid changes and afflictions. Reform Judaism and Zionism are both dead-ends: Neither has realized its messianic promise.

Samuel Terrien, *The Elusive Presence: The Heart of Biblical Theology* (San Francisco: Harper & Row, 1978).
The presence and reality of God (rather than covenant) as basis for ecumenical theology. Interplay of a vision of the ultimate and a passion for the service of humanity as the core of scripture.

Chapter Four
CHRISTIANITY: FORGIVENESS AND FREEDOM

Robert Farrar Capon, *The Parables of Grace* (Grand Rapids, MI: Eerdmans Publ. Co., 1988).
A follow-up to his book on the parables of the kingdom. Fresh and provocative analysis of several parables, including that of the prodigal son, setting it into its immediate context and into the wider biblical context and message of grace.

John Dominic Crossan, *The Dark Interval: Towards a Theology of Story* (Niles, IL: Argus Communications, 1975).
Distinguishes between mythical religion (which gives the final word about "reality" and thereby often excludes authentic experience of mystery) and parabolic religion (which continually and deliberately subverts final words about "reality" and thereby introduces the possibility of transcendence).

John C. Dwyer, *Church History: Twenty Centuries of Catholic Christianity* (Mahwah, NJ: Paulist Press, 1985).
Highly condensed picture of the church in its historical reality and ambiguity, judged from the standpoint of Jesus' original revelation. Criticism of the Crusades, neglect of Reformers' legitimate concerns, and recent popes. Emphasizes the role of theology in the life of the church.

Paul Johnson, *A History of Christianity* (New York: Atheneum, 1980).
The story of the rise, greatness, and decline of Christianity, based more on politics, economics, and social and cultural factors than on theology. Shows how the varied themes of Christianity repeat and modulate themselves through the centuries.

John Koenig, *New Testament Hospitality* (Philadelphia: Fortress Press, 1985).
Examines the ministry of Jesus, the missionary practice of Paul, and the lifestyle of the community in Luke-Acts to show how hospitality and openness to strangers were crucial to the life of the early Christians.

William G. Thompson, *Paul and His Message for Life's Journey* (Mahwah, NJ: Paulist Press, 1986).
Shows how Paul's message can help people find coherence and meaning in life through an inductive and experiential consideration of Paul's themes of dying and rising in Christ, God's plan of action in the world, and communities in the new age.

Mary Jo Weaver, *Introduction to Christianity* (Belmont, CA: Wadsworth Publ. Co., 2nd ed., 1991).
A nuts-and-bolts presentation of the background, history, and issues of Christianity as a religion. Unity in diversity and diversity in unity. An introduction to contemporary issues, and a summary of Christian commonality by way of worship.

Chapter Five
ISLAM: SUBMISSION AND MARTYRDOM

Kenneth Cragg, *The Pen and the Faith: Eight Modern Muslim Writers and the Qur'an* (London: George Allen & Unwin, 1985).
Deep themes of Muslim religious thought and experience from contemporary Muslim writers. Shows a great diversity of Qur'anic understanding and how Qur'anic guidance is applied to critical situations in the modern world.

Frederick Denny, *Islam and the Muslim Community* (San Francisco: Harper & Row, 1987).
Combines the historical and the topical into a convenient introduction to the Islamic tradition and the worldwide Muslim community. Pays special attention to the doctrines, spirituality, and institutions of Islam, and provides ready understanding of world events involving Muslims.

Shams al-Din, Shaykh Muhammad Mahdi, *The Rising of Al-Husayn: Its Impact on the Consciousness of Muslim Society* (Boston: Routledge & Kegan Paul, 1985).
Surveys literary and religious sources from the earliest periods to modern times, showing how the rising and martyrdom of Husain has affected the spiritual life of Shiite Muslims. Martyrdom as the highest degree of self-sacrifice for sake of religious principles.

John L. Esposito, *Islam: The Straight Path* (New York: Oxford University Press, 1988).
Helps understand contemporary developments in Islamic world. Depicts the emergence of the Muslim community, the varieties of Muslim beliefs and practices, the tensions between tradition and modernity, and the Islamic resurgence of recent years.

Marshall G.S. Hodgson, *The Venture of Islam: Conscience and History in a World Civilization*, 3 vols. (Chicago: University of Chicago Press, 1974).
Traces and interprets the historical development of Islamic civilization from

before the birth of Muhammad to the middle of the twentieth century. A magnificent introduction to Islamic civilization.

Jacques Jomier, *How to Understand Islam* (New York: Crossroad, 1990).
Examines Muslim beliefs, religious observance, and ethics alongside everyday piety and Islamic mystical literature. Outlines the history of Islam, particularly its penetration of Africa below the Sahara, and shows how Islam considers Christianity.

Annemarie Schimmel, *And Muhammad Is His Messenger* (Chapel Hill: University of North Carolina Press, 1985).
Depicts how pious Muslims have venerated Muhammad through the centuries. Cites poetry, legends, and miracles that show a deep love and warm trust for Muhammad.

Chapter Six
HINDUISM: DETACHMENT AND INITIATION

Christopher J. Chapple, *Karma and Creativity* (Albany: State University of New York Press, 1986).
A short and useful work that argues for the efficacy of human action in the pursuit of liberation. Studies classical Hindu texts to shift the Western understanding of karma (action) from connotations of determinism and fatalism to connotations of creative freedom and purposeful action.

Paul B. Courtright, *Ganesa: Lord of Obstacles, Lord of Beginnings* (New York: Oxford University Press, 1985).
An outstanding analysis of Ganesa mythology and worship. The major themes of the Ganesa story—birth, beheading, restoration, thresholds, obstacles—are developed within the context of field experience.

Diana L. Eck, *Banaras: City of Light* (Princeton, NJ: Princeton University Press, 1982).
An introduction to how Indian religion is actually lived. Analyzes the art and architecture, geography, history, and anthropology of Banaras and describes its elaborate and thriving rituals, its myths and literature.

John Stratton Hawley and Donna Marie Wulff (eds.), *The Divine Consort: Radha and the Goddesses of India* (Boston: Beacon Press, 1986).
An appreciation of the feminine aspect of divinity. An anthology on several female divinities from all over India and the theology that surrounds them (e.g., divine duality, play, power, and consorts).

David R. Kinsley, *The Sword and the Flute (Kali and Krsna, Dark Visions of the Terrible and the Sublime in Hindu Mythology)* (Berkeley: University of California Press, 1975).
Shows Hindu openness to a divine dimension of reality that both intoxicates and terrifies. Conveys the depth, complexity, and inexhaustible apprehen-

sion of the sacred in human experience, helping us discern the meaning of
Hindu spirituality.

Klaus K. Klostermaier, *A Survey of Hinduism* (Albany: State University of New
York Press, 1989).
Comprehensive survey of India's past and present religious life and
thought, dealing with the Hindu worldview, paths to liberation, major
branches, social order, and its efforts to deal with modernization.

Robert Minor (ed.), *Modern Indian Interpreters of the Bhagavad Gita* (Albany: State
University of New York Press, 1986).
Ten papers on the manner in which the spiritual teachings of the Gita have
been understood by both modern Indians and by critical historians of religions.

Chapter Seven
CHINA: HUMANENESS AND NATURALNESS

Julia Ching, *Confucianism and Christianity: A Comparative Study* (Tokyo: Kodan-
sha International, 1978).
Philosophical assessment of the Confucian heritage and its ultimate viability
in today's world. Consideration of prayer and meditation, mysticism and
ritual, of religion that unites ethics with politics and worship with rulership.

Chang Chung-Yuan, *Creativity and Taoism* (New York: Harper & Row, Colo-
phon edition, 1970).
Presents Taoist ideas in a systematic way. Manifestations of the invisible Tao
in different areas, such as sympathy, creativity, peace, poetry, and painting.
Points out ways of self-cultivation toward the ultimate goal of enlightenment.

Herbert Fingarette, *Confucius—The Secular as Sacred* (New York: Harper Torch-
books, 1972).
Emphasizing the universality of the Confucian ideal of ritual (li), he argues
that the Confucian perception of society as the holy rite makes the presump-
tion of an inner psyche superfluous.

David Hall and Roger Ames, *Thinking through Confucius* (Albany: State University of New York Press, 1987).
A critical interpretation of Confucius's philosophical reflections, based on
the famous saying from the Analects: "At fifteen my heart-and-mind were
set upon learning; at thirty I took my stance; at forty I was no longer of two
minds; at fifty I realized the ming of t'ien (will of heaven); at sixty my ear
was attuned; and at seventy I could give my heart-and-mind free rein without overstepping the mark."

Victor Mair (ed.), *Experimental Essays on Chuang Tzu* (Honolulu: University of
Hawaii Press, 1983).

Diverse methodological approaches to Chuang Tzu by many non-experts in Chinese culture. A testimony to the vital power of his words and ideas to stimulate thought in our own time.

Tu Wei-Ming, *Confucian Thought: Selfhood as Creative Transformation* (Albany: State University of New York Press, 1985).
A sustained deliberation on the Confucian concept of person and the transformation of the self. Studies Confucianism as social philosophy, a philosophy of practice and engagement with the moral affairs of the world.

Holmes Welch, *Taoism: The Parting of the Way* (Boston: Beacon Press, 1965).
A comprehensive discussion of Taoism, Lao Tzu, and the Tao Te Ching. Treats the period of religious syncretism, the interior gods, hygiene school, alchemy, and development of the Taoist pantheon.

Chapter Eight
BUDDHISM: COMPASSION AND MEDITATION

Allan Hunt Badiner (ed.), *Dharma Gaia: A Harvest of Essays in Buddhism and Ecology* (Berkeley: Parallax Press, 1990.)
Ties together the teachings of Buddha and ecological consciousness. A guide for living in the emerging environmental era, stressing balance between humans, all other forms of life, and the true mother, the Earth.

William Theodore de Bary (ed.), *The Buddhist Tradition: In India, China, and Japan* (New York: Modern Library, 1969).
Excerpts from the basic Buddhist sacred texts and major writings of Buddhist thinkers, with necessary background essays, providing a commentary on the mainstream of Buddhist thought and practice.

Ruben L.F. Habito, *Total Liberation: Zen Spirituality and the Social Dimension* (Maryknoll, NY: Orbis Books, 1989).
Shows how Zen sustains a socially active role in the world by leading to involvement and struggle against violence and oppression. Expands Zen contemplation and the personal growth dimension to embrace all of creation.

Albert Low, *The Iron Cow of Zen* (Wheaton, IL: Theosophical Publ. House, 1985).
Shows Zen as a completely existential discipline, relating the koans to everyday experience. Discusses the causes and forms of the dilemmas and ambiguities of human condition.

Aloysius Pieris, *Love Meets Wisdom: A Christian Experience of Buddhism* (Maryknoll, NY: Orbis Books, 1988).
Finds elements of redemptive love and salvific knowledge in most major religious traditions. Argues that the major benefit of interreligious encounter is that it can promote the retrieval of suppressed elements of one's own tradition.

Robert S. Ellwood, Jr., *An Invitation to Japanese Civilization* (Belmont, CA: Wadsworth Publ. Co., 1980).
Looks at Japanese history, modern education, business, religion, and philosophy. Explains the delicate and aesthetic interweaving of skill and nature in sculpture, painting, the dramatic arts, and literature.

D. T. Suzuki, *Zen and Japanese Culture* (Princeton, NJ: Bollingen, 1959).
Considers in detail how various aspects of Japanese art and life, e.g., the cult of swordsmanship, the tea ceremony, the haiku form of poetry, and the Japanese love of nature, lead to the satori which is the awakening of self-realization and seeing into one's own being.

Chapter Nine
MAYA AND UGANDA: SACRIFICE AND DEATH

David Carrasco, *Quetzalcoatl and the Irony of Empire: Myths and Prophecies in the Aztec Tradition* (Chicago: University of Chicago Press, 1982).
Sketches out the lines of force that related the central shrines and sacred symbols associated with Quetzalcoatl to the social and historical processes that animated the sacred cities in Mesoamerican culture.

Kwesi Dickson and Paul Ellingworth (eds.), *Biblical Revelation and African Beliefs* (London: Lutterworth Press, 1969).
The attempt to find the correlation, if any, between the biblical concept of God and the God of African traditional beliefs. Chapters by different African theologians on priesthood, sacrifice, human destiny, ethics, and eschatology.

Joseph G. Donders, *Non-Bourgeois Theology: An African Experience of Jesus* (Maryknoll, NY: Orbis Books, 1985).
Captures the symbolism, mood, experience, dreams, and vision of the people in their rapidly urbanizing East African environment. Chapters on God, family, human life, time, community power and institutional impotence, suffering, and prayer as power.

John S. Mbiti, *African Religions and Philosophy* (New York: Praeger, 1969).
A scholarly survey of African religion: on God, death, morality, the religious orientation of various rites and social relationships. Includes his stimulating interpretation of the traditional concept of time in East Africa.

Benjamin C. Ray, *Myth, Ritual, and Kingship in Buganda* (New York: Oxford University Press, 1990).
Describes and interprets the myths, rituals, shrines and sacred regalia of the kabakaship (kingship) within the changing contexts of the pre-colonial, colonial, and post-independence eras in Uganda.

John Roscoe, *The Baganda: An Account of Their Nature, Customs and Beliefs* (London: Macmillan, 1911).

Describes the social and religious life of the Baganda in the days before Uganda came under European influence. Treats rites of passage, relationships, clans and their totems, the kabakaship, government, warfare, and subsistence methods. Chapters on the myths of Kintu and the marriage ritual.

Dennis Tedlock (trans.), *Popol Vuh: The Mayan Book of the Dawn of Life* (New York: Simon & Schuster, 1985).
Includes an excellent introduction to this extraordinary document of the human imagination, from the primeval deeds of Maya gods to the radiant splendor of the Maya lords who founded the Quiché kingdom in the Guatemalan highlands.

J. Eric Thompson, *Maya History and Religion* (Norman: University of Oklahoma Press, 1970).
Ethnological approach to Maya history, studying written records and archaeological discoveries, to show how worship (prayers, sacrifices, and other rites), major gods, and creation myths mirror the character and mentality of the Maya.

INDEX